Understanding Second Language Process

SECOND LANGUAGE ACQUISITION
Series Editor: Professor David Singleton, *Trinity College, Dublin, Ireland*

This series brings together titles dealing with a variety of aspects of language acquisition and processing in situations where a language or languages other than the native language is involved. Second language is thus interpreted in its broadest possible sense. The volumes included in the series all offer in their different ways, on the one hand, exposition and discussion of empirical findings and, on the other, some degree of theoretical reflection. In this latter connection, no particular theoretical stance is privileged in the series; nor is any relevant perspective – sociolinguistic, psycholinguistic, neurolinguistic, etc. – deemed out of place. The intended readership of the series includes final-year undergraduates working on second language acquisition projects, postgraduate students involved in second language acquisition research, and researchers and teachers in general whose interests include a second language acquisition component.

Other Books in the Series
Language Acquisition: The Age Factor (2nd edn)
  David Singleton and Lisa Ryan
Focus on French as a Foreign Language: Multidisciplinary Approaches
  Jean-Marc Dewaele (ed.)
Second Language Writing Systems
  Vivian Cook and Benedetta Bassetti (eds)
Third Language Learners: Pragmatic Production and Awareness
  Maria Pilar Safont Jordà
Artificial Intelligence in Second Language Learning: Raising Error Awareness
  Marina Dodigovic
Studies of Fossilization in Second Language Acquisition
  ZhaoHong Han and Terence Odlin (eds)
Language Learners in Study Abroad Contexts
  Margaret A. DuFon and Eton Churchill (eds)
Early Trilingualism: A Focus on Questions
  Julia D. Barnes
Cross-linguistic Influences in the Second Language Lexicon
  Janusz Arabski (ed.)
Motivation, Language Attitudes and Globalisation: A Hungarian Perspective
  Zoltán Dörnyei, Kata Csizér and Nóra Németh
Age and the Rate of Foreign Language Learning
  Carmen Muñoz (ed.)
Investigating Tasks in Formal Language Learning
  María del Pilar García Mayo (ed.)
Input for Instructed L2 Learners: The Relevance of Relevance
  Anna Nizegorodcew
Cross-linguistic Similarity in Foreign Language Learning
  Håkan Ringbom
Second Language Lexical Processes
  Zsolt Lengyel and Judit Navracsics (eds)
Third or Additional Language Acquisition
  Gessica De Angelis

For more details of these or any other of our publications, please contact:
**Multilingual Matters, Frankfurt Lodge, Clevedon Hall,
Victoria Road, Clevedon, BS21 7HH, England**
http://www.multilingual-matters.com

SECOND LANGUAGE ACQUISITION 25
Series Editor: David Singleton, *Trinity College, Dublin, Ireland*

Understanding Second Language Process

Edited by
Zhaohong Han

In collaboration with
Eun Sung Park, Andrea Révész, Charles Combs
and Ji Hyun Kim

MULTILINGUAL MATTERS LTD
Clevedon • Buffalo • Toronto

Library of Congress Cataloging in Publication Data
Understanding Second Language process/edited by ZhaoHong Han, in collaboration with Eun Sung Park ... [et al.].
Second Language Acquisition: 25
Includes bibliographical references and index.
1. Second language acquisition. I. Han, Zhaohong II. Park, Eun Sung.
P118.2.U53 2007
418–dc22   2007020108

British Library Cataloguing in Publication Data
A catalogue entry for this book is available from the British Library.

ISBN-13: 978-1-84769-014-2 (hbk)
ISBN-13: 978-1-84769-013-5 (pbk)

Multilingual Matters Ltd
UK: Frankfurt Lodge, Clevedon Hall, Victoria Road, Clevedon BS21 7HH.
USA: UTP, 2250 Military Road, Tonawanda, NY 14150, USA.
Canada: UTP, 5201 Dufferin Street, North York, Ontario M3H 5T8, Canada.

Copyright © 2008 ZhaoHong Han and the authors of individual chapters.

All rights reserved. No part of this work may be reproduced in any form or by any means without permission in writing from the publisher.

The policy of Multilingual Matters/Channel View Publications is to use papers that are natural, renewable and recyclable products, made from wood grown in sustainable forests. In the manufacturing process of our books, and to further support our policy, preference is given to printers that have FSC and PEFC Chain of Custody certification. The FSC and/or PEFC logos will appear on those books where full certification has been granted to the printer concerned.

Typeset by Techset Composition Ltd.
Printed and bound in Great Britain by MPG Books Ltd.

Contents

The Contributors vii

Preface xi

1 Revisiting the Role of Consciousness with MOGUL
  Michael Sharwood Smith 1

2 Multi-Competence: Black Hole or Wormhole for Second Language Acquisition Research?
  Vivian Cook 16

3 Transfer Appropriate Processing as a Model for Classroom Second Language Acquisition
  Patsy Martin Lightbown 27

4 On the Role of Meaning in Focus on Form
  ZhaoHong Han 45

5 The Efficacy of Visual Input Enhancement in Teaching Deaf Learners of L2 English
  Gerald P. Berent and Ronald R. Kelly 80

6 Learner Spontaneous Attention in L2 Input Processing: An Exploratory Study
  Eun Sung Park and ZhaoHong Han 106

7 Working Memory and L2 Processing of Redundant Grammatical Forms
  Nuria Sagarra 133

8 L2 Learners' Interpretation of Operator-Variable
   Binding in VP Ellipsis
   Hong Guang Ying 148

9 Metasyntactic Ability in L2: An Investigation
   of Task Demand
   Daphnée Simard and Véronique Fortier 160

10 Prosody Acquisition by Japanese Learners
   Tomoko Shibata and Richard R. Hurtig 176

11 Recognition and Production of Formulas
   in L2 Pragmatics
   Kathleen Bardovi-Harlig 205

References 223

Index 254

The Contributors

Dr Kathleen Bardovi-Harlig is Professor of Second Language Studies at Indiana University. Her books include *Tense and Aspect in Second Language Acquisition* (2000), *Interlanguage Pragmatics: Exploring Institutional Talk* (with Beverly Hartford) (2005) and *Pragmatics and Language Learning* (with César Félix-Brasdefer and Alwiya Omar) (2006). She has published in *Language Learning, Studies in Second Language Acquisition,* and *TESOL Quarterly,* and is a former editor of *Language Learning.*

Dr Gerald P. Berent is Professor at the National Technical Institute for the Deaf and Rochester Institute of Technology. He conducts research on deaf learners' acquisition of English grammatical knowledge and the efficacy of specific methodologies in English teaching to deaf students. His multidisciplinary research draws on second language studies, theoretical linguistics, and English language teaching with a research focus also on language-learning disabilities and attention deficit disorders in deaf learners. Dr Berent teaches English grammar to deaf college students and graduate teacher training courses and also provides professional development to teachers of English to deaf students. His recent research explains parallel interlanguage development in deaf and hearing learners and explores English language factors that impede deaf students' development of mathematical knowledge.

Dr Vivian Cook is Professor of Applied Linguistics in the School of Education, Communication and Language Sciences at the University of Newcastle upon Tyne in England, where he teaches on the MA and PhD programs. He is mostly known among applied linguists for his work developing the idea of multicompetence and for his books on Chomsky and on the applications of SLA to language teaching. Recently he has also taken up writing books on writing systems and a popular book on spelling. His current research interest is the study of bilingual cognition. He was a founder and first President of the European Second Language Association.

Véronique Fortier is currently a PhD Candidate at Université du Québec à Montréal, where she also teaches French grammar for second language learners. Her research interests focus on the role of metalinguisitc reflection in second language acquisition among elementary school learners in a submersion context.

Dr ZhaoHong Han is Associate Professor of Linguistics and Education at Teachers College, Columbia University. Her research interests include second language learnability, second language teachability, and second language reading processes. She has published in a variety of TESOL and applied linguistics journals and books. She is the author of *Fossilization in Adult Second Language Acquisition* (Multilingual Matters, 2004) and co-editor (with Terence Odlin) of *Studies of Fossilization in Second Language Acquisition* (Multilingual Matters, 2006).

Dr Richard Hurtig is Professor of Speech Pathology and Audiology in the College of Liberal Arts and Sciences at the University of Iowa. He is the chair of the American Sign Language Program. He also serves on the faculty of the University of Iowa Neurosciences PhD Program and the FLARE PhD program in Second Language Acquisition. Professor Hurtig's research and teaching responsibilities are in the area of psycholinguistics and speech perception. His research on early literacy development is funded by the Institute of Educational Sciences, U.S. department of Education.

Dr Ronald R. Kelly is Professor at the National Technical Institute for the Deaf and Rochester Institute of Technology. He conducts research on learning processes in deaf and hard-of-hearing students. His multi-disciplinary research focuses on the mathematical problem-solving skills of deaf learners, including associated language and cognitive processing in analytical tasks. His collaborative research has examined deaf learners' morphological knowledge, their understanding of universal quantifiers and other relational language, their command of visual–spatial relational representation, and their mental calculations – all pertinent to analysing and solving mathematical problems. His recent research has also involved the comparison of specific methodologies for teaching English grammatical knowledge to deaf learners. He teaches graduate courses on technology applications for deaf learners and the psychology of teaching and learning.

Dr Patsy Martin Lightbown is Distinguished Professor Emeritus (Applied Linguistics) at Concordia University in Montreal. The principal area of her research is second language acquisition in the classroom, particularly the complementary contributions of communicative and form-focused activities. With Nina Spada, she co-authored *How Languages are Learned* (Oxford University Press), an introduction to second language acquisition research for teachers that is now in its third edition. She lives in Massachusetts, where she continues to do research, consulting, writing, and teaching about language teaching and learning.

Dr. Eun Sung Park is a Visiting Professor in the Graduate School of Language and Educational Linguistics at the Monterey Institute of International Studies, where she teaches in the MATESOL/TFL program. Her interests are in the areas of input and attention in SLA, and the interface of theory and practice in language learning and teaching. She received her EdD in Applied Linguistics from Teachers College, Columbia University in May 2007, where she also taught graduate courses in the TESOL program. Her dissertation entitled *Learner-generated noticing of second language input* explores what learners are prone to notice in the input on their own, when left to their own devices.

Dr Nuria Sagarra is Assistant Professor at Pennsylvania State University. Her research concentrates on the processing of morphosyntactic cues by second language (L2) learners and bilinguals from a psycholinguistic perspective, as well as on the role that working memory plays in L2 comprehension and grammar/vocabulary development. She also examines the effect of computer-delivered feedback, input modification (simplification and enhancement), and instruction on L2 acquisition in adults. She investigates these topics by means of quantitative experiments, using on-line techniques, such as eyetracking and moving window. In addition, she is the director of the Spanish Basic Language Program and the Spanish Technology Project at Penn State.

Dr Mike Sharwood Smith works at Heriot-Watt University in Edinburgh where he teaches linguistics, applied linguistics, TESOL, and advanced EFL. He has over a hundred publications in one or other of these areas. His research interests are in cognitive processes in second language development. He is currently working with John Truscott (National Tsing Hua University, Taiwan) on their new theoretical framework for investigation language acquisition and performance called MOGUL. He is founding editor of *Second Language Research* and runs the web-based International Commission on Second Language Acquisition. His books include *Second Language Learning: Theoretical Foundations* (1994) and *Aspects of Future Reference in a Pedagogical Grammar of English* (1975).

Dr Tomoko Shibata is a lecturer at Princeton University. She received her MA in Japanese pedagogy at the University of Iowa in 1999 and her PhD in second language acquisition at the University of Iowa in the autumn of 2005. Her dissertation title is *Prosody Acquisition of Japanese as a Second Language: An Integrated Approach*. Her research interests include Japanese prosody acquisition, phonology, phonetics, Japanese pedagogy, and language strategy instruction.

Dr Daphnée Simard is Professor at the Université du Québec à Montréal. She teaches courses in language acquisition. Her research focuses on the role of attention and metalinguistic reflection in SLA. She has taught ESL at various levels and under different conditions (enriched, individualised, regular) and French for specific purposes.

Dr. H.G. Ying is Associate Professor of Applied Linguistics at the University of Colorado at Denver and Health Science Center. His research interests are in second language acquisition/processing and the interface between syntax and pragmatics. He has published articles in *Language Learning, Second Language Research, International Review of Applied Linguistics, Language Sciences, Semiotica* and *International Journal of Applied Linguistics*. He is the author of *Investigating Reconstruction in a Second Language* (2003).

Preface

The field of second language acquisition (SLA) research, since its inception, has been inextricably intertwined with pedagogical concerns. For many, if not all, researchers, the goal of SLA research is to produce insights and develop instructional strategies that may eventually improve the efficacy and efficiency of learning, something that learners at large have proven to be lacking. Although numerous strategies have indeed been developed over the years, the empirical research that has undergirded them, in the main, enacts and perpetuates a tradition that values learning as a product rather than a process. In that vein, the efficacy of the strategies has been construed and/or measured in terms of overtly manifested – oftentimes, superficial and form-oriented – changes in learners' behaviour (cf. Philp, 2003; Truscott, 1998). Often, though not always, statistical results are adduced to support one strategy over another. Individual-level, qualitative analyses of the linguistic data are, on the other hand, sparse, but when and where such analyses are undertaken, the results tend to show divergence rather than convergence (cf. Bardovi-Harlig, 2006a; Ellis & Larsen-Freeman, 2006; Larsen-Freeman, 2006a). The overall understanding that then ensues is one replete with contingency – the strategies are helpful for some learners but not for others, or they are helpful sometimes but not always. Nothing conclusive can therefore be said about any of them, and speculations have come in abundance.

Some of the speculations have even turned into clichés. For example, nowadays it is often said that second language (L2) learning is 'a complex enterprise'. Another impending cliché is that it is learners themselves, and not any external agents (i.e. a teacher, a researcher, or a textbook developer), who control the learning process. Importantly, such clichés are vacuous, empirically, for there has been little direct empirical proof of them. As a result of the product orientation in research referred to above, there has been a persistent absence in the literature of a fine-grained understanding of many fundamental issues pertaining to L2 learning as a process. These issues include, but are not limited to, the following:

- the genesis and ontogenesis of linguistic and metalinguistic abilities;
- the extent to which a multilingual mind influences cognition in general, and the processing of L2 input and generation of output in particular;
- the process by which learning transfers from one context to another;
- the extent to which L1 interferes with L2 meaning – form mapping;
- the extent to which learner attention can be externally manipulated;
- the default process and strategies by which learners analyse input;
- learners' working memory capacity for processing input for form and meaning;
- the extent to which Universal Grammar (UG) constrains the processing of grammatical ambiguity;
- the extent to which tasks differ in identifying metalinguistic ability;
- the extent to which various aspects of L2 (e.g. prosodic features, pragmatic formulas) are acquired;
- the relationship between perception and production.

This book tackles these issues and many more, through theoretical analyses and/or empirical research. The book contains eleven chapters, the first four of which are conceptually orientated and the remaining seven of which are empirical studies, conducted with a variety of target languages, including Korean, Chinese, Spanish, French, English, and Japanese, and with hearing and/or deaf learners. Although not a comprehensive treatment of process in L2 learning, as the title of the book indicates, the book provides much food for thought, particularly for second language instruction. Each chapter conveys a message for classroom learning, but the messages are not always consistent. This scenario aptly mirrors the diversity of current convictions about what would bring about the most effective instruction, and it, in turn, points to the need to increase the amount of further, systematic research by both researchers and practitioners.

Since Corder's (1967) seminal distinction between input and intake, it has never been clearer that instruction cannot be effective unless it directly addresses learners' processing needs (e.g. Doughty, 2001, 2003; VanPatten, 1996, 2004a). Doughty (2003: 298) has convincingly argued that 'the goal of L2 instruction should be to organise the processing space to enable [learners] to notice the cues located in the input ...'. Even so, exactly what that entails and how that may be achieved in the classroom requires concerted effort to elaborate. This book, at it were, provides a point of departure for the collective endeavour.

The book resonates with an increasingly stronger call from the 'applied linguistics quarter' of SLA research for a paradigmatic shift from product to process. Ellis and Larsen-Freeman (2006a) have emphasised:

[A]ttested data cannot tell us what transpired in the language up until the construction of the text, nor where it is destined. While this may seem obvious, and forgivable, from a complexity theory perspective, by limiting our investigations to attested language, we miss the perceptually changing, perceptually dynamic nature of language.

In her recent paper in *Applied Linguistics*, Larsen-Freeman (2006a) underscores the need for researchers to adopt an 'emic' perspective on second language development (cf. Hauser, 2005) and provides a clear demonstration of the level and depth of understanding that may result from pursuing a focus on the learner rather than on the target language. This is doubtless a promising direction for future research to take.

Along a similar line, many authors in this book have pleaded earnestly for longitudinal research to document the dynamics of the L2 process. In light of the currently abundant cross-sectional research, it appears that cross-sectional research, although capable of capturing group tendencies, is inadequate to reveal the multifaceted complexity of the learning process per se, unless it is balanced by ontogenetic research. Although many of the logistics of the learning process tend to be 'eclipsed' in phylogenetic research, they can be elucidated by research examining learners as individuals (Bardovi-Harlig, 2006). It follows, then, that not only should case studies be promoted in future SLA research, but a within-group design must also be encouraged in group-based research.

This book would not have been possible without the dedicated work of its authors and their cooperation and patience with the process. We are indebted to them all. Our thanks also go to the reviewers, whose critical feedback and constructive comments are essential in helping authors achieve and maintain clarity. Lastly, we wish to express our appreciation to Michael Feyen and Kristen Loesch at Teachers College, Columbia University and Tommi Grover (and his colleagues) at Multilingual Matters for their support and efficiency.

The book is intended for second language researchers, graduate students, and bilingual and/or second language practitioners.

ZhaoHong Han
(In collaboration with Eun Sung Park,
Andrea Révész, Charles Combs, and Ji Hyun Kim)
New York

Chapter 1
Revisiting the Role of Consciousness with MOGUL

MICHAEL SHARWOOD SMITH

Thirty years of research has not produced any really hard evidence that making people aware of formal features of the second language (L2) has any significant long-term effect on their grammatical development. However, people still have a persistent feeling that metalinguistic ability in the L2 is more than just a luxury extra or, viewed more pessimistically, more than a distraction and an encumbrance. It is surely a prerequisite for any proper research into such issues that we have a much more fine-grained explanation of the mechanisms involved in metalinguistic ability than has been the case so far. At the least, we need to develop a coherent theoretical model of this ability that we can use to generate interesting research questions about such issues as input enhancement (see Berent & Kelly, this volume) and focus on form (see Han, this volume). You might say that, although there has been no dearth of empirical research, not all that much has happened in this theoretical arena since the 1970s. The MOGUL[1] framework being developed by Sharwood Smith and Truscott aims, among other things, to rekindle the search for more coherent conceptualisations of the problems involved.

MOGUL is a processing model that is devised in such a way as to engage coherently with research across a variety of domains. Following proposals by Ray Jackendoff, it involves a recognition of the existence of a separate, modular language faculty, containing the core phonological and syntactic systems. It also recognises the crucial importance of 'conceptual structure', which includes the vital semantic and pragmatic dimensions of language that, in this framework, lie outside this core and allow for the possibility of conscious introspection. In fact, it is in the conceptual domain that metalinguistic ability is anchored, allowing the language user to construct fragmentary or even quite sophisticated metagrammars that co-exist with the inaccessible grammar(s) processed inside the core language modules. Although accessible to conscious awareness, these metalinguistic systems can in principle be recruited in performance skilfully and quite spontaneously.

MOGUL has a way of explaining the relationships between these two types of grammar and the way they may develop and interact, which takes us well beyond the original innovative and widely disputed model proposed by Stephen Krashen and in ways that accord with current research into cognition. It also places metalinguistic ability in a wider context as something that is a regular part of everyday use in both first language (L1) and L2, that is, both in and outside the classroom.

The Early Years

At the close of what might be called the first years of L2 acquisition starting with Corder's seminal paper on error analysis and ending with Dulay, Burt and Krashen's *Language Two* in 1982, three basic ideas had been introduced to the field (Corder, 1967; Dulay *et al.*, 1982):

(1) The learner system;
(2) The 'developmental imperative'; and
(3) Dual Knowledge Hypothesis.

The first of these was the idea that language learners operate a non-native version of the target language, which one could regard in some sense as systematic and autonomous, in other words, as not merely an ill-assorted collection of correct and incorrect ideas, rules or principles concerning the properties of the L2 in question.

The second basic notion was what one might call the 'developmental imperative', namely that the L2 grammar, or a goodly part of the morphosyntax, unfolds in the learner in pre-ordained ways, usually to be interpreted as a pre-ordained *sequence* or perhaps a set of sequences, such that no intervention by either teacher or learner could influence the course of events, provided that the learner continued to be exposed to the L2. It is as though there is a programmed sequence of steps that needs only exposure to the appropriate input to trigger growth. Aspects of the learner's system must develop in their own time and in a manner much constrained by in-built principles (not provided by the environment) – it is the role of SLA research to determine the nature and scope of these principles. Although the idea of fixed sequences is not a Chomskyan notion nor is it necessarily implied by the existence of principles of universal grammar, the basic idea fits in neatly with the general assertion, familiar from generative linguistics, that because mother tongue (L1) grammatical development unfolds without the need for correction or introspection, it must therefore in some way be helped along by innately given principles. The claim put forward by various L2 researchers was, of course, that L2 development is driven by essentially the same principles, although their implementation might in practice encounter more obstacles on the way.

The third and perhaps most contentious notion was that learning language in a conscious, analytic manner resulted in a kind of knowledge that was quite distinct from that which underlies spontaneous language use. *Knowing* the language is not the same as *knowing about* the language. SLA theory must account for the characteristic discrepancy between the two.

The nub of the problem

The most contentious part of the dual knowledge idea was Krashen's assertion that there was no 'interface' between consciously and subconsciously gained grammatical knowledge (Krashen, 1976, 1978, 1985; Sharwood Smith, 1981). Conscious rules could not be converted into subconscious ones, no matter how hard one practised. If this were so, then the developmental sequences could easily be subverted and, all other things being equal, particular training programmes could dictate the actual sequences in which learners gained control over given areas of the L2 grammar. The research carried out during this early period suggested that conscious learning could not interfere with the pre-ordained sequences of development and only made the learners more knowledgeable about the nature of the 'errors' they committed. The best thing was to focus on the meaning and not the form of the message (Dulay *et al.*, 1982).

Looking back on these early days from a 21st century perspective, one can see that these three basic ideas have stood the test of time. Even the conscious/subconscious distinction as presented in Krashen's various publications is still a live issue, and it took until 1998 for a collection of studies to come out that signalled a concerted attempt to find support for drawing learners' attention to formal aspects of the L2, and this included explicit reference to (or 'focus on') form as opposed to meaning (Doughty & Williams, 1998a; Long & Robinson, 1998). Moreover, Doughty herself, in a state-of-the-art paper in 2003, expresses great reserve about the role of consciousness, that is, 'metalinguistic' knowledge in grammatical development (Doughty, 2003:298). Although Schmidt claims that no learning can take place without noticing, the precise nature of noticing, whether it involves some degree of conscious awareness – without necessarily implicating analytic understanding (Schmidt, 1990) – is constantly under scrutiny and is no way decided (Carroll, 2001; Truscott, 1998).

After so many years of empirical research, one senses in the SLA literature a growing trend to refine the conceptual basis for making claims about how an L2 develops over time and, in particular, how the basic ideas outlined above accord with contemporary research in sister disciplines. In the discussion that follows, the idea surrounding 'metalinguistic' ability and its role in L2 development will be revisited, this time using the MOGUL framework, the aim behind which is precisely to achieve the required increase in theoretical precision and cross-disciplinary validity.

Dual knowledge: The essentials

Krashen's conscious/subconscious learning distinction can be explicated as follows:

(1) Conscious learning produces 'technical' ('meta') knowledge about the target language.
(2) Using this knowledge requires the operation of a conscious mental editor called the 'Monitor'.
(3) The Monitor is a grammatical 'first aid kit'. It is
   (a) linguistically unsophisticated (for most learners);
   (b) available only for non-spontaneous use; and
   (c) not always used anyway, even in optimal circumstances.

What are the consequences for language learners (and teachers)? Put in its most extreme form, the advice to learners is to throw away the grammar book and just try to listen, read, and understand. Learning words and phrases, in the sense that this is focusing on meaning and not on the systematic aspects of L2, is the only guaranteed way in which a conscious approach to L2 learning will bring benefits. In short, the role of conscious learning is given at most a very peripheral role.

In the 1970s, the evidence for the no-interface hypothesis was not solid and hence open to considerable scepticism. However, despite the failure to establish a strong empirically backed foundation for conscious learning in defiance of the no-interface hypothesis, people continue to have a persistent feeling that metalinguistic ability in the L2 is more than just a luxury extra that is of no real relevance to L2 development. This may be justified, but where is the hard evidence for this feeling? Thirty-five years of research has not produced any substantial proof that making people aware of formal features of the L2, whether by means of correction or explanation or both, has any long-term effect, at least where basic morphosyntax and phonology are concerned.

Note that it is important to mention what aspects of the language we are talking about, because when talking about 'the' language or 'the' L2, people sometimes ignore substantial aspects of language that (1) have not been as well researched as syntax and phonology and (2) may by their very nature be amenable to manipulation by external agents, either teachers or the learner 'outside' the inaccessible parts of language, that is, by the conscious learner (see relevant discussion in Sharwood Schwartz, 1999; Smith, 1994). The role of 'conscious' learning *outside* core syntax and phonology has never been explicitly denied but the issue has remained vague and relatively unexplored. It also depends on what you mean precisely by 'lexical' and 'pragmatic' aspects of L2. You certainly need a proper linguistic theory to determine this: the empirical data will not tell you and traditional grammatical categories are notoriously vague and unreliable. Is the English definite article 'the' a functional/grammatical phenomenon or a lexical one, for instance? The category 'article', or 'determiner' or *Det* are functional terms but the particular items in English that actually fulfil this morphosyntactic function can easily be called lexical, and the selection of which article should go in which context may well be dictated by semantic or pragmatic principles. In sum, the question of conscious awareness and what aspects of language it has absolutely no access to remains a problematic and complex issue that requires both linguistics and other disciplines to be brought to bear on it.

Alternatives to dual knowledge

There are various theoretical perspectives that allow for different modes of knowledge but deny total separation between them (DeKeyser, 2003; Hulstijn, 2002). Development in one area may contribute to development in the other, as knowledge is 'automatised' or reformatted for real-time processing. There are also theoretical perspectives that would, in addition, account for language development without resorting to notions like 'knowledge' or 'internal representations' of language at all (N. Ellis, 2003). Realistically, these approaches still have to make their case and provide enough evidence to discredit their rival and more established approaches concerning the acquisition of the core language system, that is, syntax and phonology. In the meantime, we have to assume they contain some interesting insights but cannot yet account for how the totality of an L2 system is acquired. In sum, the jury is still out.

Limits of Krashen's explanations

Whereas Krashen could have referred us to linguistic theory as far as subconscious knowledge of language was concerned, he could not say much about the mechanisms of conscious learning given the relative dearth of research then in this still thorny area of cognitive science. He also appeared to assume a sharp, black-and-white distinction between conscious and non-conscious modes of processing.

Monitor Theory was an interesting but sketchy claim about how we gain and use conscious knowledge and it was, so its critics asserted, substantiated only by a bare minimum of hard and hotly contested evidence. Also, as regards development, developmental sequences were pretty much magic; no overall explanation was forthcoming at the time. We had to wait for researchers working on German migrant worker data for the first attempt to really explain sequences (e.g. Clahsen, 1984; Meisel *et al.*, 1981; Pienemann, 1984). On the credit side, Krashen's claims were at least interesting, relevant and made a wide impact at the time, and so they have posed useful challenges for researchers that are still unanswered at the time of writing.

Other approaches to metalinguistic ability

Various researchers expressed critical views concerning Krashen's claims. In 1981, for example, Sharwood Smith responded by saying that what he called grammatical 'consciousness-raising' (C-R) as presented by Krashen was too simplistic and that research into the effectiveness or non-effectiveness should proceed with a more fine-grained conceptualization that defined C-R not as a rigid dichotomy but as a range of options along two dimensions: one which had to do with degrees of *explicitness* ranging from the very subtle, indirect cues that might attract the learner's attention to the very explicit, where grammatical forms were pointed out and talked about, and another dimension, namely *elaboration*, which described how much time and space was devoted to the C-R activity by teacher or textbook. Only when research had investigated all the various possibilities allowed by this scheme could we say definitely that drawing the learner's attention to grammar rather than meaning was always ineffective. Sharwood Smith also speculated that learners might be able, metalinguistically, to generate their own input by consciously constructing L2 utterances, use them to communicate, and then acquire the grammar subconsciously according to principles as outlined by Krashen alongside other grammatical forms that were embedded within utterances addressed to them by other speakers (or writers), that is, L2 input in the standard sense of the term.

Later, in 1993, Sharwood Smith proposed that C-R should be replaced by input enhancement in that it focused on what we know, namely that we have manipulated the visible or audible input in some way (any of the ways described along the two dimensions of explicitness and elaboration), and did not presume to describe in advance the actual psychological effect on the learner: what is salient in the input and salient for the observer will ultimately depend on internal mechanisms *in* the learner.

The 1990s

As evidenced by the Doughty and Williams (1998a) book of readings, research into these issues finally got under way in earnest in the second half of the 1990s. The terminology adopted by many for this was based on Long's formulation of the difference between *focus on form(s)* and *focus on form*, the former being the traditional explicit and elaborate focus on grammar and the latter being a strategic and sporadic focus, presumably relatively unelaborated and with varying degrees of explicitness, firmly embedded within a communicative, that is, meaning-oriented, approach to language instruction (Long & Robinson, 1998).

The limitations of explicit focus on form

Despite the promise of breakthroughs, research into focus on form has been plagued with methodological obstacles: for example, too many variables, absence of late post-tests, and so on (see the critique in Trenkic & Sharwood Smith, 2002). It is possible to say in general that some form of explicit instruction has been shown to facilitate learning with regard to given areas of the L2. In fact, the research literature is full of encouraging signals and 'promissory notes' that would appear to go beyond the objective experimental findings, but without a better theoretical backing, researchers risk generalising from short-term effects to long-term success. Varying degrees of doubt have certainly been voiced. Truscott, for example, concludes in 1997 that 'research on form-focussed instruction has produced essentially no evidence that it is helpful and has produced considerable evidence that it is ineffective (though the latter is not entirely conclusive)' (Truscott, 1996, p. 121) and Doughty (2003) concludes her review of instructed SLA with a proposal advocating an indirect, implicit approach to focusing on form, saying that instruction should help to 'organise the learner's processing space' (2003: 298) so that the (adult) learner can pick up on the cues the same way young learners can.

MOGUL: An Overview

Conceptual structure and cognition in general

The MOGUL framework being developed by Sharwood Smith and Truscott aims, among other things, to fill this gap. MOGUL is a real-time processing model that is devised in such a way as to engage coherently with research across a variety of domains.

Following proposals by Ray Jackendoff, it involves a recognition of the existence of a separate, modular language faculty, containing the core phonological and syntactic systems, each of them also being modular in character. It also recognises the crucial importance of 'conceptual structure', which includes the vital semantic and pragmatic dimensions of language, which, in this framework, lie outside this core and allow for the possibility of conscious introspection. Conceptual structure, which provides the support system for our complex mental life (e.g. Jackendoff, 1987; Pinker, 1997), is also linked with representations that have their basis in the senses: sounds, tactile and olfactory sensations, and visual images. All of this is best illustrated by considering dreams where not only thoughts are invoked, but also a multitude of sensations that have no basis in what is happening outside us. In other words, sounds and images have an independent existence in our minds and the virtual sensory experiences we have must be supported by something that triggers them from 'inside' rather than from outside in the external environment. The necessary perceptual (visual, auditory, and so on) representations that fulfil this role will be crucial when the issue of metalinguistic knowledge is considered.

Constraints imposed upon conscious introspection

First, the basic ways in which we process and acquire language according to MOGUL will be briefly considered (for a fuller account, see Truscott & Sharwood Smith, 2004a, 2004b). It should be stressed that the MOGUL account draws on a range of existing research findings and research proposals from various disciplines; this is why it is perhaps more of a unifying 'framework' than a theory in its own right. The important thing at this juncture is that we have conscious access, and can attend to the contents of conceptual structure that encompasses much of what is normally understood as semantics and pragmatics, and also as the perceptual structures that derive from our perceptual/sensory systems. By the same token, we have no conscious access to and cannot attend to any aspect of what happens within the core phonological and syntactic modules any more than we can inspect what is happening during perceptual processing. The question then is what is happening when we talk about, and think about grammar?

Processing and growth in MOGUL

The core systems that lie at the heart of the language faculty are the phonological and syntactic modules. In processing terms, these each contain a processor that manipulates structure, and a 'database' or memory store of structures that, when activated and placed in working memory, become accessible to the processor. The two systems just referred to are linked by an interface processor, which has the job of putting a syntactic structure and a phonological structure 'in registration' with each other. As with everything else in the core language system, interface processing is, and can only be subconscious. The net result of this particular interface process is a chain of two structures: a PS (phonological structure) from phonological memory ('sublexicon' as it were) and an SS (syntactic structure) from syntactic memory, which form two elements of a tripartite structure familiar from the traditional lexical entry. Hence, a chain consisting of /hit/ and $[V^{transitive}]$, say, needs just a CS (conceptual structure), from the memory store of meanings, to supply its semantic and pragmatic characteristics. Whereas a traditional lexical item or entry integrates these three aspects of structure, in a Jackendoff system these are isolated in separate modules so that the interface systems that link modules are not converting or translating anything, because PS code is unintelligible to the syntactic module and SS code is unintelligible to the phonological module. That is why the term 'registration' is used (Jackendoff, 1987). This shows briefly how modularised is the core of linguistic system. In other words, we do not just have a single 'language module', but rather a set of two modules, each of which is autonomous so that phonological processing is done in phonological code, which is 'unintelligible' not only to processes beyond the core language system but is also unintelligible to its sister, syntactic module. In exactly the same way, the phonological module cannot make sense of syntactic code. The syntactic module just tries to 'make sense of', that is, it builds larger structures out of, whatever syntactic structures happen to come into syntactic working memory as a result of activity in the phonological module. This means that you can never have hybrid structures built out of different codes but rather chains linking different types of structures. The job of the interfaces is simply to identify that a structure in one module should be chained with a structure in an adjoining module. At the end of the line, in input processing terms, is a flow of conceptual structures popping into conceptual working memory, thanks to the operation of the interface between syntactic and conceptual systems. Conceptual structures, once triggered, do impact upon consciousness, so we may become aware of meanings without any access to the elaborate phonological and syntactic activity that has brought them into being. We have access only to the output of conceptual activity. This is, of course, just the basic idea; the precise details of how consciousness works still eludes even the finest minds.

Four basic aspects of the system as a whole are important to keep in mind. First, processing is *bidirectional*, not only accounting for both comprehension and production but also for repeated attempts to build representations for a complex or unfamiliar piece of input, involving going back and forth through the modules, until a satisfactory representation is found. Secondly, the processors will attempt to build a representation for input *in any way they can*, even if this means mixing language systems and putting in structures that are not perceived but ought to be there to make an intelligible, well-formed construction. Thirdly, *processing directly affects growth*; every representation that is achieved for familiar or unfamiliar input will result in acquisition of some sort, that is, the creation of new structures in the memory stores referred to above or the reinforcing of predicting structures (Truscott & Sharwood Smith, 2004a, 2004b). Growth may be transitory if there is no repeated experience to build it up further. What has been 'acquired' may only be acquired for a fleeting moment. It is a 'use-it-or-lose-it' system. Finally, (phonological and syntactic) structures are created for unfamiliar input in a way that is constrained by the architecture of the language faculty, so Jackendoff, and hence MOGUL, subscribes to the notion of *universal grammar constraints*.

This, very briefly, is the way in which acquisition and language growth is conceived in MOGUL. The processing of PSs and SSs takes place beyond the range of conscious introspection and so any attempt to influence its operations directly, by explicit input enhancement, say, is doomed to failure, and so far this is supported by mainstream research in SLA. What then should we make of the psycholinguistically fuzzy notion of metalinguistic knowledge?

Building the metagrammar

As any introductory course in linguistics will tell its students, assuming the primacy of speech, grammar is a way of systematically associating sounds and meanings. If this process is normally done by the system as described above to develop mental grammars of the L1 and any subsequent language through exposure to utterances in the relevant language, then what are the sounds and meanings involved in metalinguistic, or metagrammatical development? By definition, they must be accessible to conscious introspection and this possibility, also by definition, has been excluded in the case of 'normal' language acquisition. Put another way, when we talk about or think about, say, the position of a word in a sentence or what ending should go on a particular verb or whether the definite article has been used correctly, it cannot be that we are consciously inspecting grammatical structure in the sense used above. The grammatical structure that our minds assemble in milliseconds on-line in order to process utterances (for production or comprehension) is absolutely inaccessible to conscious introspection. On might say that it just has to be so for extremely fast and efficient language use to be possible. And it should be added, however slowly and phlegmatically an utterance is produced, there is still no conscious access to its fine phonological and syntactic structure. All this strongly suggests that the kind of grammar we can talk and introspect about is a different kind of grammar entirely and must be plausibly accounted for in a quite different way. How then are sounds and meaning associated systematically to enable us to actually talk about and consciously analyse linguistic structure?

The processing of different types of sound

It is important in any linguistic analysis to distinguish various stages between the moment when sound strikes the ear and the phonological structure of a word like /hit/. One stage in MOGUL is auditory structure, which is a generic sound structure that, in addition to supporting actual physical stimuli emanating from the environment, also supports illusions of sounds, sounds conjured up intentionally or unintentionally in one's thoughts or dreams and of which we can become aware. Auditory structure (AS) might constitute a preliminary stage prior to the matching of non-linguistic sound to linguistic (i.e. phonological) structure (PS). Another possibility is that the auditory-acoustic stage of processing leads two ways.[2] Anything that can be matched up with PS is matched up, while, at the same time, auditory structure is derived from the self-same source to produce non-linguistic sound structures that can, in turn, be linked up with conceptual structures reflecting 'breaking glass', 'creaking door', and so forth.[3] From this it will be seen that, either way, a word like 'hit' has an auditory structure separate from the PS /hit/. If the listener does not know English, 'hit' may retain its character of an unfamiliar auditory structure until that learner has managed to associate it with some PS. In fact, we can become most intensely aware of a word's auditory structure when we do not in fact understand it. When we do understand it, we may still have some awareness of how it sounds, its AS in other words, but one thing is certain: we have no access to its linguistic (phonological) structure, its PS. It follows from this that we cannot consciously manipulate our linguistic knowledge of its sound structure in any direct fashion, because both PS and SS are inaccessible to conscious introspection. This explains why attempts to raise the learner's awareness of the phonological structure of a word do not produce any guarantee of phonological development, and, of course, the same goes for the development of syntax.

In short, every word has a sound of which we can become aware, and this sound is not to be confused with its phonetic and phonological structure. This distinction is important when we come to accounting for how metalinguistic grammars are built up in the mind. Whereas we cannot become aware of the linguistic structure underlying a word or string of words, which is processed within the closed-off phonological and syntactic modules, it seems that we *can* become aware of its auditory structure, to the extent we can describe the word(s) as 'hissing' or 'buzzing' or 'sing-song' or 'loud' or 'quiet' or 'creaky', and so forth, the very same types of terms we might use to describe some non-linguistic sound.

Associating sounds and meanings

MOGUL offers a principled account of how sounds and meanings can be consciously manipulated for the purposes of grammatical structure. Metagrammars are developed by systematically associating the *auditory structure* of words with *conceptual structures*, both of which are accessible to conscious introspection. A new system has to be assembled where sounds (and letters) are coupled systematically with meanings to create a grammar linked up with but outside the core language system. In addition, new conceptual structures are needed, that is, metalinguistic concepts, which will be manifested in the way we think and speak about grammar and also in the need for new words. For even a rudimentary metagrammar, we also need a terminology, for example, WORD and WORD ORDER, as well as the pre-existing conceptual structures like 'LAMP' 'UNDER'. Some of these terms will reflect metalinguistic processes needed to arrange these into complexes like 'UNDER + THE' + ' LAMP' rather than 'LAMP' + 'THE + UNDER' as appropriate. In this way, we end up with two grammars in MOGUL: one impenetrable system or set of systems that grows naturally in response to language input and is constrained by processes that are beyond our direct, conscious control, and the other, which develops via conscious processes and which is accordingly open to manipulation either by ourselves or others influencing us in a very conscious and deliberate manner (see related discussion in Sharwood Smith, 2002).

Note that we can also, by enlisting the help of our metagrammar, assemble or interpret utterances and texts in a manner that exceeds the resources of our core language system. This is most graphically illustrated by what is possible with a dead language such as Latin or Ancient Greek, where sophisticated sentences can be produced by a meticulous application of consciously learned rules of grammar to selected lexical items, sentences that would probably not emerge in spontaneous production nor would they be successfully interpreted if uttered by a (ghostly) native speaker (Sharwood Smith, 1996). However, it should also be added, and this complicates the picture somewhat, that although it is intuitively appealing, metagrammatical knowledge, like any other knowledge open to conscious introspection, is subject to automatisation such that it can be fluently used. In other words, speakers can become metalinguistically fluent. Indeed, metalinguistic fluency to some extent is a defining characteristic of all literate language users, although high degrees of such fluency are reserved for the specially gifted, such as orators, stand-up comedians, and successful writers, whereas fluency in the sense of rapid, efficient use of our subconscious, core language system core language abilities is the preserve of virtually everybody, although it will obviously be less impressive where someone is not especially coherent in the way they put their thoughts together, in other words, people who are not particularly conceptually fluent. The main point here is that, to the extent that one can become skilful in at least some areas of metagrammar, the MOGUL account departs from the Krashen account where Monitor use is typically dysfluent.

Conclusion

As suggested at the outset of this chapter, MOGUL promises a more fine-grained explanation of the mechanisms involved in metalinguistic ability than has been the case so far. It is one that meshes with much research into the possibilities and limitations of intervention in L2 grammar instruction. What, in sum, *is* metalinguistic knowledge within the MOGUL perspective? It is a conceptual system built up via introspection and (often) some training. It follows the same principles as any other conceptual system (can be implicit, explicit, declarative, procedural). It is quite separate from dedicated modular systems that interface with the outside world (sound, touch, smell, vision), and the workings of these systems are not directly accessible to conscious introspection. It is, however, necessarily *connected* with (interfaced with) the modular system that lies at the heart of the language faculty. In a sense, it is parasitic upon it, as are all metalinguistic functions, including the ability to produce a fine after-dinner speech and a complex sentence in Ancient Greek. You cannot possess metalinguistic knowledge in the absence of any linguistic knowledge. In L1 acquisition, linguistic development must necessarily precede metalinguistic development. Also, as we actually use metalinguistic knowledge, the subconscious language system cannot possibly stay dormant. The reverse is not true. We can be metalinguistically ignorant but still able to use our core language system to communicate, and we can use our core language system without necessarily activating any metalinguistic knowledge we might possess. We are also free to attribute to metalinguistic development the theoretical concepts that have been developed in cognitive psychological models that do not themselves acknowledge the domain specificity of language, as long as we appreciate that such development, however skilful the learners may become, takes place outside the core language system and is not guided or constrained by it. The extent to which this metalinguistic development complements, extends, or inhibits core language development is another important issue that will, for the moment, have to be left until another occasion.

Notes

1. MOGUL stands for Modular On-line Growth and Use of Language (Truscott & Sharwood Smith 2004a, 2004b; Sharwood Smith 2004).
2. This was suggested to me by John Truscott and is the version we both favour now. So, as we hear the sound of a word, we process it *simultaneously* as

sound and as a string of phonological structures. In other words, the auditory processors and the phonological processors both feed off the acoustic information coming in at the same time, independently. One stage does not precede the other.
3. The same type of solution is worth considering with respect to the processing of music.

Chapter 2
Multi-Competence: Black Hole or Wormhole for Second Language Acquisition Research?

VIVIAN COOK

The purpose of this chapter is to present some of the basic ideas and research associated with the multi-competence view of second language acquisition (SLA). If these are taken seriously, much of existing SLA research could disappear into a black hole, as its methods and results are partial, suspect, or irrelevant. Perhaps, however, there is a wormhole through which SLA research can escape to another universe...

Multi-Competence

The common-sense belief about people speaking a second language is that they are imperfect imitations of native speakers, embodied in a typical Chomsky quotation:

> We do not for example say that the person has a perfect knowledge of some language L similar to English but still different from it. What we say is that the child or foreigner has a 'partial knowledge of English' or is 'on his or her way' towards acquiring knowledge of English, and if they reach this goal, they will then know English. (Chomsky, 1986: 16)

The goal of SLA is then to acquire the language as spoken by the native speaker; 'English' or 'Spanish' is what native speakers know so all second language (L2) learners can do is try to become like them.

The first challenge to this was the concept of the 'independent language assumption' that learners are not wilfully distorting the target system, nor arbitrarily selecting bits of the system, but are inventing a system of their own, mooted by McNeill (1966) and others in the 1960s for the first language (L1) and captured in the term 'interlanguage' (Selinker, 1972) for the second language. L2 learners do indeed speak interlanguages that do not correspond to established languages such as Spanish or English, with unique grammars, phonologies, and so on. These are not just 'partial' grammars of the L2 any more than the three-year-old child's L1 grammar is a partial grammar; rather, they are grammars with their own properties, created by the learners out of their own internal processes in response to the L2 data they receive. Klein and Perdue (1997), for instance, demonstrated that L2 users of five L2s speaking six L1s produced the same basic interlanguage grammar. Figure 2.1 represents this interlanguage as independent from both L1 and L2 and related to a host of other factors and processes internal to the learner's mind.

The concept of multi-competence originally arose out of what seemed an anomaly, with Figure 2.1 considered in the context of the poverty-of-the-stimulus argument (Cook, 1991). The L1, the interlanguage, and the other mental processes are all internal to the L2 learner; the L2 is, however, known by someone else, a native speaker of that language. Hence the figure is obscuring a major difference in its components. For it to make sense we needed a name for a complex mental state including the L1 and the L2 interlanguage, but excluding the L2. Hence the term multi-competence was originally coined to reflect this totality in one mind, originally expressed as 'the compound state of a mind with two grammars' (Cook, 1991), as shown in the redrawn Figure 2.2. However, the word 'grammar' led to some confusion, as it was used in the Chomskyan sense of the total knowledge of language in the mind rather than just syntax. Hence multi-competence is usually defined nowadays as 'knowledge of two languages in one mind', to make it clear that it is not restricted to syntax.

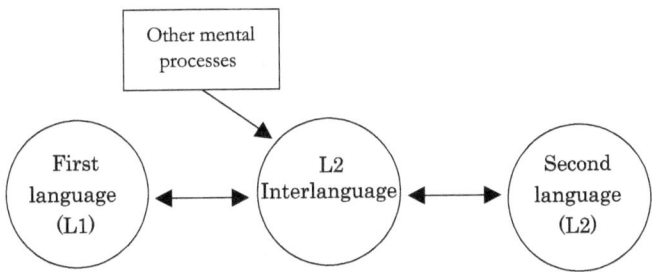

Figure 2.1 The learner's independent language (interlanguage)

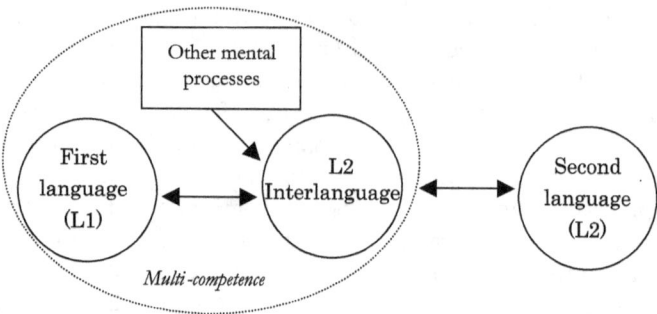

Figure 2.2 Multi-competence

Development of the Multi-Competence Idea

Once multi-competence had been proposed, it gradually became clear that it had a number of repercussions for SLA research. These have developed over the past 15 years into a solid set of research and ideas that start from the point that the mind of the L2 user is different from that of the monolingual native speaker.

Re-evaluating the native speaker norm

Cook (1999) asked why, if the L2 user's interlanguage is independent, it should be measured against the native speaker? In SLA research it was common to speak about the learner as a failure for not being like a native speaker. To take three representative quotations: 'When human beings later in life try, sometimes very hard, to acquire these very same abilities, most will not succeed, and they will be betrayed by their non-native accent' (Sebastián-Gallés & Bosch, 2005: 68); 'After all, the ultimate goal – perhaps unattainable for some – is, nonetheless, to 'sound like a native speaker' in all aspects of the language' (González-Nueno, 1997: 261); 'Relative to native speaker's linguistic competence, learners' interlanguage is deficient by definition' (Kasper & Kellerman, 1997: 5). So, showing L2 learners have access to Universal Grammar means demonstrating that they possess identical knowledge to that of native speakers (Cook & Newson, 2007). Even with the interlanguage assumption alone, the relationship with the native speaker's competence is indirect, because the L2 is simply one part in the equation rather than the necessary target. With multi-competence, the competence of a monolingual native speaker became in a sense irrelevant; it was the competence of the successful L2 user that mattered. Of course, this begs the question of the difficulty of defining exactly what a successful L2 user might be, perhaps as chimerical as the native speaker, as several people have pointed out (e.g. Han, 2004a). This issue is debated further in Cook (2006a, 2006b) in terms of the de Saussurean combination of the social and psychological faces of language: 'Le langage a un côté individuel et un côté social, et l'on ne peut concevoir l'un sans l'autre' (de Saussure, 1976: 24).

This argument was extended in Cook (1997) to the methodology of SLA research. Virtually all the L2 research techniques employed to date relied on the native speaker, such as:

- Error Analysis, which normally defines error as deviation from native speaker norms;
- obligatory occurrence, defined as when native speakers would usually produce something;
- grammaticality judgements, defined against native speakers; and
- elicited imitation, measured against what native speakers produce.

There is no reason why one thing cannot be compared to another; it may be useful to discover the similarities and differences between apples and pears. SLA research can use comparison with the native speaker as a tool, partly because so much is already known about monolingual native speakers. The danger is regarding it as failure not to meet the standards of natives: apples do not make very good pears. Comparing L2 users with monolingual native speakers can yield a useful list of similarities and differences, but never establish the unique aspects of second language knowledge that are not present in the monolingual; moreover, there is a potential trap of being too dependent on comparison as a research tool (Han, 2004a, 2004b). Hence, to respect the multi-competence idea, we can never regard an L2 user as an unsuccessful native speaker, only as a different kind of person in their own right, an extrapolation of Labov's argument about difference between speakers not entailing deficit (Labov, 1969). So the term 'L2 user' often became preferred to 'L2 learner', because it allows the person to achieve a final state rather than to be a perpetual 'learner' always on the way to native speaker status, but doomed never to get there.

Seeing transfer as a two-way process

The next development in work on multi-competence was to look at the relationship between the L1 and the interlanguage in the mind of the L2 user. Weinreich (1953) had talked about interference as 'those instances of deviation from the norms of either language which occur in the speech of bilinguals as a result of their familiarity with more than one language'

(Weinreich, 1953: 1). A large industry of SLA research traced the properties of the interlanguage back to the learner's first language. Contrastive Analysis attempted to predict interference when the systems of the two languages were different and sometimes when they had slight but crucial differences. Error Analysis retained the L1 as probably the strongest source of errors. Researchers in the early 1970s, however, tended to take a position closer to interlanguage by insisting that sequences of acquisition such as grammatical morphemes development did not depend on the first language, as indeed was shown by Klein and Perdue (1997) in a very different approach.

Yet people had not really absorbed a crucial part of Weinreich's message: interference goes in two directions. The L2 interlanguage affects the L1 as well as the L1 affecting the L2. The exception was the tradition of attrition research, defined, say, as 'dysfluency and the inability to retrieve lexicon, the inability to pronounce the L1 with a NS pronunciation, the production of syntax that would not be acceptable to NSs and the inability to make judgments of grammaticality in the same way that NS monolinguals would' (Seliger, 1996: 606). From a multi-competence perspective, this assumes that L1 changes are a matter of loss and 'inabilities', not arising from the complexity of a new combined system. The usual dictionary definition of attrition involves 'the action of grinding down, by friction', particularly in 'war of attrition'. Why is this considered loss? Because this is not how a native speaker would do it. Changes in the L1 can only be for the bad.

Reconceptualised as the influence of the L2 interlanguage on the first language transfer, sometimes known as 'reverse transfer', it became an exciting new research question, as shown in the papers in Cook (2003), based on a paradigm of comparing L2 users with monolinguals in their L1, not with native speakers of the L2. A later section will present some of the evidence for this from different angles. Overall, it became clear that the L1 in the mind of an L2 user was by no means the same as the L1 in the mind of a monolingual native speaker. Although it is hard to make value judgements, many of the changes were to the benefit of the L2 user, such as helping L1 reading development (Yelland *et al.*, 1993), raising the standards of L1 essays (Kecskes & Papp, 2000), and increasing creativity (Lambert *et al.*, 1973).

Looking at the L2 user's mind

A further shift in multi-competence research has been to take in other aspects of the L2 user's mind under the banner of 'bilingual cognition'. The 1990s saw a revival of the debate over how language is linked to thinking. Levinson (1996) produced startling results that there were groups that used absolute direction based on points of the compass rather than relative direction based on the speaker's own body. Roberson et al. (2000) showed that people from Papua New Guinea looked at colours differently from other groups. Everett (2005) discovered that Pirahã speakers had no idea of number. In other words, human beings from different cultures and from different first languages in some respects think differently. Often, of course, this is a matter of preference for a particular way of thinking rather than absolute inability: Norenzayan et al. (2002) established that Chinese people preferred intuitive reasoning rather than formal reasoning.

So what happens if someone speaks two languages or has two cultures? Perhaps the thinking style is so engrained in their minds that they continue to use the same style after acquiring a second language. Perhaps they switch, thinking in one style or another depending on situation. Or perhaps they have some merged intermediate style that is neither the first nor the second but something in between – an 'intercognition' if you like. Raising this question has led to a new wave of research comparing the thought processes of L2 users and monolinguals. As well as contributing to SLA research, this may also provide a way of tackling the culture versus language divide by seeing whether a change of language without a cultural change leads to a change of thinking.

Applying multi-competence to language teaching

Over time, the implications of the multi-competence approach for language teaching have become clearer. One aspect was the use of the first language in the classroom. The traditional view of language teaching going back to the late 19th century had insisted that the L2 was learnt in isolation from the L1: the model was always of complete separation. Hence, despite their other differences, teaching methods from the Direct Method to the audiolingual method to task-based learning were united in ignoring the first language already present in all the learners' minds invisibly in the classroom.

Yet, despite the official advice from the authorities to minimise L1 use, teachers continued to make use of it while teaching, while harbouring feelings of guilt, as Macaro (1997) documents. If there are many possible relationships between the two languages as well as separation, if the L2 interlanguage is indissolubly wedded to the L1 in most L2 learners' and users' minds, separation is a misguided common-sense view of SLA rather than something to be imposed upon all learners. Cook (2001) called for a rational evaluation of the ways in which the L1 could be used in the classroom, such as providing a short cut for giving instructions and explanations where the cost of the L2 is too great, building up the interlinked L1 and L2 knowledge in the students' minds, carrying out learning tasks through collaborative dialogue with fellow students, and developing L2 activities such as code-switching for later real-life use.

This leads into the fundamental issues of the purpose of language teaching and of the target that the learner is aiming at (Cook, 2007). The crucial point is basing the target on what learners are going to be, L2 users, not on what they can never be, monolingual native speakers of the L2. L2 users have distinctive uses for language, such as translating and code-switching; they can do more with language than any monolingual. Although some L2 users may need to speak to native speakers of the L2, they rarely need to pass as natives, even though this may still be a personal goal for many. For languages like English and French, however, the need is often to speak to fellow L2 users. English is a useful lingua franca for much of the globe. Sometimes, indeed, speakers of the same L1 may choose to use an L2 to each other, as happens with Arabic-speaking businessmen communicating in English e-mails between countries. Language teaching goals, teaching methods, and coursebooks need to look at the achievable goal of creating L2 users. Hence, as the papers in Llurda (2005) attest, the day of the native speaker teacher may be over; the NS teacher is not a good model of an L2 user who has got there by the same route that the students will take and *ceteri paribus* does not have the appropriate experience or insight into the students' situation. Indeed, 'in the new rapidly emerging climate native speakers may be identified as part of the problem rather than the source of a solution' (Graddol, 2006: 114). Further discussion of multi-competence in language teaching will be found in Cook (2007, in press).

Differences of the L2 User from the Monolingual Native Speaker

As the discussion so far will have made obvious, the core concept is the L2 user – 'any person who uses another language than his or her first language (L1), that is to say, the one learnt first as a child' (Cook, 2002: 1). L2 users can be airline pilots communicating with the control tower in an L2, opera singers singing in another language, reporters for CNN, children translating for their parents in medical consultations, Samuel Beckett writing in French, refugees in camps, diplomats in embassies ... In other words, they are as diverse as any other arbitrary collection of human beings and probably outnumber the monolingual native speakers of the world.

The term 'L2 user' was originally intended to counteract the implication that people with a second language are learners for life and to give them an equal status with people with an L1. This is not to say that the same person cannot be both an L2 learner in a classroom and an L2 user in the street outside. Nor are 'multi-competence' or 'L2 user' related to a level of success in the second language, certainly not reserved either for 'balanced bilinguals' or for 'native passers'. Doubtless both of these exist, but they do not seem characteristic of the broad mass of L2 users; far too much time has been spent on this select few in the past.

The previous section alluded to some of the characteristics of L2 users that set them apart from monolinguals in the first language. Let us now try to give a brief overview of some of these.

The lexicon

Considerable research effort has gone into the question of how the L1 and L2 lexicons are related, primarily within the psychological tradition (De Groot, 2002). The usual question is how many lexicons are involved – one lexicon for the first language, one for the second, a single lexicon for both, or various amounts of overlap between the languages. In terms of word recognition, 'a large majority [of results is] in favour of a bilingual model of visual word recognition with an integrated lexicon in which access is language non-selective (parallel access to words of both languages)' (van Heuven, 2005). That is to say, when English L2 users of French read the word *chat*, they do not at first know whether it is the English word meaning 'talk' or the French word meaning 'cat'. For our purposes, the crucial point is that neither of the two lexicons is ever completely off-line, but is always present at some level of activation, whichever language is actually being used. Spivey and Marian (1999) tracked the eye movements of bilinguals naming pictures in their L1, showing they moved to distractors that had similar forms to L2 words. The L2 user has a different vocabulary network in their mind, which at some level combines both languages; hence neither L1 nor L2 lexicons will be the same as those of monolingual native speakers of the L1 or L2. Reaction time for a word is sensitive to the frequency of its cognate in a second language (Caramazza & Brones, 1979). Laufer (2003) documented the effects of L2 Hebrew on L1 Russian vocabulary; for example, *telephone* in Russian became wrongly connected with *close*, since in Hebrew you *close the telephone* when you hang up on someone.

Pragmatics

The way that people convey meanings through the first language is also affected by the second language they know. For example, English speakers of Japanese use *aizuchi* (nodding for agreement) when talking English (Locastro, 1987). Pavlenko (2003) asked L1 speakers of Russian in Russia and the United States to describe films, finding *inter alia* that 'L2 influence on L1 prompted some study participants to frame emotions linguistically as states, rather than as active processes, violating both semantic and syntactic constraints of Russian'. She quotes the Polish–English writer Eva Hoffman as saying 'When I speak Polish now, it is infiltrated, permeated, and inflected by the English in my head. Each language modifies the other, crossbreeds with it, fertilizes it. Each language makes the other relative' (Hoffman, 1989: 273).

Phonology

Perhaps the most studied area of L2 influence on L1 is phonology. The study of voiced onset time (VOT) for plosive consonants has shown that the timings of L2 users neither match the target language VOTs fully nor retain their first language VOTs completely, supported by research ranging over Spanish/English (Zampini & Green, 2001), Hebrew/English (Obler, 1982), and German/Spanish (Kehoe *et al.*, 2004). Indeed, the original VOTs for monolinguals often come from bilingual subjects in the United States tested in their L1 and hence are inaccurate as a measure of monolingual native speaker (Kato, 2004). More recently, similar effects have been found for intonation. There are differences in the intonation patterns in Dutch of Dutch people who speak Greek (Mennen, 2004) and in German of German children who speak Turkish (Queen, 2001).

Syntax

A variety of studies from different approaches have shown that the L1 grammar of L2 users is no longer the same as that of monolingual native speakers. Within the UG approach, Tsimpli *et al.* (2004) looked at the effects of learning an L2 that does not allow null subjects (non-pro-drop) on an L1 that allows them (pro-drop); 'near-native' Greek learners of English produced far more definite preverbal subjects in Greek than monolingual native speakers, similar to what Cook *et al.* (2005) found for Japanese users of English judging sentences with and without subjects. Balcom (2003) studied how French speakers who know English react against French sentences using the middle voice *Un tricot de laine se lave à l'eau froide* (A wool sweater washes in cold water) compared to those who do not know English. Using a Competition Model paradigm (MacWhinney, 2005), Cook *et al.* (2003) found that Japanese, Greek and Spanish speakers of English prefer the first noun to be the subject of the sentence in *The dog pats the tree* (translated into their respective languages) to a greater extent than those who do not know English. Whether measured in a principles and parameters model of competence or the Competition Model of processing, the L2 user's knowledge of the L1 differs from that of the monolingual.

Writing system

So far, the impact of learning a second writing system (L2WS) on the first language has been little studied. L2WS readers of English are better at detecting word-final silent <e>s in text than English L1WS readers (Cook, 2004). Italian readers of L2WS English are less affected by phonological foils than English L1WS readers in English word recognition tasks (Sasaki, 2005). Chinese L2 users of English segment 'words' differently in Chinese compared to L1WS Chinese (Bassetti, 2004). In addition, some research has uncovered general beneficial effects on L1 literacy; English children taught Italian learn to read English faster (Yelland *et al.*, 1993) and Hungarian children who were taught English learnt to write better essays in Hungarian (Kecskes & Papp, 2000).

Concepts

An active new area of L2 user research is the area of bilingual cognition research, building on the 1990s wave of research into whether language is related to thinking mentioned above. In the area of colour perception, Athanasopoulos (2001) showed that Greek L2 users of English had a different perception of the colour 'blue' from monolinguals, Athanasopoulos *et al.* (2004) claimed that Japanese L2 users of English distinguished between two 'blue' and two 'green' colours differently from monolingual native speakers. Cook *et al.* (2006) looked at categorisation of shapes and substances, finding that Japanese subjects who had been in England longer than three years categorised objects more in terms of shape than Japanese who had been there less than three years. Athanasopoulos (2006) turned to number to show that Japanese learners of English move with level of English towards the English preference for counting objects rather than substance. Using another language means your thinking is changed in some respects.

Conclusions

At one level, then, little of the current SLA research is acceptable to a multi-competence perspective, essentially because of the insidious presence of the native speaker in the imagined target of SLA and in the methodology of research. If we are interested in L2 users and L2 acquisition rather than closeness to native speakers, we need to start from the mind of the L2 user in all its richness and complexity.

Multi-competence ideas have spawned new research questions about the nature of the L2 and the L1 and the relationships between them. Sometimes current or past areas of SLA research can be reinterpreted from a multi-competence perspective, for example, attrition. Multi-competence is a liberating process for SLA research in that it opens many doors and establishes SLA not only independently of the language of native speakers but also as the core case of language acquisition, of which monolingual acquisition is a pale and limited version. SLA research is being destroyed by the black hole, but is coming out the other side through a wormhole reconstituted into something else – the central area concerned with human acquisition of languages. As Julia Kristeva once remarked, 'Speaking another language is quite simply the minimum and primary condition for being alive'.

Chapter 3
Transfer Appropriate Processing as a Model for Classroom Second Language Acquisition

PATSY MARTIN LIGHTBOWN

Research in cognitive psychology is increasingly influential in second language acquisition (SLA) studies. It is one source of valuable guidelines for research in the classroom, helping us to shape the questions we ask about how language is learned, processed, remembered, used, and, in some cases, apparently forgotten. Psychological research on learning and retrieving what we have learned can provide insights into the processes underlying the learning that occurs in different types of second/foreign language instruction.

In this chapter, some psychological perspectives on memory – learning and retrieving information – are examined for their relevance to second language acquisition and instruction. The emphasis is on *transfer appropriate processing* (TAP). The fundamental tenet of TAP is that we can better remember what we have learned if the cognitive processes that are active during learning are similar to those that are active during retrieval (Blaxton, 1989; Morris *et al.*, 1977). On the one hand, this suggests that learning to use language in a communicative context may improve the ability to retrieve it in such contexts (Segalowitz & Lightbown, 1999). On the other hand, TAP may also offer a way of explaining why learners in communicative, content- and task-based language learning environments have difficulty in the acquisition of some features of the target language (e.g. Barcroft, 2006; Trofimovich, 2005; VanPatten, 1990).

To be sure, we cannot simply transfer the findings of research in cognitive psychology to second language classroom practice. Studies in psychology, linguistics, general education, and even some SLA research can help us form questions about how languages can be taught most effectively, but we can understand the real relevance of this research only by carrying out studies in classrooms where languages are taught and learned (Lightbown, 2000). Carefully controlled conditions for studies in cognitive psychology are very different from the conditions that are typical of classrooms. More importantly, perhaps, the *objects* of learning in those studies are often extremely simple when compared to the complexity of a natural language, which is the object of second and foreign language learning. It is one thing to learn a list of words or phrases and remember the items on that list a few minutes later. It is quite another to learn second language words or phrases and then retrieve them in the middle of an ongoing conversation, correctly integrated into a morphosyntactic frame within a pragmatically and sociolinguistically complex interaction, before the conversation moves on to another topic. And language learners want to be able to do this days, weeks, or months after the material was learned in the classroom.

Mismatches between the conditions in which learning takes place and the conditions in which learning is used or assessed have been the focus of transfer appropriate processing research. Even though the findings from laboratory studies do not directly parallel language acquisition that takes place in classroom environments, the research can be helpful in understanding the effectiveness of different types of instruction for learning different language features and for the retrieval of what has been learned in different situations.

Matching Conditions for Language Learning and Language Use

For more than 30 years, pedagogical practice and second language research have emphasized the value of language learning that takes place in situations where learners are actually engaged in using language rather than in learning word lists and grammar rules in anticipation of using the language at some future time. This includes instructional models such as content-based instruction or a version of communicative language teaching in which there is essentially no form-focused language teaching and students are expected to learn language 'incidentally', while their attention is focused on meaning (Howatt, 1984; Snow *et al.*, 1992). Form-focused instruction that is *isolated* from communicative language use has become rare in many classrooms (Lightbown & Spada, 2006). The preference is to *integrate* form focus into a communicative context (Long & Robinson, 1998). One approach to language teaching that has been strongly criticised is the kind of mechanical drill in which students repeat sentences that are related only by the fact that they share some grammatical pattern (Lightbown, 1985; Long, 1991; Wong & VanPatten, 2003). DeKeyser (1998: 53–54) makes this point particularly well when he says, 'Drills make sense only if they are defined in terms of behaviors to be drilled ... but [audiolingual methodologists] forgot to define the behaviors they wanted to establish ... *conveying personal meaning*'.

There is wide agreement that when language form is learned in isolation, it is not readily available for use in communicative interaction. There is less agreement about a related hypothesis: that language features that are first learned as explicit, declarative knowledge can, through practice, *become* proceduralised and accessible for communicative use, that is, retrieved automatically, without conscious attention to the declarative knowledge. Some SLA researchers conclude that it cannot (Krashen, 1982), but others contend that the jury is still out (N. Ellis, 2005, for a review). DeKeyser (2003: 329) contends that '... there is no evidence in the SLA literature that explicit learning and practice *cannot* lead to automatized procedural knowledge, only a dearth of evidence that it can ... Absence of evidence is not evidence of absence'.

One of the reasons for the lack of evidence is that, in both teaching and research settings, success continues to be measured in terms of discrete points of language in isolated explicit test situations rather than in contexts calling for automatized procedural knowledge of language in spontaneous language production. There are good reasons for this – both practical and theoretical. In practical terms, it is far easier for teachers and researchers to ask students to fill in the blanks or make a choice between grammatical and ungrammatical sentences than it is to solicit (and record and transcribe and analyse) samples of spontaneous speech. The theoretical reasons to prefer discrete point measures come from the importance in hypothesis-testing research of ensuring that the conditions for assessment are as nearly identical as possible across the groups being compared. But there can be a cost to using explicit, discrete point types of measures. They may not adequately answer questions about the extent to which different kinds of instruction prepare learners to use the language under other conditions. Doughty (2003) reviewed the studies that were included in Norris and Ortega's (2000) comprehensive meta-analysis of research on the effect of instruction and concluded that the studies overwhelmingly used 'explicit' assessment instruments, even when the researchers' intention was to assess an 'implicit' approach to instruction. As Norris and Ortega point out, the evidence suggests that the predominance of explicit testing may not be solely responsible for the finding that explicit instruction appeared to be more effective.

Nevertheless, TAP suggests that limiting assessment to this kind of testing may fail to capture at least some of what has actually been learned.[1]

Levels of Processing and Transfer Appropriate Processing

TAP can be understood within a broader framework of information processing theory. It is often contrasted with the *levels of processing* (LOP) approach to research on learning and retrieval (Craik, 2002; Lockhart, 2002; Roediger *et al.*, 2002). Both approaches include the assumption that the human mind has a limited capacity for processing information: we cannot notice, pay attention to, process, or remember everything we are exposed to. Thus, in any given learning event, we encode (store in long-term memory) some information, while other information goes unencoded or, in any case, is encoded less effectively, making it less available for retrieval. Some of what we encode will be what we intended to learn. However, sometimes to our advantage and sometimes to our disadvantage, other information will be encoded incidentally, while our intentional efforts are focused elsewhere. Thus, although the sum total of what is learned in a classroom represents only a subset of the information that is present in the learning environment, it is not always the subset that the teacher intends for students to learn that is actually internalised.

Research on LOP has a long and rich history in the study of learning and retrieving what we have learned. A paper by Craik and Lockhart (1972) established a framework for this line of research, and scores – possibly hundreds – of studies have been carried out within it. For example, Craik and Tulving's (1975) study exemplifies the kind of research in this approach. In that study, participants were asked 'orienting' questions such as 'Does the word rhyme with train?' or 'Is the word a type of flower?' before seeing the words in a list. When the orienting question drew attention to the form of a word (e.g. whether it rhymed with *train*), participants were not very good at remembering whether they had seen the word before when they were asked – unexpectedly – to identify the words they had seen in the experiment and those they had not seen. When the orienting question drew attention to the semantic properties of a word (e.g. whether it was a type of flower), participants were more likely to remember it. This was interpreted as showing the superiority of 'semantic' encoding.

In one of the first publications introducing the TAP perspective, Morris *et al.* (1977) questioned the conclusion that a semantic orientation during learning would always produce better results. They carried out a series of studies in which they varied not only the type of processing used to learn words, but also the type of processing required in the retrieval task. Using a methodology similar to the one described above for LOP studies, Morris *et al.* found that when they asked participants to identify new words that rhymed with words they had seen in the learning condition, those who had experienced orienting questions that drew attention to rhyme were more successful than those who had been oriented to meaning. This led them to conclude that semantic processing was not always superior. Rather, the most successful retrieval was achieved when the retrieval conditions were similar to the learning conditions. TAP suggests the hypothesis that what matters most is not how we learned something in the first place, but whether the learning processes are easily transferred to the retrieval processes and conditions (Franks *et al.*, 2000).

Although LOP research initially focused on the importance of processing the semantics – the meaning – of items, subsequent research showed the importance of other components of the learning situation. These included

- *Frequency* – numerous encounters with language features are almost always required for effective memory encoding (e.g. N. Ellis, 2002).
- *Distribution and spacing* – in general, long-term retention is better if there are multiple, spaced exposures rather than a single study session, even if the overall time devoted to learning is the same (e.g. Dempster, 1996).
- *Generation* – it is usually helpful for learners to produce as well as hear or see the item during the learning phase, especially if they must retrieve it from memory and use it to express their own meanings (e.g. DeKeyser, 1998; Jacoby, 1978; Slamecka & Graf, 1978).
- *Elaboration* – linking the item to be learned to multiple aspects of form and meaning, as well as to related ideas, will increase the likelihood that it will be retrieved successfully (Laufer & Hulstijn, 2001).

Eventually, the studies led to the general conclusion that semantic processing was only one of several factors contributing to the depth of processing that would lead to more successful retrieval of learned material.

In a review article, Nairne (2002) discusses both TAP and LOP research and concludes that the multiple associations that are characteristic of deeper processing make it possible for what was encoded to be 'tapped by a range of different retrieval cues' (2002: 394). This is compatible with both TAP and current connectionist views of language learning in that it suggests that the more connections there are to a word or phrase – or the greater the number of matches between learning processes and retrieval processes – the greater the likelihood of retrieval (N. Ellis, 2001). Nairne also argues, however, that the importance of matching learning and retrieval processes may not be as great as ensuring that the retrieval cue has some unique relationship to the item we are trying to remember. That is, if the retrieval cue matches too many possible items, it will be less effective for triggering an accurate memory of a particular item (Lockhart, 2002).

Type of Processing and SLA

A considerable amount of research has explored how depth of processing affects the learning of second language words (e.g. Brown & Perry, 1991; Mondria & Wit-de-Boer, 1991; and for reviews, N. Ellis, 2001; Hulstijn, 2001, 2003). Most language teachers are familiar with the idea that we remember language better when we process it 'deeply' – with frequent exposure, attention to meaning, opportunities for generation and elaboration – than when we process it 'shallowly' – that is, with attention primarily on the surface form and without the opportunity or the need to generate meaningful utterances that contain the material being learned. Communicative language teaching is implicitly based on this idea. TAP is also consistent with the idea that the most effective preparation for understanding and producing language in communicative environments will occur in contexts where learners gain experience in understanding and producing language in communicative environments. Segalowitz and Lightbown suggested that

> ... according to the principle of transfer appropriate processing, the learning environment that best promotes rapid, accurate retrieval of what has been learned is that in which the psychological demands placed on the learner resemble those that will be encountered later in natural settings. (Segalowitz & Lightbown, 1999: 51)

However, some language features appear difficult to learn when they are encountered only in environments where there is competition for attention, especially where those language features are difficult to perceive in natural speech, communicatively redundant, or misleadingly similar to the L1 (Doughty & Williams, 1998b). Years of experience with meaning-focused approaches to language teaching (communicative, content-based, and task-based instruction) have led to the conclusion that good content teaching may not always be good language teaching (Pica, 2002; Swain, 1988), and as Skehan and Foster (2001: 189) observe, 'If a task demands a lot of attention to its content (...), there will be less attention available to be devoted to its language'.[2] This suggests that free-flowing, communicatively rich interaction may not always create the most favorable conditions for learning certain language features. There are several proposals for helping learners make the most of such conditions.

One approach to communicative language teaching that draws explicitly on research on cognitive processing was developed by Gatbonton and Segalowitz (1988, 2005; Trofimovich & Gatbonton, 2006). Their proposal creates opportunities for extended form–meaning mapping practice in which learners make use of a limited number of expressions that must be used repeatedly to accomplish the classroom task. This form–meaning mapping practice is followed by a consolidation activity in which learners have opportunities to focus more explicitly on these forms and the meanings they carry, but in activities that remove the communication pressure of the earlier activities. Finally, students participate in tasks in which there is a high likelihood of the practised phrases being used, but in exchanges that are more open-ended than those in the earlier phases of instruction. The focus in this integrated instructional model is on automatisation, based on repetition and practice of language that expresses the learners' own meanings. This approach provides the kind of practice that DeKeyser (1998: 59–60) referred to in saying that '... learners should be encouraged to use in more open-ended activities what they have practiced in the more structured activities such as communicative drills'. The notion of 'communicative drill' sounds like an oxymoron to many SLA researchers and teachers. However, although learners in such 'drills' make repeated use of a small sample of utterances, they do so in situations where *they* have to choose the utterance that fits the meaning *they* wish to convey.

Another approach to improving the effectiveness of communicative language teaching is the provision of feedback on form while learners are engaged in communicative interaction or content-based learning (Doughty & Varela, 1998; Lightbown & Spada, 2006; Long, 1991). This is also consistent with TAP as a framework for matching classroom learning processes to the processes that will be used outside the classroom. That is, feedback is likely to be most effective if it occurs when learners know what they are trying to express and the feedback helps them say it better (Lightbown, 1998; Han, this volume, for the importance of ensuring that the feedback accurately reflects a learner's intended meaning). Some years ago, I reported on a series of classroom observations and studies in which we saw a teacher successfully teach French-speaking learners of English to use *be* where they had previously used *have* as a presentational form, saying, for example, 'In this picture you have a boy ...' rather than 'In this picture, there's a boy'. The teacher told me that she had 'drummed it into their little heads!' She said that she was 'so tired of hearing "you have a this; you have a that"' that she had made a joke of it and when the students said 'you have' rather than 'there is'. She looked all around as if taking seriously their claim that she 'had' something in her possession that they could see. Her students learned to use the presentational form correctly and, even a year later, they were more likely to do so than comparable groups of students (Lightbown, 1991).

I have often regretted reporting that teacher's characterization of her focus on this language feature as 'drumming it into their heads', because some readers interpreted this as evidence that she engaged in the kind of mindless drill and repetition that led Wong and VanPatten (2003) to conclude that 'drills are out'. The reality was that this teacher had provided integrated instruction and feedback, specifically focused on form-meaning mapping. When students said, for example, 'you have a boy', she showed them, by her humorous searching around, that they were not conveying the meaning they intended to convey. She encouraged them to try again, using the language form that did say what they meant. Such feedback and opportunities for self-correction were crucial for the students in a class where everyone used exactly the same incorrect interlanguage form. Sustained, spaced, integrated feedback on form–meaning mapping and opportunities for 'modified output' (McDonough, 2004; Swain, 1995) had a long-term effect on the students' use of this language feature.

We found something similar in another study, with another teacher who got very good results in teaching questions by integrating the form focus into ongoing communicative activity (Spada & Lightbown, 1993). Her feedback was gentle and sometimes humorous, but it was explicit and sustained in communicative activities over many class periods. Even so, the classroom observation evidence showed that students did not lose interest in the communicative activities themselves. These corrective interventions were small asides, and the students quickly returned to the content at hand.

TAP and Form-Meaning Connections

Instruction that integrates the learning of specific language features within communicative interaction is consistent with TAP as a framework for classroom practice. The above examples of approaches to communicative language teaching are compatible with TAP in that learning takes place in the kind of interactive communicative environments in which learners will later wish to retrieve what they have learned. It appears, however, that some language features are extremely difficult to learn within these environments. Furthermore, if the goal is precise, accurate knowledge of particular language features, learning that relies entirely on communicative interaction will almost certainly be incomplete. This leads to the possibility that a more focused type of instruction may sometimes be necessary. This may appear to contradict the suggestion that the most effective learning will take place in conditions that emulate the natural communicative situations in which language will later be used. It is noteworthy, however, that in their early outline of TAP, Morris *et al.* (1977: 519) asserted that '... particular acquisition activities are never inherently "superficial" or "nonmeaningful"'. Instead, task meaningfulness must be defined relative to particular learning goals'. This suggests that there is still an important role for some of the types of instruction that have fallen out of favour – teaching activities in which learners' attention is drawn to 'superficial' form itself.

TAP does indeed suggest that what is learned in communicative interaction will be more easily retrieved in similar 'noisy' environments but also that *meaning-focused* processing may not be 'transfer appropriate' if what we seek to *retrieve* requires memory for language *form* or specific *form–meaning connections* (Barcroft, 2006). It is also the case that there are elements in the language that learners are exposed to in communicative interaction that they will rarely or never notice or learn. This is in part because of the difficulty students have in perceiving certain low-frequency or low-salience features, as well as those that are misleadingly similar to the L1 (Doughty & Williams, 1998b; Harley, 1993; Spada *et al.*, 2005). It is also due to the fact that learners have a limited capacity for processing information. A primary or exclusive focus on meaning may make it difficult to notice formal features of the language (VanPatten, 1990). Furthermore, students are not the only ones who cannot focus on everything at once. Teachers are also limited-capacity processors. This may account for the ambiguity of feedback provided to students in content-based instruction such as immersion, where the teacher is responsible not only for students' language learning but also (or, indeed, primarily) for their learning of subject matter (Lyster, 1998). In content-based instruction, when students in a math lesson get both the math and the grammar wrong, the teacher is likely to attend to the former rather than the latter. Similarly, in communicative language teaching, teachers are often wary of interrupting the flow of conversation or embarrassing students and negatively affecting their motivation if they provide explicit form-focused feedback (Raimes, 2002).

VanPatten (1990) showed how difficult it is for second language users to notice certain language forms while their attention is focused on getting the meaning from a text. His research has also emphasized how learners tend to process second language input as if it conformed to patterns they were already familiar with from their L1, thereby failing to perceive important patterns in the new language (VanPatten & Cadierno, 1993). When sentences containing the problematic patterns occur in meaningful or communicative interaction, learners can usually interpret the meaning correctly by using their general knowledge or contextual cues. For example, when English speakers encounter sentences in Spanish in which the word order is Object–Verb–Subject rather than the Subject–Verb–Object order they are familiar with, they may successfully guess the meaning if there is only one possible context. However, if the context is ambiguous, they will tend to rely on the L1 (Subject–Verb–Object) pattern in processing the sentence for meaning.

VanPatten (2004a) developed an approach called 'processing instruction' in which learners' attention is drawn to exact form–meaning connections in conditions where only an understanding of the language forms themselves can disambiguate the meaning. For example, participants must choose which picture best corresponds to a Spanish sentence such as 'Him-follows-the girl' by recognizing that although the pronoun is in the sentence position where English speakers would expect to find the subject, the form of the pronoun shows that it is the *object* rather than the subject of the verb. Furthermore, in processing instruction there is no pressure to produce language (thus removing another burden on processing capacity).

This line of research has shown that it is possible for learners to improve their ability to process second language input by engaging in activities in which a language feature is taken out of its 'normal' communicative context and presented through more structured input (Wong, 2004a). When the assessment of learning emphasizes the ability to interpret the form–meaning connections in Object–Verb–Subject sentences, learners who have been explicitly trained to do that perform better than those whose instruction in the language has focused on their ability to produce sentences based on a model that is presented to them for practice. Processing instruction may lay a good foundation for learners to be able to interpret the Spanish word order patterns in subsequent learning activities, leading eventually to their ability to produce these patterns fluently and correctly following opportunities for additional practice in communicative situations.

TAP and Priming Effects

Another way of laying the foundation for subsequent processing may be seen in research on priming effects in second language pronunciation. Trofimovich (2005) investigated how the possible benefits of word priming were altered when participants paid attention to different properties of spoken words. The basis for this study is the clear evidence from innumerable studies by cognitive psychologists that when something that was recently seen or heard, it is processed more quickly than something that is novel or, at least, not recently seen or heard.[3] In this study, English native speakers who were low-proficiency learners of Spanish listened to recorded lists of words, both Spanish lists and English lists. Although the participants had low levels of Spanish proficiency, Trofimovich made sure that the words on the Spanish lists were words that were familiar to them. Each group of participants experienced the lists in different ways. One group (Just Listen) were told simply to listen to the words. A second group (Semantic) were told to think about each word and assign it a rating according to its 'pleasantness'. The third group (Auditory) were instructed to focus on the quality of the recordings and to give each word a rating according to the clarity of the sound. After exposure to the words in one of these three conditions, each participant heard lists of words again. This time they were asked to repeat each word as quickly and accurately as possible after they heard it. They heard both 'primed' words (those that were on the original lists) and 'new' words (familiar words that were not on the original lists). The analysis involved a comparison of the speed (measured in milliseconds) with which the participants repeated the words after hearing them. The effects of priming were assessed in terms of the difference between how quickly participants began their repetition of *primed* versus *new* words.

Trofimovich found the expected benefit for priming for English (L1) words, no matter what instruction participants had been given when they first heard them. That is, they repeated the primed words faster than the new words. In the participants' second language, priming also resulted in faster repetition for the Just Listen and Auditory groups. However, the Semantic group, who had been told to focus on the pleasantness of the words, did not repeat the primed words significantly faster than new words. Trofimovich interprets this finding as evidence that the processing capacity that participants had devoted to word meaning and word associations had detracted from their focus on the actual sound of the words. He suggests that this focus on meaning, which is the hallmark of interpersonal communication and communicative language teaching, may provide a partial explanation for the fact that adult language learners are often so much better at learning the meaning of words than they are at pronouncing them correctly. In any case, this study provides further evidence for the important relationship between the cognitive processes that are engaged during learning and those that are called on in the retrieval context. Emphasis on listening to what the words sounded like led to more rapid retrieval of their acoustic properties than did emphasis on the words' meaning (for more details, Trofimovich & Gatbonton, 2006).

Barcroft (2002, 2004) has carried out a series of studies that further show how what is in focus during learning can predict what second language learners will most easily or most accurately remember during retrieval. He developed what he calls the Type of Processing – Resource Allocation (TOPRA) model. This model emphasizes the competition for cognitive resources that results when learners try to learn different things at the same time (VanPatten, 1990). Some of Barcroft's research involved participants in tasks that required attention primarily to form *or* meaning while learning new words. He typically found that when participants used cognitive resources to focus on meaning, they sacrificed some of their ability to remember aspects of language form. In investigating how different types of processing affect the learning of *new* words, Barcroft proposed a third dimension of processing, suggesting that the learning of 'form–meaning mapping' requires a specific kind of processing. In one study, second language learners of Spanish saw a sequence of computer screens showing a simple drawing (e.g. a kite) and the noun form that labelled the picture (chiringa). All participants were told to 'try to learn' these new words. One group were told simply to study the picture/word pairs; the other group were instructed to write each word as they saw it. On the retrieval task participants were to write each word when the associated picture appeared on the screen. It comes as a surprise to most teachers that the group who wrote each word were *less* successful at the retrieval task than those who merely 'studied' the words and pictures. Barcroft sees this result as consistent with the TOPRA model. In focusing their attention on the strictly formal aspects of each word (how it was written), participants had been less able to focus on the form–meaning connection that linked the words and pictures (Barcroft, 2006).

Processing Research and the L2 Classroom

The language classroom needs to provide conditions in which learners have opportunities to use their cognitive processing to focus on meaning, on formal features of the language, and on form–meaning mapping for new or poorly learned language elements. There should also be provision for frequent repetitions of partially learned language, in contexts where the meaning of these elements is clear and, ideally, originates with the learner.

Bjork (1994) brings together a background in research on *memory* within cognitive psychology and *instruction*, especially the teaching of science. Bjork's interpretation of research on memory – on encoding and retrieval – has led to the suggestion that the most effective instruction introduces 'desirable difficulties' into classroom learning (Bjork & Linn, 2006). He contends that learning tasks and activities that make it difficult for learners to perform successfully in the classroom may be more effective for learning than those in which the learner appears to 'succeed' easily. In some sense, this is counterintuitive. When students perform well in classroom activities, we tend to see this as evidence for successful learning. However, Bjork points out that memory research shows that when the environment includes situations that challenge learners to work harder during learning, the result can be better long-term retention.

It is easy to see how this might relate to TAP and to language learning. It may be difficult to use language in complex communicative situations outside the language classroom if classroom experience involved repetitive drill, imitation of a recent model, memorized dialogue, or communicative interaction where the simplicity of language and/or the support offered by the context made both comprehension and production as easy as possible. Language produced under conditions that require more effort, more retrieval from long-term memory, and more competition for processing resources may be a better preparation for using language in new situations. Thus, Bjork's proposals are worthy of consideration as they may apply to second language instruction. The five desirable difficulties are (1) vary the conditions of practice, (2) create contextual interference during learning, (3) distribute or space study and practice, (4) reduce feedback to the learner, and (5) use tests as learning events.

Vary the conditions of practice

Both LOP and TAP approaches to memory suggest that the greater the number of situations in which language features are encountered, the greater the likelihood that there will be adequate triggers for retrieval in different situations. From the perspective of TAP, we can interpret this as suggesting that learning under varying conditions of practice may result in richer, more contextualized representations of the learned material. When the material learned this way is needed later, in a communicative context, the conditions of language use will resemble one or more of the conditions encountered during the learning activity, serving as a retrieval route for accessing the learned material. Furthermore, the research on practice suggests that the effects of practice may be specific to the mode of practice. That is, comprehension practice may improve comprehension, while speaking practice is necessary to improve speaking (De Keyser, 2007; N. Ellis, 2005).

Another reason for varying the conditions of practice is that practice that is always predictable and always draws on the same cognitive processes is likely to be less effective in reaching students with different learning styles and preferences. Finally, another benefit of variety is simply that it stimulates interest. In his extensive work with teacher education, Fanselow (1987, 1992) has urged teachers to 'try the opposite', observing that, over time, teachers tend to include *less* rather than more variety in their instructional activities. Varying the types of processing that the learning activities require may increase both the depth and the transferability of learning (Lyster & Mori, 2006).

Provide contextual interference during learning

Bjork also refers to this as 'interleaving'. This is one of the most obvious ways in which new approaches to language teaching are different from the kinds of drills and lessons that were typical of language teaching approaches such as grammar translation and audiolingual drill, which tended to be based on teaching one language element until it was well learned, then going on to another, often without any apparent link between the different elements. For example, we observed students who spent weeks practising sentences with verbs in the progressive form, only to have that form disappear from classroom language when the next lesson introduced the simple present (Lightbown, 1983). With contextual interference, the pattern of instruction is, for example, ABCAB-CABC rather than AAABBBCCC. One element is highlighted, then another – possibly related – one, then another before returning to a focus on the first. In language instruction, the A, B, and C could represent not only different grammatical structures or lexical items, but also different aspects of language use, such as accuracy and fluency. Inevitably, when language is used in communicative activities, a variety of language features will be needed. Not all language features will come up as frequently or with the necessary salience to make them learnable through such activities, however, and language instruction will still be enhanced by the intentional inclusion of activities that focus on rare or non-salient language features (Lightbown & Spada, 2006).[4]

Distribute/space study and practice

This has been referred to as '. . . one of the most robust and general findings in learning research' (Dempster, 1996). Time and again, studies in laboratories and classrooms have shown that material that is learned in multiple brief study sessions is remembered better than that which is studied intensively in a single learning session (Seabrook et al., 2005). There are a number of reasons why spacing contributes positively to the likelihood that there will be additional depth and transferability of processing. Because of the priming effect material may be more readily accessible when it is encountered again. In addition, the learner may have acquired additional knowledge with which to anchor and integrate the new knowledge. The learner may have reached a new developmental level in which the material is more easily incorporated (Lightbown, 1998; Mackey & Philp, 1998). Distributing the focus on particular elements over time (ABC, ABC, and so on) allows learners to review and reintegrate previously learned material and it gives them time for internalization, restructuring, and 'off-line' processing, which further improve the ease with which they can access these elements. This is also clearly related to the previous recommendation for interleaving material (providing contextual interference) in instruction.

Reduce feedback

This suggestion seems surprising. Should learners not know when they are getting it right? Yes, they should. But if there is constant external feedback, learners may cease to notice it in the teacher's language, especially if the general learning environment is one in which there is pressure to focus on meaning rather than language form. On the other hand, in classes where students have developed the expectation that the teacher will always provide a corrected version of their attempted language use, there is little need for self-monitoring or effortful generation of knowledge that is known but not yet automatized (Schmidt et al., 1989, for evidence of the negative effects of too much feedback[5]). When feedback is focused on a limited number of objects or available in some classroom activities but not in others, learners can take greater responsibility for creating and monitoring their own output.

Using tests as learning events

Learning activities need to include a 'test' element, that is, the requirement for effortful retrieval of previously learned material. Test situations require that students make an effort to retrieve information from long-term memory. Such retrieval can create a genuine learning event as the generation and practice of learned material further strengthens the memory of it. This may account for the evidence that, in some classroom situations, prompts provide more effective feedback than recasts for second language learning because learners are not given the correct form but must retrieve it from their own memory (Lyster, 2004).

In a classroom, tests as learning events may have the added benefit of providing diagnostic information about what students have learned and what they still need help with. Unfortunately, actual tests are sometimes designed in ways that lead to frustration and failure rather than to opportunities to consolidate knowledge. This brings us back to concerns for ensuring that tests accurately assess what students have learned.

Conclusion

Understanding the complexity of language learning in particular and of human learning and memory in general will always provide new challenges for researchers in linguistics, cognitive psychology, and education. As Roediger and Karpicke (2005: 486) caution, 'Memory does not refer to a single, unitary property of the mind, and dissociations among measures of retention indicate that several different memory processes and systems work together to produce the complexity of human memory'.

The TAP framework emphasizes the importance of a match between the processes and conditions that are present during learning and those that are present at the time of retrieval. If the task for retrieval requires memory for the semantic elements of the stimulus, then semantic encoding may be more effective than encoding that focuses instead on some perceptual feature of the stimulus – how it is spelled or pronounced or what it rhymes with, for example. On the other hand, if the retrieval task requires us to remember just those things – spelling, pronunciation or rhyming words – then an encoding task that emphasizes those aspects will be more effective than a semantic encoding task. The hypothesis is that, in the former case, processing effort or 'space' is taken up with the semantic encoding, leaving less or no room for attention to the perceptual features. The opposite would also be true. An encoding task focused on perceptual features will give poorer results when the retrieval task requires semantic knowledge. This harkens back to the criticism of drill in which the learners' task is to repeat or manipulate language forms without tying them to what DeKeyser called 'personal meanings'. Learners who have not had experience in retrieving language from memory while engaged in communicative interaction will be less well prepared to use language outside the classroom.

Second language learners need to know many different things and be able to do many different things with their knowledge. They may need to know how words are pronounced and spelled, what their nuanced meanings are, how they are combined to form longer units of language, and that meanings vary in different social and linguistic contexts. It is not possible to learn all these things at once, and instruction that is based on an assumption that the same instructional practices will be most effective for everything from pronunciation to pragmatics is implicitly placing an almost impossible burden on both learners and teachers. Transfer appropriate processing offers insight into the value of identifying – and helping learners to identify – the intended target of an instructional event. As a high school student, I learned to type. That typing class is one of the very few classes in which I was conscious of the teacher's instructional strategies. In every lesson, our exercises alternated between speed and accuracy. Sometimes we typed as fast as we could and worried less about our accuracy; other times, we typed as carefully and accurately as possible, not concerned with speed. Over time, our speed typing became more accurate and our accurate typing became faster. Such alternation of attention in the language class may also help learners achieve greater accuracy in fluent speech and greater fluency in accurate speech. Learning a language is more difficult and more complex than learning to type. Nevertheless, as we come to better understand how learning takes place, it seems likely that alternating between a primary focus on general meaning in interactions, tasks, reading, or listening activities and a primary focus on form or on form–meaning connections in more limited contexts will allow learners eventually to use the knowledge acquired in one setting and apply it in new ones. Along the way, however, assessments – especially those that are used to determine a learner's educational achievement – should reflect the instructional focus.

Transfer appropriate processing is one framework for understanding how learning occurs and how it can be accurately and fairly assessed. TAP helps to explain why learners are not always able to mobilize the knowledge they have acquired in certain situations when they face new ones. TAP suggests that an important part of the solution to this mismatch is an increase in the number of settings and processing types in which learners encounter the material they need to learn. Classroom-based research on form-focused instruction in communicative, content-based, and task-based instruction provides evidence to support this approach. Nevertheless, considerably more research will be needed if we are to strike the right balance between opportunities to focus on form, on meaning, and on form–meaning connections in classroom interaction. Such research should include both observational and experimental studies carried out by researchers in classrooms as well as action research by individual teachers or groups of teachers to seek to understand the needs of their own students.

Acknowledgements

I am grateful to the colleagues who provided information and encouragement during the preparation of this chapter. I would particularly like to thank Norman Segalowitz for starting me thinking about how TAP might be relevant to an understanding of instructional approaches to SLA. In addition to providing valuable references and feedback on interpretations, Pavel Trofimovich and Joe Barcroft allowed me to report on work that was still unpublished. Nick Ellis, ZhaoHong Han, Norman Segalowitz, Nina Spada, and Pavel Trofimovich offered feedback on earlier versions of the manuscript. The limitations and errors in the chapter are, of course, my own.

Notes

1. Transfer appropriate processing is only one basis for arguing for the importance of improving the match between instruction and testing. Another might be termed 'educational fairness'. I recently observed an example of mismatch in a second-grade class in a dual language bilingual education program. Each class is made up of both Spanish-dominant and English-dominant students, and students have learned to work in teams, to collaborate, to help each other. Thus, when they work in their second language, students can always work with others who are more proficient. Teachers have been trained to emphasize this kind of cooperative learning. At the end of second grade, students were tested on reading and writing in each of their languages. They were required to put up little screens to ensure that no one could see their paper and that they could see no-one else's. Several students who were able to function successfully in their second language in a variety of classroom activities ended up with scores of zero, suggesting that they had learned nothing. The cognitive processes required in the testing context were utterly different from those required in the learning context, and these students were not yet able to transfer their knowledge for use in the new context. The assessment was neither a learning opportunity for them nor a useful diagnostic tool for their teachers.
2. For extensive discussion of how task demands may limit or enhance attention to, and retention of, language features, see Robinson (2003).
3. Priming has also been shown to affect the likelihood that learners will use certain language forms, including syntactic structures (McDonough & Mackey, 2006).
4. It is worth noting that language features that are 'rare' in classroom interaction are not necessarily 'unimportant'. A striking example was provided by Merrill Swain (1988), who found that verbs in the past tense were rare in French immersion history class. Similarly, Lyster (1994) found that students in French immersion had little opportunity to learn the contrast between *tu* and *vous*, the familiar and polite second person pronouns in French. Such language features would seem to be quite basic for a second language learner's knowledge, but students in these classes had few opportunities to learn them in the ongoing content-based instruction they experienced.
5. I thank ZhaoHong Han for drawing this article to my attention.

Chapter 4
On the Role of Meaning in Focus on Form

ZHAOHONG HAN

Over the last 25 years, focus on form (Long, 1991) has emerged as a leading paradigm for second language acquisition (SLA) research on the interface between theory and practice. Numerous studies have been conducted to assess its efficacy as it is implemented in a variety of instructional settings. The findings, on the whole, point to the understanding that focus on form selectively facilitates second language (L2) development in some linguistic domains, with others such as inflectional morphology not quite susceptible to its influence.

In this chapter, I use the role of meaning in focus on form as a lens through which to identify conceptual and empirical problems that may have contributed to its relative lack of efficacy for L2 morphosyntactic learning. First, I will provide some general background for focus on form. Then, I will review the main tenets of focus on form and examine one of its instantiations, recasts, with a view to revealing the gaps between the theory and the research. After that, I will advance the argument that meaning is a learnability problem. Finally, building on the insights gained from the preceding analysis, I will present a pedagogical model for recasts that may increase their efficacy for morphological restructuring.

Some Background

Second language acquisition, like first language acquisition, proceeds largely through functions, featuring the primacy of communicative meaning.[1] Semantics appears to take precedence over syntax and morphology, and pragmatics, in turn, takes priority over semantics (Lightbown & Spada, 2006; Skehan, 1998; Slobin, 1973; VanPatten, 1996). This seeming commonality notwithstanding, the outcome of second language learning is almost always different from that of first language learning (passim the L2 literature). 'In fact, it can be argued that it is the enormous contrast between the two phenomena that needs explaining, rather than either of the two phenomena per se' (DeKeyser, 2005: 1). Accounts of the disparity in achievement have indeed been sought, and in fact, well established, in cognitive and biological terms (for review, Han, 2004c).

Cognitively, by general understanding, the initial state of second language learning is *tabula repleta*, and not *tabular rasa* as characterising first language learning (N. Ellis, 2006a). Specifically, second – not first – language learners come to the learning task with minds already entrenched in the knowledge and experience of a prior linguistic system (i.e. the L1) (MacWhinney, 2001, 2006). This cognitive state, henceforth, functions as a constraint and filter in L2 input reception and output generation, the key processes of acquisition. For the majority of L2 learners, the learning of a second language begins in post-pubescent years; that is, it happens, biologically, after the close-off of the neurologically based critical period (Lenneberg, 1967). In consequence, the 'developmental sharpening' (Doughty, 2003), which figures in first language acquisition, only has a weak presence in second language acquisition. Second language learners lack the capacity and efficiency they had when learning the first language to respond to environmental stimulation; that is, they exhibit low sensitivity and flexibility on encounters with L2 input. As Doughty puts it,

> An unfortunate drawback to the extreme efficiency of L1 processing, in particular to the developmental sharpening that it entails, is that adults are rendered 'disabled second-language learners later in life' (Cutler, 2001). This is because speech-processing abilities are altered, through experience with the native language, so that adults acquiring their L2 typically process input with mechanisms already attuned to their L1. (Doughty, 2003: 284)

Due to conspiracy between biological and cognitive constraints, second language learning, uniquely, displays (1) 'lack of equipotentiality' (Schachter, 1996), (2) local impairments or 'fossilisation' (Han, 2004c; Han & Odlin, 2006; Selinker, 1972), and (3) lack of implicit learning, among other disadvantages. In terms of lack of equipotentiality, learners tend to react differently to different target languages, depending on the typological proximity between the native and the target language. When the distance between the two languages is small, the target language feels easy to acquire (see, however, Kellerman, 1983), but it feels difficult when the distance is large (Schachter, 1996). Another manifestation with respect to the lack of equipotentiality is that learners' acquisition of some linguistic features is easy, but difficult when it comes to others.

As regards local impairments, certain linguistic features either consistently evade L2 learners' attention or are systematically processed in an idiosyncratic, biased manner, leading to persistent non-targetlike representations and behaviour. These features include, but are not limited to, grammatical morphemes (e.g. DeKeyser, 2005; N. Ellis, 2006a; Han, 2004c; Sagarra, this volume) and the so-called 'interface structures' that involve interaction between morphosyntax and other domains such as semantics and pragmatics (e.g. Geeslin & Guijarro-Fuentes, 2006; Sorace, 2005; Strauss *et al.*, 2006).

A third ubiquitous phenomenon is that L2 learners generally have an attenuating capacity for implicit learning. Simultaneous processing of natural, communicative input for meaning (i.e. semantic information) and form (i.e. linguistic code feature) rarely happens. Instead, learners' processing of input is largely – if not solely – orientated to constructing meaning, viz., comprehension (Gass & Selinker, 2001; Lightbown, 2000 and this volume; Sharwood Smith, 1986; Skehan, 1998; VanPatten, 1996, 2004b), and this is often accomplished through resorting to nonlinguistic cues (cf. Lightbown, this volume), resulting thereby in (1) little attention to how form encodes meaning (i.e. intake), (2) biased processing of form (VanPatten, 1996, 2004b), and/or (3) 'shallow processing' (Clahsen & Felser, 2006) – all adverse to acquisition.

To mitigate these tendencies, over the past 25 years, a considerable number of L2 researchers have set out to identify compensatory strategies, strategies that may increase learners' metalinguistic sensitivity to input. This line of research was undergirded by cognitive theory of attention in general, and its SLA derivations in particular (Robinson, 1995; Schmidt, 1990, 1994, 2001; Tomlin & Villa, 1994). For example, Schmidt's noticing hypothesis – that there is no intake without conscious attention – has motivated an array of pedagogically orientated proposals. Among them three proposals are particularly popular, namely, input enhancement (Sharwood Smith, 1991, and this volume), processing instruction (VanPatten, 1991), and focus on form (Long, 1991), all, contextualized in meaningful use of language, attempting to draw learners' attention to select features of input by, respectively, (1) enhancing their salience, (2) instilling an explicit understanding of form–meaning relations, and (3) providing implicit corrective feedback. The three proposals have each led to a flurry of empirical research into their efficacy, and the resultant findings were mixed (for reviews, see Norris & Ortega (2000) on focus on form, Han (2005) on input enhancement, and VanPatten (2004a) on processing instruction). The remainder of this chapter is concerned with one of the proposals, focus on form, in part because this proposal has spawned the greatest number of empirical studies to date, and hence established itself as a leading paradigm for theory and research on effects of instruction on learning, but, more importantly, because it is in this widely pursued proposal and its follow-up empirical research that meaning is found to have been inadequately treated.

Focus on Form

'Focus on form' was introduced by Long (1991) to contrast with a traditional, structural approach to instruction which he termed 'focus on forms'. In his words,

[W]hereas the content of lessons with a focus on forms is the forms themselves, a syllabus with a focus on form teaches something else – biology, mathematics, workshop practice, automobile repair, the geography of a country where the foreign language is spoken, the cultures of its speakers, and so on – and *overtly* draws students' attention to linguistic elements as they arise *incidentally* in lessons whose overriding focus is on meaning or communication. (Long, 1991: 45–46; emphasis added)

For Long, the overt but incidental focus on form in a meaningful context may constitute an effective strategy to redress learners' natural – and often persistent – tendency not to notice, process, and learn communicatively redundant, perceptually non-salient, or infrequent and rare forms in input (cf. Doughty, 2003; Schmidt, 2001), and hence, may be beneficial for continued interlanguage (IL) development (Long & Robinson, 1998).

For the purposes of this chapter, it is interesting to note that in this initial definition of focus on form, meaning was accorded a very general sense, referring to the content in focus, content that is made clear from the context. This context referent of meaning is reaffirmed seven years later by Long and Robinson:

Focus on form refers to how focal attentional resources are allocated ... During an otherwise meaning-focused classroom lesson, focus on form often consists of an occasional shift of attention to linguistic code features – by the teacher and/or one or more students – triggered by perceived problems in communication. (Long & Robinson, 1998: 23)

It is clear, then, that in the theoretical conceptualization of focus on form, form is the pedagogical target, meaning providing 'the cognitive processing support' to it (Doughty & Williams, 1998a, p. 3). Simply put, meaning occupies the background and form the foreground. In attentional terms, focus on form requires a temporary shift of focal attention *away from meaning* to form (Doughty, 2003; emphasis added). Given so, the relation between form and meaning is loose, at best.

However, there appears to be a closer tie between form and meaning in Long's more recent characterization of focus on form, as seen in the second definition above, where 'perceived problems in communication' is noted as the trigger of focus on form. This thereby narrows down the scope of possible incidence of focus on form to only those cases where there is (or is likely to be) a comprehension/production failure, implying that focus on form should be reactive in nature, and not preemptive (see, however, Doughty & Williams, 1998a). On this conception, a typical event of focus on form should, then, have the following sequence shown in Figure 4.1. As generally paraphrased in the literature, such a sequence means that communication breakdown prompts negotiation for meaning, which, in turn, results in focus on form (negotiation of form), thereby providing the learner with an opportunity to acquire a particular form.

This sequence reveals that form is ultimately responsible for 'perceived problems in communication'. Thus, again, it is form that is at the foreground. Moreover, the sequence predicts that negotiation of form, prompted by negotiation for meaning, will, of necessity, involve certain items to the exclusion of others (cf. Foster & Ohta, 2005; Skehan & Foster, 2001). In all likelihood, and as has indeed been empirically attested (e.g. Brock *et al.*, 1986; Day *et al.*, 1983), those items are mostly lexical words (the so-called 'content words'), which are able to contribute essential semantic information to communication, as opposed to grammatical morphemes (the so-called 'functors'), which are semantically light,

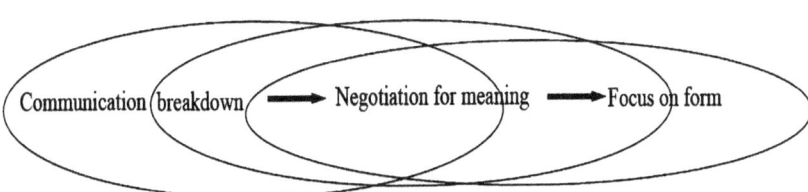

Figure 4.1 Sequence of a focus on form event

communicatively redundant, and perceptually non-salient. Nonetheless, the latter are precisely the ones that focus on form initially set out to target, because they have long been empirically established as hard to acquire by learners with or without instruction (e.g. DeKeyser, 2005; N. Ellis, 2006a; R. Ellis, 1994; Sagarra, this volume; Terrell, 1991; VanPatten et al., 2004; Young, 1991).

One problem arises: If focus on form ends up directing learners' attention and noticing to lexical items rather than morphosyntactic features, it not only makes itself redundant, but, more profoundly, it may potentially have an adverse impact on learning by reinforcing a natural bias, as noted earlier, for meaning in L2 input processing. According to VanPatten (2004b, p. 14), the processing bias entails, *inter alia*, (1) that 'learners process input for meaning before they process it for form', (2) that 'learners process content words in the input before anything else', and (3) that 'learners ... tend to rely on lexical items as opposed to grammatical form to get meaning when both encode the same semantic information'. This bias functions not only in L2 written input processing, but also in oral input processing, as the next section will show.

In sum, focus on form, as Long has conceptualized it, hinges on a communicatively meaningful environment in which it exclusively targets surface form. It is based on two tacit assumptions: (1) that form-meaning mapping will, *ipso facto*, occur for the learner as long as the pedagogical act is embedded in a meaningful context, and (2) that learning difficulty lies in form, not in meaning. Long's more recent definition (Long & Robinson, 1998), which designates communication breakdown as the trigger of focus on form, has a built-in prediction that focus on form will direct attention to meaning-laden forms to the exclusion of meaningless forms, even when the latter are its intended targets.

In the next section, I turn to the empirical dimension of focus on form by examining one of its popular instantiations, recasts. I will illustrate how meaning is treated there, and in so doing, demonstrate that the underlying assumptions of focus on form are problematic, and that as practised, focus on form is low in efficacy and reinforces the natural bias for meaning in L2 input processing.

Recasts: A Case in Point

The L2 literature of the last 15 years has seen an exponential growth of studies of recasts (for summaries, see Gass, 2003; Long, 2007; Nicholas et al., 2001). This interest, still in ascendance today, was largely kindled by Long's (1996) interaction hypothesis and its pedagogical corollary, focus on form, but also by an observational study by Lyster and Ranta (1997) showing, among other things, that recasts are the most frequent type of feedback in L2 French immersion classrooms, in spite of their 'ineffectiveness at eliciting student-generated repair' (1997: 37). In his recent review, Long (2007) has, nevertheless, claimed that 'Of all the many ways negative feedback is delivered in and out of classrooms ... , *implicit* negative feedback in the form of corrective recasts seems particularly promising'(2007: 76; emphasis in original).

Long (2007) defines a corrective recast as 'a reformulation of all or part of a learner's immediately preceding utterance in which one or more non-target-like (lexical, grammatical, etc.) items is/are replaced by the corresponding target language form(s), and where, throughout the exchange, the focus of the interlocutors is on *meaning*, not language as object' (2007: 77; emphasis in original). Long further notes that 'unlike various traditional pedagogic procedures for delivering "error correction," the "corrections" in recasts are implicit and incidental'.

Although definitions of a recast have not been identical from one researcher to another, most of them have, to a greater or lesser extent, adhered to the following properties. A recast (1) is adjacent to an ill-formed utterance, (2) reformulates it, (3) expands it in some way, and (4) retains its central meanings. These are illustrated in [1] and [2] (Han & Kim, in press).

[1]
1 S: I did not know I hurt her feeling.
2 T: *You hurt her feelings.*
3 S: Yes, but I didn't know.

[2]
1 S: I cannot get angry easily to others.
2 T: *I don't get angry easily. I don't get angry easily ... If you don't get offended easily, you're 'thick skinned'. Thick skinned.*
3 S: We have same idiom.

In [1], the student's utterance in Turn 1 is immediately followed by the teacher's recast (Turn 2), which reformulates the utterance by making a grammatical change to 'feeling'. In [2], the student's utterance in Turn 1 leads to a recast by the teacher (Turn 2) who not only reformulates the trigger utterance by changing 'cannot' into 'don't', but also expands it with additional utterances. Thus, in light of the four properties of recasts, the recasts in [1] and [2] are both reformulations of an ill-formed utterance, but differ in that [2], but not [1], expands on the trigger utterance. Incidentally, in the literature [1] is known as an isolated declarative recast and [2] an integrated declarative recast (e.g. Lyster & Ranta, 1997). With regard to properties (3) and (4), it appears that [1] retains the meaning of the trigger utterance, but [2] both retains and expands it. Finally, both [1] and [2] are adjacent to the trigger utterance.

Long (2007) hypothesizes that recasts may potentially contribute to acquisition because

> [They] convey needed information about the target language *in context*, when interlocutors share a *joint attentional focus*, and when the learner already has *prior comprehension* of at least part of the message, thereby facilitating form–function mapping. The learner is *vested* in the exchange, as it is his or her message that is at stake, and so will probably be *motivated* and *attending*, conditions likely to facilitate *noticing* of any new linguistic information in the input. The fact that the learner will already understand all or part of the interlocutor's response (because it is a reformulation of the learner's own) also means that he or she has additional freed-up *attentional resources* which can be allocated to the form of the response, and, again, to form–function mapping. Finally, the *contingency* of recasts on deviant learner output means that the incorrect and correct utterances are juxtaposed. This allows the learner to compare the two forms side by side, so to speak, and to observe the contrast, an opportunity not presented by non-contingent utterances, i.e., models. (Long, 2007: 77–78; emphasis in original)

According to this statement, recasts should only concern forms in the learner's utterance, not their meaning, because the meaning, as set forth in the definitions, should be retained. In other words, what corrective recasts essentially do is re-encode the meaning of the learner utterance by correcting its grammatical violation(s). In a nutshell, where acquisition is conceived of as a form–meaning connection process, recasts deal with problems in form, leaving meaning, on the other hand, intact, or taking it for granted.

Although the general thrust of the existing empirical research has been to examine the nature of recasts and their efficacy, descriptive and confirmatory studies have been undertaken to assess and understand the impact on learners' representations and behaviour of recasts as a function, internally, of their varied configurations (e.g. length, complexity, single vs. multiple errors), externally, of contextual demands, or of their interaction with individuals' cognitive differences. Although many of the findings are still largely contingent (for reviews, see Long, 2007; Nicholas *et al.*,

2001; for recent collections of studies, see the special issue of *Studies in Second Language Acquisition* [SSLA] edited by Mackey & Gass, 2006; also Mackey, 2007), the jury being still out on Long's hypothesised advantages, there is at least one categorical finding: learners are better at recognising and utilising information contained in phonological and lexical recasts than in morphosyntactic recasts (e.g. Braidi, 2002; Carpenter *et al.*, 2006; Kim & Han, 2007; Lyster, 1998; Lyster & Ranta, 1997; Mackey *et al.*, 2000; Nabei & Swain, 2002; Oliver, 1995; Pica, 2002; Sheen, 2004), notwithstanding the fact that the latter type of recasts far outnumbered the former types, an interesting paradox. Furthermore, even where morphosyntactic forms were the exclusive focus of the study, recasts appeared to be more helpful for some (putatively simple), but not for other (putatively hard) forms (Doughty *et al.*, 1999, cited in Long, 2007; Iwashita, 1999; Leeman, 2003; Long *et al.*, 1998; Ortega & Long, 1997). Long (2007; see also Leeman, 2003) attributes the latter finding to the differential salience of different linguistic forms, and surmises that 'conversation was *selectively facilitative* of acquisition' (emphasis in original), echoing Sato (1986). He calls for further research to assess the impact of perceptual salience and/or other qualities of the target forms on the efficacy of recasts, rationalizing that

> Knowing which classes of problematic target language features can be addressed successfully via implicit negative feedback, and which, if any, require more explicit treatment would be both theoretically important, because it could help explain how recasts work, and pedagogically useful. (Long, 2007: 110)

In much the same vein, I believe that an equally (if not more) important piece of the recast puzzle to solve is the first, more generic finding, viz., the above noted paradox of learners' low perception of morphosyntactic recasts against their high frequency in the communicative environment, to which I now turn.

In a recent study, Kim and Han (2007) offered a detailed analysis of learners' interpretation of the recasts provided by their native-speaking teachers in intermediate, communicative English as a Foreign Language (EFL) classes, taking account of the possible influence of (1) the type of teacher intent (corrective or communicative), (2) the type of addressee (direct or indirect), (3) the type of linguistic target (morphology, syntax, phonology, or lexis), and (4) the form of recast (declarative or interrogative). Results from analyses of 20 students' stimulated recall protocols on 68 audio-recorded recast episodes yielded, among other things, an inverse relationship, particularly for the complex recasts (i.e. targeting

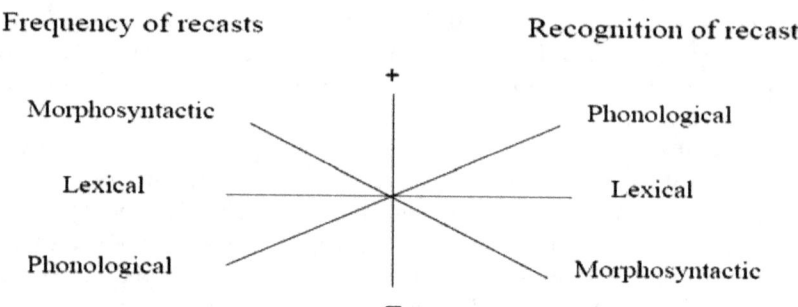

Figure 4.2 Recasts: A paradoxical finding

more than one error), between the frequency of the recasts and students' ability to recognize gaps between the recasts and the trigger utterances, as schematically illustrated in Figure 4.2. Figure 4.2 shows that of all forms of recasts (morphosyntactic, lexical, and phonological), morphosyntactic recasts were the most frequent, as indicated in the left column, and yet, the students were the least able to recognize gaps between them and the trigger utterances, as shown in the right column.

Interestingly, the same pattern, independently, emerged from two other studies, one study on beginner-to-lower-intermediate English as a Second Language (ESL) and Italian as a Foreign Language learners (Mackey et al., 2000) and one on advanced ESL learners (Carpenter et al., 2006). Mackey et al. (2000), investigating learners' perceptions about interactional feedback, showed that although morphosyntactic recasts were more frequently provided to ESL learners than lexical and phonological recasts, they were the least correctly perceived, as judged from students' recall protocols. Morphosyntactic recasts also elicited the least amount of uptake, as measures of the students' immediate responses to the recasts indicated. Likewise, Carpenter et al. (2006: 210) reported that 'morphosyntactic recasts were less accurately recognized than phonological or lexical recasts', even though the former were greater in number than the latter.

The observed paradox thus appears to be consistent and pervasive, transcending learning contexts, proficiency levels, and target languages. In an interesting way, it demonstrates the earlier noted input processing bias. In this case, the bias occurred in the processing of oral negative input (i.e. oral recasts). Several explanations have been proposed for the phenomenon. One explanation invokes the intrinsic communicative value of the lexical and phonological items versus that of morphosyntactic forms, arguing that because lexical and phonological items carry more communicative value than morphosyntactic forms, the former are more salient than the latter, and hence more noticeable (e.g. Carpenter *et al.*, 2006; Mackey *et al.*, 2000). Another account draws on the observation that lexical and phonological recasts tend to be shorter than morphosyntactic ones, and from a processing perspective, it is argued that the former are more salient and easier to process than the latter (Carpenter *et al.*, 2006). Also among the explanations is that the former are often accompanied by negotiation, whereas the latter seldom are, and negotiation helps draw attention to the language (Mackey *et al.*, 2000), a point I return to later.

Given the mounting evidence and the existing explanations, it will only seem logical to conclude that recasts are not the most effective for treating morphosyntactic errors in communicative language environments.[2] Mackey *et al.* (2000: 493) assert that 'using recasts to provide morphosyntactic feedback may have been suboptimal' (see also Lyster, 2004; Panova, 2005). Similarly, reviewing a sample of the existing studies, Long (2007: 112) concludes that 'It is quite possible that future research will support what current findings already suggest: recasts or other delicate, unobtrusive forms of corrective feedback work satisfactorily for some linguistic targets, for example, meaning-bearing items, better than others, but that more explicit, more intrusive, intervention is required for communicatively redundant, acoustically non-salient forms' (see also Lightbown, this volume). Indeed, such claims would seem plausible were it not for the fact that there are several discrepancies between the theory and empirical research on focus on form that have hitherto remained out of the general purview. These discrepancies, two of which are singled out and discussed below, might give us cause for rethinking the observed paradox.

Gaps In and Between Theory and Research

As noted previously, according to Long's focus on form proposal, breakdowns in communication should be what trigger pedagogical interventions; that is, any focus on form incidence must arise from negotiation for meaning. Instead, the majority of recasts were not actually occasioned by communication breakdowns, and consequently, there was lack of negotiation for meaning at the time of recasting (cf. Mackey *et al.*, 2000). For one thing, following Long's proposal, one should expect to see more communicative recasts (i.e. naturally resulting from negotiation for meaning as in [3]) than corrective recasts (i.e. artificially contrived to focus the learner's attention on language as in [4]) (e.g. from Brock *et al.*,

1986). In contrast, the empirical research reports that there is greater deployment of corrective recasts as in [4] than of communicative recasts as in [3] (cf. Hauser, 2005). This is one gap between the theory and the research.

[3] Communicative recast
1 NNS: I goed to New York yesterday.
2 NS: *You went yesterday?*

[4] Corrective recast
1 NNS: I goed to New York yesterday.
2 NS: *You went.* (declaratory intonation)

Another gap, related to the first, pertains specifically to the conceptualisation of recasts in contrast to the research on recasts. On the one hand, Long's conception is that any recast should be incidental and implicit such that 'throughout the exchange, the focus of the interlocutors is on *meaning*, not language as object' (Long, 2007: 77), and that recasts (or any implicit feedback, for that matter) should address the issues the learner is struggling with at the time of interaction (Long, 1996). On the other hand, a preponderance of the existing empirical studies has featured an explicit, intentional focus on forms. In these studies, morphosyntactic recasts – typically delivered in the manner illustrated in [4] – outnumber lexical and phonological recasts, notwithstanding the fact that morphosyntactic forms, because of their relative lack of semantic content, are usually the forms the learner is least likely to struggle with during communicative interaction.

Thus, there exists a conflicting picture concerning the theory, research, and efficacy of focus on form, as illustrated in Figure 4.3. Outlined in

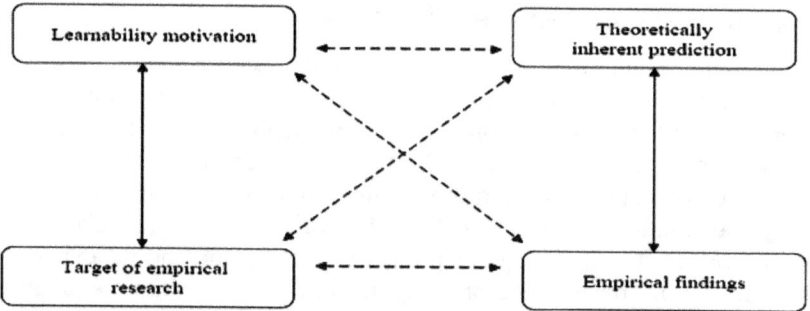

Figure 4.3 Conflict among theory, prediction, and empirical research

Figure 4.3 are four aspects of focus on form, indicated by the boxes. The upper-left box represents the theoretical motivation of focus on form, the lower-left box the target of empirical research on focus on form, the upper-right the default prediction of focus on form, and the lower-right empirical findings. In addition, the two double-arrowed solid lines indicate congruence and the four double-arrowed broken lines suggest incongruence. A detailed explanation follows.

As shown in Figure 4.3, on the one hand, focus on form is motivated by the pedagogical desire to address those forms that the learner is not likely to learn on his/her own (e.g. morphosyntactic forms), a learnability concern, and the ensuing empirical research has indeed targeted them. On the other hand, focus on form – as a theory – has an inherent prediction that negotiation for meaning, triggered by communication problems, will direct the learner's attention to lexical and phonological items, and this has indeed been borne out by research indicating that learners perceive lexical and phonological recasts better than morphosyntactic recasts, regardless of the abundance of the latter in their communicative environment.

This picture points up a number of difficulties with focus on form as an SLA innovation. A first difficulty is that at the theoretical level, there is a discrepancy between the learnability motivation for focus on form and its inherent or default prediction. A second difficulty lies at the interface between theory and research. There is a discrepancy between the learnability motivation of focus on form and the empirical findings suggesting a shortfall of its desired efficacy. A third difficulty, the focus of the remainder of the chapter, resides in the empirical research itself showing a departure from the theoretical tenet of focus on form and for that matter, the interaction hypothesis: morphosyntactic recasts are typically delivered in the absence of negotiation, as pointed out in Mackey *et al.* (2000). However, unlike Mackey *et al.*, who viewed the role of negotiation as serving largely as an attention-getting device, I contend that lack of negotiation entails that meaning is, wrongly, ruled out as a learnability concern, to which I now turn.

Meaning as a Learnability Problem

Meaning maintenance in recasts

In Long's accounts of focus on form, meaning retention serves as the lynchpin of the hypothesized acquisitional benefits. In the case of recasts, it is what motivates and enables the learner (by releasing attentional resources) to attend to input contained in recasts and to subsequently make cognitive comparisons, a process crucial for representational restructuring (Nelson, 1987; Saxton, 1997). The meaning maintenance mechanism, however, does not seem tenable in the face of the observed paradox, as discussed above. In particular, it does not explain away why morphosyntactic recasts, despite their high frequency, nevertheless tended to go unnoticed by the learner, importantly, when meaning seemed to have been held constant, as illustrated in [5] (Mackey et al., 2000):

[5]   Morphosyntactic episode
1   NNS: There is a three bird my picture.
2   NS: Three birds in your picture?
3   NNS: Three bird yeah.

What, then, explains the NNS's lack of sensitivity to the corrective input on the plural form -s? Although several factors – including the salience and communicative value that were mentioned earlier (see also Sagarra, this volume, on working memory) – may have played a role, none of them, alone or in combination, appears to be adequate enough to account for the lack of sensitivity, and more generally, for the widely noted pervasive and persistent lack of processing and acquisition among L2 learners of grammatical morphemes. Salience, for example, is increasingly proposed as a major predictor of difficulty (e.g. DeKeyser, 2005; N. Ellis, 2006a, 2006b), and yet it cannot explain a very simple fact, namely that instructed learners, of all proficiency levels, have trouble with grammatical morphemes for which they have received abundant explicit instruction. Apparently, instruction-induced salience has little impact on their acquisition.

By way of illustration, let us look at a segment of conversation in a Korean EFL classroom, drawn from the same database as [1] and [2] (Kim & Han, 2007).

[6]
1   T: Good, we'll be preparing ... okay ... Chapter three ... so ... question is what is the most unusual dish you've ever eaten? What is the most unusual dish you've ever eaten? The most unusual ...
2   S1:   Grasshopper fried snack.
3   T: What? What is that?
4   S1:   Snack.
5   T: Snack?
6   S1:   They were ... are made of grasshopper.
7   T: *They are grasshoppers?*

8	S1:	Yes.
9	S2:	Where?
10	S1:	In Thailand.
11	T:	Thailand.
12	S1:	They look ... they looked like real grasshopper, but it was fried.
13	T:	It was deep fried, wasn't it?
14	S1:	Yeah, deep fried, and it was very crispy.
15	T:	Really?
16	S1:	Yes, it was very delicious.
17	T:	Delicious?
18	S1:	Yes [Laughing]
19	S1:	I can see their leg.
20	T:	*I could see their legs.*
21	S1:	I could see. [...]
22	T:	[...] I don't think I've had deep fried grasshoppers. What do deep fried grasshoppers taste like?
23	S1:	It is like corn-chip.
24	T:	*Corn-chips?*
25	S1:	Yes no taste. No smell. If you don't see their appearance, you don't know if this is grasshopper.

The segment of interaction above involves a teacher (T) and two students (S1 and S2). As illustrated, S1's production showed lack of acquisition of the plural -s. Her utterance in Turn 6 was immediately followed by the teacher's recast, which reformulated S1's utterance by attaching -s to 'grasshopper'. However, as shown several turns later, in Turn 12, S1's production continued to feature zero use of the plural -s. In the subsequent interaction, S1 had a few more opportunities to notice the plural -s. In Turn 19, her utterance triggered another recast (Turn 20), which changed the original singular form 'leg' into 'legs', but, again, as shown in Turn 21, S1's production did not incorporate the correct form. In Turn 22, T's utterance contained two models of the plural form. In Turn 23, S1's non-use of the plural -s triggered a third recast changing 'corn-chip' into 'corn-chips'. In spite of the multiple, contextualized learning opportunities, Turn 25 shows that none of them had a noticeable impact on S1's production[3]. The recasts, therefore, did not have any discernable efficacy, even though they all seemed to have retained the original meaning of the learner's utterance.

This raises several questions. First, when S1 produced the singular, instead of the plural, did she really have a plural meaning in mind, as T construed? Second, what was S1's conception of 'grasshopper', 'leg', and 'corn-chip'? Do they represent concrete or abstract entities to her? Third, are these nouns subject to plural marking in her native language? Finally, how would she say these things in a similar situation in her L1?

Contemplating these questions might open up alternative avenues for understanding the function of recasts. For example, if the answer to the first question turned out to be negative, then the teacher may have imposed his own meaning on the learner's utterance – different from what the learner had intended. Conversely, if the answer turned out to be affirmative, the teacher was, then, right in supplying the plural form through his recasts. Either way, it seems clear that without an investigation of the intended meaning of the learner, there will not be a definitive answer. Language, as Hauser (2005: 310) notes, is inherently ambiguous, and, likewise, 'the meaning of a turn is ambiguous, indexical, and open to negotiation and renegotiation'.

Focusing on the coding criteria deployed in the L2 empirical research on recasts, Hauser (2005: 294) objects to the narrow conception of meaning, embedded in those criteria, as 'propositional content and/or the speaker's intention, separate from both its context and linguistic encoding'. Drawing on Bilmes's (1986) two-folded conception of meaning as propositional content and as action, Hauser argues that the practice of coding has relied on the former, 'the criteria ostensibly used to code particular turns as "corrective recasts" treat[ing] the propositional content of the "error turn" and the "corrective recast" as readily identifiable and identical' (2005: 296), while ignoring the latter (i.e. meaning as action), resulting in 'the transformation of the data that obscures what is happening in the interaction' (2005: 295). Although Hauser's criticisms are directed at the off-line conception and application of the coding criteria, they are clearly relevant to the on-line delivery of recasts.

Driven by the theoretically circumscribed need to maintain the central meaning of the learner utterance, recasts contain grammatical changes made according to some norms of the target language, and more importantly, on the basis of one's intuition about what the propositional content ought to be, 'what the interlocutor perceives to be the learner's intended message' (Mackey & Philp, 1998: 342). As a result, it is possible that the re-encoding (i.e. recasting), although targetlike, may deviate, at times, from the original meaning, hence distorting the learner's intention. A case *par excellence* is where a recast is provided in response to a learner's utterance made up of disjointed and incoherent words and/or phrases such that it is impossible to decode, not even with the help of the local context, let alone re-encoding it accurately (e.g., Hauser, 2005, Segment 1). Compounding the difficulty of maintaining the learner's meaning is that an error turn (i.e. the trigger utterance) may be recast in more than one way (e.g. Hauser, 2005, footnote 20), thus giving additional cause for the potential existence of perverted recasts. Furthermore, from a linguistic relativity point of view, reformulation of others' words may have implications for meaning. All these amount to suggesting that, regardless of whether the learner's utterance is discrete or continuous, insofar as the forms chosen for the utterance are carriers of any idiosyncratic meaning and intention (e.g. Bardovi-Harlig, this volume; von Stutterheim & Klein, 1987), meaning maintenance can be elusive in practice, and hence, that while providing target samples, recasts may lose their corrective efficacy.

Such, I believe, is the case with recasts of grammatical morphemes, and, as I will argue below, it is both unjustified and unjustifiable – given the relative lack of efficacy of morphosyntactic recasts noted earlier – to attribute morphosyntactic errors exclusively to inadequate acquisition of certain grammatical norms of the target language. Doing so is fallacious, too, because it conceals the fact that acquisition may equally – and possibly to a greater extent – be hindered by the lack of a targetlike semantic and/or conceptual system (for evidence, see, Coppieters, 1987; Ioup et al., 1994).[4] As von Stutterheim and Klein (1987: 193) have aptly pointed out, 'A structural analysis will overlook or cannot cope with the majority of those cases where learners have built up a system of their own by using L2 structures with meaning or function other than those of the L2'.

Meaning as a source of difficulty

Meaning is receiving increasing attention from L2 researchers, as seen in the recent literature. VanPatten *et al.* (2004: 4), in their opening chapter to a volume entitled *Form–Meaning Connections in Second Language Acquisition*, state that 'L2 forms can ... be connected to meanings that are not L2-like' (see also Odlin, 2003).

In an attempt to deconstruct the notion of grammatical difficulty, DeKeyser (2005) explicitly identifies and tackles several constituents, including complexity of form, complexity of meaning, and complexity of the form–meaning relationship (cf. Larsen-Freeman, 2003). Where complexity of meaning is concerned, he claims, on the basis of available empirical evidence, that novel and abstract meanings, such as those encoded by grammatical morphemes, are particularly 'hard to acquire for native speakers of L1s that do not have them or that use a very different system', and that 'these elements are even strongly resistant to instructional treatments' (DeKeyser, 2005: 5).

Similarly, Selinker (2006: 204) asserts that those elements 'easily get fossilized', on the grounds that they 'appear impervious to correction in the contexts where they occur' and are permeable to transfer effects (Selinker & Lakshmanan, 1992). Citing diary data of spontaneous L2 utterances by native speakers of Italian and Spanish, such as [7] and [8], Selinker illustrates how very advanced speakers of L2 English can still flounder over grammatical morphemes, making non-targetlike form–meaning mappings.

[7]
That happened all over the places.

[8]
If you do your best, she said, I will keep your name in the play.

Subjected to a surface analysis, [7] is flawed because it shows overuse of the plural -s, and [8] is flawed, because of a redundant article, *the*, hence the conclusion that the speakers have not acquired the morphemes. A deeper analysis, considering not only the linguistic environment of the errors but also extra-linguistic factors such as the speakers' amounts of experience with the target language and the level of sophistication of their linguistic and academic performance in other discourse domains, however, suggests otherwise. The driving force for the errors is not any lack of knowledge of the morphemes per se, but rather the semantic and conceptual system that the speakers possess, a system different from that underlying the target expressions. The errors concern English idiomatic expressions 'all over the place' and 'in play', whose syntax is fixed or frozen, so to speak. By inserting the grammatical morphemes in [7] and [8], the speakers gave literal meanings, resulting in referential ambiguity. In this case, the speakers appeared to have mapped their idiosyncratic meanings to the expressions.[5] But exactly what those meanings are needs to be empirically determined. As Selinker (2006: 204) has emphasised, 'since interlanguage data [are] often ambiguous, one must find out systematically what the intended interlanguage semantics is'.

In an interactional setting, negotiation, needless to say, is the default way to identify interlanguage meanings. Nevertheless, it is equally clear that not every meaning can be clarified through negotiation, and this may be particularly true of errors involving grammatical morphemes. For want of any empirical research yet to confirm this, I speculate, based on the general findings on recasts, that even if those errors are open to negotiation, it is unlikely that the ongoing communication will not be disrupted, a designated pedagogical advantage of recasts, nor is it likely that the brief on-line negotiation will shed much light on the learner's semantic system – more likely, perhaps, on a transient meaning. Yet, what is transient must be differentiated from what is systematic – a classic insight from Corder (1967).

It would seem, then, that a fundamental understanding of grammatical morphemes as a pervasive and persistent acquisition problem cannot derive from anything other than a crosslinguistic analysis of the semantics of the interlanguage and the native language.

Interlanguage as a function of NL semantic influence

DeKeyser and Selinker, as mentioned above, both have underscored the interference of the native language in the acquisition of form–meaning mappings of grammatical morphemes, wherein, to be sure, it is not so much the target forms themselves, but rather their meanings that are interfered with by the L1. Indeed, such insights have long existed in the literature, dating back to the early era of L2 research (e.g. Hakuta, 1976; Hakuta & Cancino, 1977). For instance, Hakuta (1976), in a longitudinal case study of Uguisu, a five-year-old Japanese girl learning English in a naturalistic environment, found that Uguisu's acquisition of English articles was not only delayed but also persistently marked by semantic deviance from the target, due to a lack of grasp of the underlying definite and indefinite contrast. In this case, the absence of similar semantic discriminations in the native language created a learnability problem for the L2 learner.

That learners depend on their L1 semantic and syntactic system for bootstrapping into L2 grammar – more so for adults than for children for apparent reasons – has been both suggested and documented in the SLA literature. Von Stutterheim and Klein (1987: 196) have stated that 'the way in which the learner organizes his utterances is heavily influenced by the conceptual structure present and by the way in which this conceptual structure is encoded in the [native] language'. This statement was advanced on the basis of an extensive study of L2 acquisition of temporality by learners of an array of L1 backgrounds, which showed, *inter alia*, that 'dominant conceptual categories – the grammatically marked ones, for instance, as well as specific structural patterns in the first language – form the "equipment" of the learner at the beginning of the acquisitional process and lead to a certain form of selectivity in dealing with the L2 input' (1987: 197). As an example, because the Turkish verbal system makes a distinction between 'near past' and 'remote past', beginning Turkish learners of German, correspondingly, developed a two-fold adverbial system 'vorher' (before) and 'ganz vorher' (very before), but this was not found in the data of beginning Italian and Spanish learners.

The 'dependence' on L1 semantics and syntax, for better or for worse, often continues into the advanced stage of L2 learning (e.g. Hopp, 2003, 2005; Sorace, 2000, 2003, 2005). A longitudinal case study of two advanced L1 Chinese speakers of English by Han (1998, 2000, 2006) indicates that in spite of the subjects' extended stay (>5 years) in English-speaking countries, the L1 topic-comment semantics and its syntactic expression remain the driving force for their production of a number of interlanguage constructions featuring over-passivisation (e.g. passivised unaccusatives) as well as under-passivisation (e.g. novel unaccusatives or pseudo-passives).

This kind of crosslinguistic influence is usually unconscious (Kellerman, 1995). The famous linguistic relativist Whorf (1940) referred to it as the 'binding power' of the native language, suggesting that explicit instruction might ease its grip on the learner (for discussion, see Odlin, 2005). There is, however, abundant evidence in the L2 literature showing that the bond can be so strong that it defies instruction, or any consciousness-raising intervention for that matter, leading to 'fossilisation' (Selinker, 1972; see also Han, 2004c). An example can be found in Odlin (2005) of the persistence of native speakers of Polish – all instructed learners, by default – in using the English pronoun 'we' to denote a singular referent, as in 'We were at the theatre with my brother yesterday', as a result of semantic and pragmatic transfer from the L1 (cf. Gotteri & Michalak-Gray, 1997). That is, the word 'bylismy', the Polish counterpart for 'we were', has a singular meaning in some discourse contexts.

Given the empirical role of L1 semantics in L2 acquisition, a brief discussion of the relationship between language and thought, within the scope of the present chapter, may shed further light on meaning as a learnability problem.

Linguistic relativity in SLA

Experience and knowledge of language develop in tandem with a conceptual system, the outcome being a language-specific world view. Such is the gist of 'linguistic relativity', commonly known as the

Sapir–Whorf Hypothesis, a linguistic theory on the proactive influence of language on cognition (see also Cook, this volume). A strong version of the theory proposes that language *shapes* thought – hence known also as 'linguistic determinism', and a weaker version states that language selectively *influences* thought such, as explained in Athanasopoulos (2006), that

> [C]ertain patterns of language may highlight certain patterns of reasoning/thinking more than others. In this respect, we are likely to pay more attention to those aspects of reality that are coded in our language than those that are not. (Athanasopoulos, 2006: 89)

In spite of the difference, both the strong and weak versions subscribe to the view that people who speak different languages conceptualise the world differently.

What implications, then, does this view hold for second language acquisition (see also Cook, this volume)? According to von Humboldt (1836),

> To learn a foreign language should ... be to acquire a new standpoint in the world-view hitherto possessed, and in fact to a certain extent this is so, since every language contains the whole conceptual fabric and mode of presentation of a portion of mankind. But because we always carry over, more or less, our own world-view, and even our own language-view, this outcome is not purely and completely experienced. (von Humboldt, 1836: 60)

Thus, a major prediction made on the premise of linguistic relativity (LR) is that acquisition of an additional language, be it a second, a third, or any, will never be complete, due to the interference of the L1-based conceptual system. In a similar vein but more concrete terms, Slobin (1996) states

> Each native language has trained its speakers to pay different kinds of attention to events and experiences when talking about them. This training is carried out in childhood and is exceptionally resistant to restructuring in adult second-language acquisition. (Slobin, 1996: 89)

Invoking the term 'thinking for speaking', Slobin underlines that it is the L1-specific system for conceptualising and verbalising experience that will serve as the semantic and syntactic substrate for L2 perception and production. Included in that system are certain grammaticised conceptual categories such as aspect, definiteness, and voice. These categories are likely to breed learnability problems in L2 acquisition – meaning that acquisition of corresponding or non-corresponding categories in the L2 will not be amenable to the influence of the usual, positive and/or negative input.

Indeed, evidence of lack of success in L2 acquisition, instructed or naturalistic, of tense, aspect, definiteness, gender, and number is extensive and robust and continues to accrue. Although the previous sections have only offered a glimpse of it, the existing research, regardless of the perspective taken, has, for one thing, uniformly pointed up the recalcitrant nature of interlanguage nominal and verbal morphology (passim the SLA literature), most, if not all, of the studies holding L1 as largely accountable for the attested persistent lack of targetlike attainment (for a recent study, see Franceschina, 2005). Even so, it can be argued that these studies have, at best, provided indirect evidence of the validity of linguistic relativity in SLA, because direct evidence of the putative relationship (or lack thereof) between language and cognition needs to come from research that investigates the performance of (ideally, the same) bilingual speakers in both linguistic and non-linguistic cognitive domains.

A study by Athanasopoulos (2006) is one such an attempt (for a review of previous studies, see Odlin, 2005). The study examined the plural marking behaviour of intermediate and advanced Japanese speakers of L2 English, against monolingual speakers of Japanese and English. Given that Japanese is a non-plural marking language and English plural marking, comparisons between L2 speakers and monolinguals of either language may attest whether L2 speakers' cognitive behaviour has changed as a result of their experience with a non-native language, and if so, in which direction the change has occurred. Fourteen English monolinguals, 28 Japanese monolinguals, and 38 Japanese speakers of L2 English (21 advanced and 17 intermediate) served as subjects. Five sets of pictures provided stimulus materials, which depicted different types of objects corresponding to the target types of noun phase (i.e. animals, implements, and substances). Subjects were tested individually by seeing five sets of pictures and subsequently judging the degree of similarity between pictures within each set and identifying the closest match between the original picture (the first in a set) and one of its five alternatives. However, the purpose of this task, as Athanasopoulos explains, 'was not to measure the participants' VISUAL ABILITY to spot the differences between the pictures, but rather to measure their COGNITIVE DISPOSITION towards changes in the number or amount of the relevant target objects in each picture' (Athanasopoulos, 2006: 93; emphasis in original). Immediately following the picture-matching task there were a grammaticality judgement task and a general proficiency test, intended respectively to measure L2 subjects' *local* linguistic knowledge (i.e. plural marking) and *global* proficiency. The main results were as follows. First, there was a correlation for the two L2 groups of their cognition, as measured by the picture-matching task, with their proficiency in the L2, as there was with their performance on the grammaticality judgement task. Second, the results from the picture-matching task demonstrated cognitive differences between the two groups of monolingual speakers (Japanese versus English), as predicted by the linguistic relativity hypothesis, but, interestingly, also between the two L2 groups, intermediate and advanced Japanese speakers of L2 English. In the latter case, the intermediate L2 speakers behaved like monolingual speakers of Japanese, on the one hand, and the advanced L2 speakers like monolingual speakers of English, on the other.

This cognitive pattern of behaviour, albeit contrastive, provides supporting evidence for the operation of linguistic relativity in SLA. The operation, thus, begins with the L1 conceptual system serving as the substrate to be then followed by a 'cognitive shift' towards the L2 conceptual system, as proficiency in the L2 advances. Crucially, in both phases, language influences cognition. In Phase 1 (as represented by the intermediate L2 speakers), the L1 is the main source of influence, but in Phase 2 (as represented by the advanced L2 speakers), the L2 is. The linguistic relativity process is schematically shown in Figure 4.4. The figure shows that when the two languages come into contact, as indicated by the L1 and L2 boxes partially overlapping, the L1 linguistic and conceptual system will initially exert a dominant impact on the L2. However, as proficiency in the L2 increases, the L1 system gradually gives way to the L2 and its attendant conceptual system, a dynamic process, as indicated by

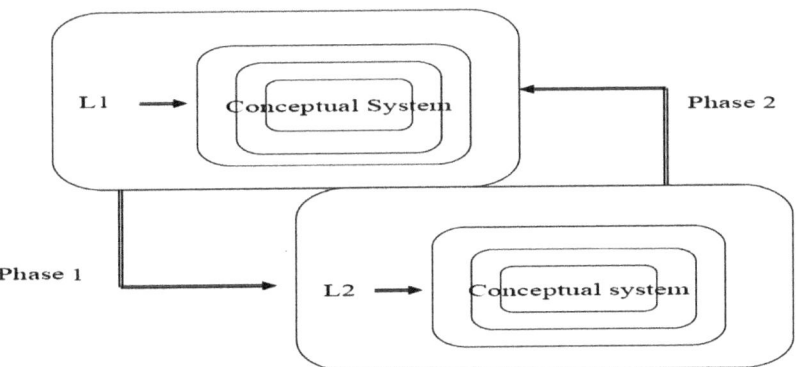

Figure 4.4 Linguistic relativity in SLA

the embedded boxes within the two big boxes representing respectively the L1 and the L2. This is not to suggest that the role played by the L1 will eventually be supplanted by the L2 system. Rather, the development of linguistic knowledge in the L2, as a result of linguistic restructuring, produces a corresponding restructuring in the conceptual system of the learner. The extent to which the restructured systems approximate the target systems might, then, vary as a function of individual differences vis-à-vis learning environment, and psychological, cognitive, and neurological conditions. Furthermore, in Phase 2, the evolving L2 conceptual system, at a certain point, may, as indicated by the arrow, 'backwash' into the L1 (e.g. Cook, 2003, and this volume).

On this LR-based account, conceptual systems are not without vicissitude, including, I believe, the L1-based semantics and conceptions underlying the L2 learner's use of grammatical morphemes. So the question now becomes 'Under what conditions might semantic and conceptual restructuring occur?' And, given the focus of this chapter, what kind of input is likely to facilitate the restructuring? More specifically, can recasts be employed for the mission, and if so, how? The next section addresses these questions.

A Pedagogical Model for Recasts

As discussed in earlier sections, focus on form faces a number of issues on both theoretical and empirical fronts, which militate against its validity and efficacy. Recasts, for one thing, have not been found as helpful for acquisition of morphosyntax as they are intended to be, much of their lack of efficacy being attributable to a problematic view of meaning and its role in the L2 form–meaning mapping process. In this penultimate section, building on my argument on meaning as a learnability problem and taking the English plural marking as an example, I will illustrate the nature and scope of its lack of learnability, challenging, therefore, the widely accepted conclusion based on morpheme order studies that the plural -s is easy and hence acquired early by L2 learners. Furthermore, highlighting the context-rich property of recasts, I will argue that recasts may improve their efficacy for morphosyntactic errors, if delivered in a certain way. Finally, I will propose a pedagogical model of how recasts may assist L2 acquisition of grammatical morphemes in general.

The English plural -s as a learnability problem

SLA research in the 1970s featured a keen interest in establishing a developmental sequence for grammatical morphemes, and comparing it to that derived from first language acquisition research. As it turned out, the orders were strikingly similar, though not identical (for review, see Goldschneider & DeKeyser, 2001). For example, the English plural -s ranked high on both the L2-based and the L1-based order, meaning that it was found to be acquired early by both first and second language acquirers (e.g. Bailey *et al.*, 1974; Dulay & Burt, 1973, for L2; for L1, see Brown, 1973; de Villiers & de Villiers, 1973). Although the observed order for L2 has not been without its challenges (e.g. Larsen-Freeman, 1975) and there has been a continued paucity of follow-up research (DeKeyser, 2005; Goldschneider & DeKeyser, 2001), the developmental sequence itself has nevertheless been widely taken for granted and indeed, has been deployed as a foundation for SLA theory and research, and even as a basis for pedagogical recommendations.

In his book-length account of task-based language instruction, R. Ellis (2003), for instance, treated the plural -s as formally simple, functionally transparent, and metalinguistically simple to explain. This view was, again, implied in the R. Ellis (2005a) empirical report on the measurement of explicit and implicit knowledge of a second language, wherein the plural -s is listed as an early acquired grammatical structure. However, there is evidence outside the body of literature on morpheme ordering indicating that the plural -s is, in fact, a long-term challenge for many learners (e.g. Lardiere, 2007; Long, 2003; Young, 1989), including those who were early starters, as demonstrated in Shin and Milroy (1999). The interlanguage forms created tend to be persistent and resistant to pedagogical interventions (see Examples [5] and [6]; see also Panova, 2005). Lightbown (2000: 451) has noted that 'Francophone students in intensive ESL classes fail to produce English plurals correctly, even when they are fairly advanced'.

Studies of grammatical morphemes often assume a particular scoring method that relies on so-called obligatory contexts for assessing acquisition accuracy. The methodological practice, as many have pointed out, may have yielded an incomplete picture, because, following Bley-Vroman (1983), a reliance on 'obligatory contexts' and hence on the target language is premised on a comparative fallacy that assumes interlanguage as a product of imitation of the target language rather than as a system in its own right (cf. Cook, this volume). Any interlanguage analysis founded on the comparative fallacy must necessarily focus on the surface, formal deviances, therefore obviating their underlying semantic and conceptual impulse (cf. Larsen-Freeman, 2006). Thus, concerning the form of the noun 'research' in [9], [10], and [11] below, an analysis based on the obligatory contexts would reveal no more than that the usages are non-targetlike.

[9]

With quite *a number of research* done on age effects (even if they are not fully conducted to strongly and absolutely support 'the earlier is better' idea), I cannot deny the fact that there is an age factor influencing second language acquisition.

[10]

Based on Pienemann's teachability hypothesis and *subsequent researches* to prove or disprove the hypothesis, Lightbown and Spada's (1999) study is intended to investigate the interaction of instruction, first language influence and developmental readiness in second language acquisition.

[11]

Bongaerts *et al.* (1997) conduct *a research* with a detail screening procedure for the selection of both subjects and judges.

In contrast, an analysis based on the linguistic relativity hypothesis would focus on the variable behaviour, sometimes 'research' being marked as plural but sometimes not. More importantly, such an endeavour would look beyond the interlanguage and into the conceptual, semantic, and grammatical properties of nouns in the native language. With regard to [9], [10], and [11], produced by an advanced Korean speaker of L2 English, an examination of the local environments surrounding the 'errors' in question, that is, 'a number of research', 'subsequent researches', and 'a research', indicates that in spite of the above noted formal variation, on the semantic level the three tokens of 'research', *invariantly,* convey a countable meaning. This consistency, in turn, mirrors a conception which, somehow, views 'research' as discrete and hence quantifiable. As it turns out, both the interlanguage semantics and the conception are accountable to corresponding representations in the L1: in Korean, *yon-gu* ('research') (1) is, conceptually, quantifiable; (2) semantically, may carry a singular or plural meaning; and (3) grammatically, has its plural meaning encoded not by morphological inflection but through, *dul,* a free morpheme known as a unitiser or classifier. For one thing, Korean allows both 'a number of research' and 'a number of researches', but semantically, the former makes a generic reference to the amount of research, and the latter a specific reference to individual studies. In sum, the cognitive impetus for (persistence of) the 'errors', as it should be clear now, was crosslinguistic semantic and conceptual differences, the influence being implicit yet powerful, referred to by Kellerman (1995) as 'transfer to nowhere'.

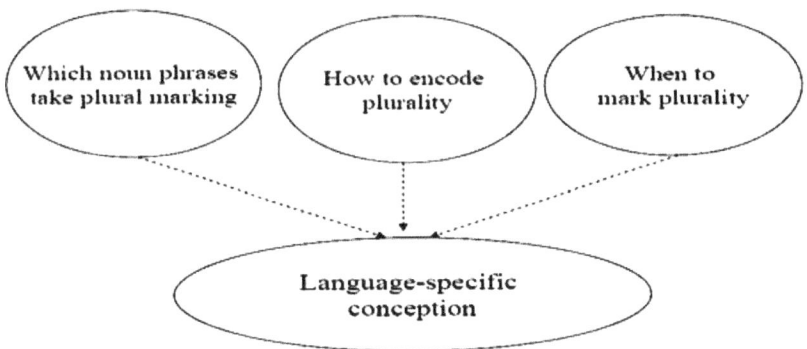

Figure 4.5 Crosslinguistic variation in plural marking

The above example elucidates that with respect to plural marking, languages may differ in, at least, three aspects: (1) what noun phrases take plural marking, (2) how to encode plurality, and (3) when to mark plurality. The choices taken by each language, in light of the earlier discussion on linguistic relativity, constitute a language-specific conceptual system, as illustrated in Figure 4.5.

Take 'hair' as in 'He has dark hair' for an example. In English, the *prototypical* use of the word 'hair' suggests that it is primarily an uncountable noun,[6] because, grammatically, it does not take the plural -s. By contrast, in Italian, the word 'capello' is countable, and grammatically, its plurality is marked by changing the word-final vowel letter 'o' into 'i' to render 'capelli'. Then, in between the two ends of the spectrum, there is Chinese, a language that treats all nouns as potentially quantifiable (or not), and grammatically, uses classifiers to quantify nouns, as in 'san1 *gen1* tou3 fa3' (three hairs). Given these differences, it is conceivable that speakers of the three languages may conceptualise 'hair' differently. So, to monolingual speakers of English, 'hair' could be non-discrete, but discrete to speakers of Italian, and to speakers of Chinese, discrete or non-discrete depending on discourse purposes.

In their discussion of form–meaning connections in SLA, VanPatten *et al.* (2004: 11) speculate that 'Words that relate to concepts that are firmly grounded in physical reality are more likely to share conceptual features from L1 to L2, but more abstract words do not necessarily share the same boundaries and may vary in attributes across languages'. Although the second part of this statement is apparently true, the above 'hair' example demonstrates (1) that even concrete words may vary cross-linguistically, and more importantly, (2) that grammatical morphemes encoding abstract concepts do not act in isolation, but rather in concert with syntactic categories such as nominal and verbal phrases. It follows, then, that assessment of morpheme accuracy should not be confined to morphemes alone; rather, it should be carried out within a larger linguistic and discourse context, including constructions that might not specifically involve the morphemes. This need is illustrated in [12] (see also [9]–[11]).

[12]
I noticed that *Coppieters and Birdsong discusses* which *grammar elements goes* under the UG umbrella, but do not question the validity of the notion [of UG] itself ...
Gass and Selinker (2001) lay out the three options we have for *counter-evidences*.

The sentences in [12] were produced by another advanced Korean speaker of L2 English. The first thing to note is that there is repeated lack of agreement between a plural subject and a verb, even though the first instance, 'Coppieters and Birdsong discusses', involves no plural -*s* morpheme. The next thing to note is the overuse of the plural -*s*, as in 'counter-evidences'. The two phenomena, although seemingly disparate, are epistemologically related in that they both stem from a lack of acquisition of semantically constrained distributional rules of the target language – owing, in turn, to the underlying L1-influenced conceptual system (cf. Bardovi-Harlig, 1992). Clearly, an understanding of this nature would be beyond the reach of any structural analysis that relies on obligatory contexts for assessing morpheme accuracy, only because formal characteristics of interlanguage plural marking are discernable at the word or sentence level, but semantic, and in particular, conceptual characteristics are evident only at the discourse level.

Of the three aspects of crosslinguistic variation identified above (see Figure 4.5), each aspect may pose some degree of difficulty for L2 learning (cf. Larsen-Freeman, 2003), but what appears to have incited the greatest difficulty is, as best shown in [12], to know when to mark plurality, the aspect where the L1 thinking-for-speaking influence proves the strongest. Simply knowing what noun phrases take plural marking and how to encode plurality does not guarantee a corresponding knowledge (in both a declarative and a procedural sense) of when to actually mark it. The example in [13], taken from Mackey *et al.* (2000), illustrates the dissociation between knowing the 'what' and 'how' and knowing the 'when.'

[13]
1   **NNS:**   Three key
2   **NS:**   Three?
3   **NNS:**   Key or keys.
[NNS's] Recall: After 'key' again, I make a little effort to say 'keys' because you have three, I was thinking try a little better English.

This interactional episode shows that the learner (NNS) underused the plural -s, not because he did not know that 'key' can take plural marking nor how to pluralize it, but because, as his/her recall protocol makes apparent, the plural -s was more or less taken to be semantically 'empty' and hence, its suppliance optional (see also Jiang, 2004). In this case, the plural -s was part of the learner's grammar, but not yet part of his/her semantic and conceptual system, a system that might still be L1-entrenched.

The discussion so far has provided for at least two understandings. First, the plural -s is semantically and conceptually related to the abstract notion of number, which, in turn, intersects with other abstract notions, such as definiteness/indefiniteness. It therefore presents itself as a learnability problem on multiple levels and in multiple dimensions. Related to this, secondly, what may eventually render the plural -s unlearnable for some learners is its distributional constraints, due to L1 semantic and conceptual interference.

What, then, does L2 acquisition of English plural marking entail? In view of Figure 4.5, the form (relating to the 'how' aspect), the meaning (the 'what'), and the function (the 'when') are the essential elements, just as Larsen-Freeman has advocated all along for grammar instruction (e.g. Larsen-Freeman, 2001, 2003), but fundamentally, as this chapter has so far made apparent, conceptual restructuring needs to occur. What instructional strategy might facilitate this process? Traditional and current pedagogical approaches have, for the most part, been discrete in nature, inasmuch as they tend to focus on one or two of the elements, a less than desirable outcome of which is that they enforce and reinforce a separation of the three otherwise interrelated elements. In the section that follows, I will propose that the recast has the potential to provide an integrated approach to facilitate the acquisition of the underlying form–meaning–function relations of grammatical morphemes through triggering conceptual restructuring.

A pedagogical model

Given what is known about characteristics of instructed learning, the acquisition of the plural -s is likely to proceed in three identifiable yet

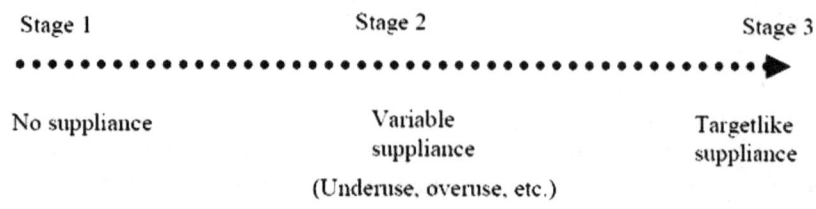

Figure 4.6 A developmental continuum

continuous stages on a developmental continuum, as illustrated in Figure 4.6. Stage 1 is marked by no suppliance of the morpheme, Stage 2 by variable suppliance, including underuse and overuse, and Stage 3 by targetlike suppliance. Linking these stages, then, to the three elements of acquisition referred to above (i.e. form, meaning, and function), the focus of learning is likely to be on form at Stage 1, on meaning at Stage 2, and on function (distributional characteristics) at Stage 3.

This view is premised on the fact that humans are limited information processors, so much so that their attention can only be selective (for discussion, see Han & Peverly, 2007; Lightbown, this volume). The three developmental stages, taken together, square with Terrell's (1991: 57) binding and access model which conceptualizes acquisition as consisting of 'the positing and storing of . . . form–meaning relationships and the restrictions on the appropriate access of these forms to express an intended meaning'.

A point was made in the last section about the potential insurmountable challenge that acquisition of distributional restrictions may present to L2 learners, for it requires restructuring of a primarily L1-based conceptual system. All too often, the challenge is compounded by a limited amount of exposure to naturally contextualised usages of the target form, a problem epitomised in English as a Foreign Language settings. Natural contexts are, nevertheless, crucial for acquisition of the distributional characteristics of linguistic forms inasmuch as they are the loci for individual form–meaning associations. Following the developmental path delineated within the framework of connectionism, spanning from individual items to low-scoped patterns and then to creative constructions (N. Ellis, 2002, 2003, 2006a, 2006b), experience with numerous contexts is likely to induce (1) an awareness and understanding of the network of rules governing the associations or distributional constraints and simultaneously (2) a restructuring of the L1-based conceptual system. On this supposition, recasts have the potential to become an effective pedagogical strategy.

Due to their non-obtrusive nature, recasts, as Doughty (2003) has noted, '[do] not detract from learners' attention to meaning, and this facilitates – rather than hinders – the mapping of form and meaning'. A related valuable property of recasts, from my perspective, is that they are context-rich, in two ways. First, as classroom research has revealed, they naturally and frequently occur in meaning-based classroom discourse. Second, they do so in response to a variety of linguistic and comprehension needs. As such, recasts have the capacity to provide numerous, repeated opportunities for the learner to see and test one form in many of its contextual manifestations. Hence, as far as acquisition of form–meaning–function relations is concerned, they are unparalleled by any explicit instruction method which is, more often than not, contextually restrictive or impoverished, limiting itself to one form–meaning association at a time and thereby inducing overuse of the target form, which may prove hard to undo later on. Furthermore, although explicit instruction faces the difficulty of converting declarative knowledge into procedural knowledge (i.e. implicit knowledge),[7] recasts directly build implicit knowledge.

However, before recasts may exercise their contextual power on the acquisition of distributional constraints on the plural -s or any other grammatical morpheme, a few pedagogical conditions must be satisfied. The most basic one is an unambiguous understanding of the meaning of the trigger utterance. As I pointed out earlier, a major problem that weakens the efficacy of recasts is the neglect of the intended meaning of the learner. Therefore, in the event of the learner utterance being ambiguous, the teacher should adopt a 'wait and see' stance until further exchange with the learner clarifies the underlying intention or, as studies of recasts have suggested (e.g. Kim & Han, 2007; Han & Kim, in press), use 'interrogative recasts' to negotiate meaning with the learner. In a connectionist or emergentist perspective, meaning is not located in a particular form; it is a function of the global state of the system, and it emerges in the interaction (Han & Larsen-Freeman, 2005; Varela *et al*., 1991).

A second pedagogical condition is that recasts must be focused, meaning that they should focus on one grammatical morpheme at a time, although not necessarily that particular form alone. As has already been suggested, in terms of triggering semantic and conceptual restructuring, recasts would be better off if they target a cohort of interlanguage constructions that represent various grammaticised ways of encoding the abstract notion.[8] Thus, in the case of the plural -s, they could be provided not only on errors concerning the application (or non) of the morpheme but also subject–verb agreement, article usages, and even a case like [14],

[14]
I have received many such letters, and I have discarded it.

where there is nothing wrong with the plural -*s* per se, but there is a problem with the anaphoric, object pronoun, *it*, and its referent, *letters*. Research on recasts has shown that focused recasts are effective in inducing restructuring – presumably because 'focused' renders the positive and negative evidence in recasts perceptually salient (e.g. Doughty & Varela, 1998; Han, 2002; Mackey & Philp, 1998).

Finally, a third condition requires that recasts be sustained, meaning that they should be ongoing (cf. Lightbown, this volume) and systematic. When recasts are systematically provided over a period of time, as opposed to randomly and one time only, they are more likely to bring about conceptual restructuring, a long, gradual, but not necessarily linear process.

A pedagogical model for recasts, in conjunction with the developmental continuum (Figure 4.6), proffers intensive recasting for Stage 1, non-intensive recasting for Stage 2, and selective recasting for Stage 3, as presented in Figure 4.7.

As shown, this model predicts that intensive recasting at Stage 1 will lead to increased sensitivity on the learner's part to the target of the recasts. As a result, the learner will become aware, and his/her output will show variable suppliance of the morpheme, and gradually, self-corrections and even hyper-corrections (Stage 2). At this point, the teacher should shift to non-intensive recasting to counterbalance the learner's

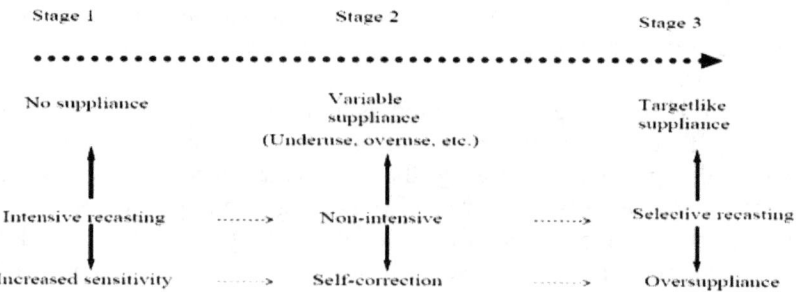

Figure 4.7 A pedagogical model for recasts

hyper-sensitivity. However, this hyper-sensitivity is likely to continue for an extended period of time, even after the learner appears able to use the target form correctly in a majority of contexts (Stage 3), in which case, the teacher should resort to selective recasting to primarily target errors of overuse.

This model, needless to say, is only an abstraction, and because of that, adjustments must be made during its implementation. Indeed, as Larsen-Freeman (2006: 198) has suggested for grammar instruction in general, 'For maximum effectiveness, the pedagogical intervention ... designed to address the particular learning challenge ... [should be] customized for the learner and the learning context. Only with optimal learning conditions will learners' full learning potential have a chance to be realized'.

Conclusions

This chapter offered an analysis of the role of meaning in focus on form. One of its main findings is that focus on form, as currently constructed and empirically applied, evinces a lack of attention to the role of learners' semantic and conceptual system in interlanguage development. As a result, its pedagogical efficacy is compromised, as the research on recasts – a popular instantiation of focus on form – has amply shown. It was subsequently argued that inasmuch as acquisition consists, broadly, of form–meaning associations, meaning can be a greater source of difficulty than form, and in that vein, grammatical morphemes encoding abstract notions are likely a long-lasting learnability problem for most L2 learners, due to the underlying interference of their L1-based semantic and conceptual systems. Drawing on the linguistic relativity hypothesis, I hypothesised that conceptual restructuring is what is ultimately responsible for targetlike acquisition of grammatical morphemes. By way of illustration, I briefly examined L2 acquisition of the English plural -s morpheme, making a case that existing morpheme order studies have erred in relying on obligatory contexts – 'a target-centric perspective' (Larsen-Freeman, 2006) – in assessing acquisition accuracy and supporting, instead, a more interlanguage-orientated approach. I subsequently proposed a pedagogical model that deploys recasts to stimulate conceptual restructuring vis-à-vis grammatical morphemes.

Admittedly, parts of my account were more speculative than I would have liked, but I hope they will provoke much empirical research. Apparently, some of the claims, such as those concerning the pedagogical model, would be best tested through longitudinal case studies. As Long (2007: 113) has speculated, 'Implicit negative feedback, such as corrective recasts, is more likely to be successful than explicit 'error correction' when applied *in long-term treatments* of hard learning targets' (emphasis added). Yet, unlike Long who believes that extended use of recasts will, *ipso facto*, lead to acquisition of the 'hard learning targets', I contend that an attention to interlanguage semantics (and conceptions, for that matter) is critical to making that happen.

SLA empirical research has yet to develop instruments sensitive to interlanguage semantics and conceptions as a state as well as a process, a domain that has been by and large ignored, due in part to the continued predominance of a form-orientated approach to SLA research, but more importantly, to the long-standing research tradition of relying on the target language in trying to understand interlanguage, this in spite of numerous theoretical claims and abundant empirical evidence on L2 acquisition being parasitic on the L1 in the literature. Overcoming the comparative fallacy (Bley-Vroman, 1983; Cook, this volume) should constitute a paramount priority for SLA research in the coming years, particularly for researchers who strive for a better understanding of any unrelenting learnability problem.

Acknowledgements

This chapter is based, in part, on Han and Larsen-Freeman's (2005) presentation at the 28th SLRF conference held at Teachers College, Columbia University, and in part, on my invited talk at Georgetown University (April 2006). Patsy Lightbown, Kathleen Bardovi-Harlig, Terence Odlin, and Alison Mackey read an earlier draft of the chapter and provided constructive critiques. Ji-Hyun Kim and Monika Ekiert assisted with the analysis of some of the examples. Any errors are exclusively my own.

Notes

1. For evidence of the functional approach, one does not have to look beyond two simple facts. Both first and second language acquirers begin by producing (1) the so-called 'telegraphic speech', that is, utterances that are devoid of grammatical functors, and (2) formulaic speech, that is, chunks of language, without knowledge of internal structure (e.g. Myles, 2004). Both types of speech have high functional value in communication (for discussion, see Hakuta & Cancino, 1977).
2. A recent meta-analysis by Mackey and Goo (2007) of 28 interaction studies reveals an interesting finding, namely that 'interaction tends to be more beneficial for lexis than grammar in the short term, but more beneficial and durable for grammar in the longer term. Recasts seem to be developmentally helpful, with large effect sizes across all posttests ...' (p. 409). At first blush,

this finding provides counter-evidence to the logical conclusion I am describing here, but close inspection of the meta-analysis soon allays the concern. In arriving at the above finding, the meta-analysis lumped the interaction studies together, without, that is, differentiating between studies involving recasts and those that did not. Hence, the extent to which recasts are effective for grammatical features is not entirely clear, nor are their putative delayed effects convincing, given that the finding is based on a small number of studies that administered short-term delayed post-tests. A further mitigating element to the finding is that, constrained by the lack of studies on different types of interactional feedback in the literature, the meta-analysis examined interactional feedback as a whole, rather than isolating and comparing different types of feedback. Accordingly, it is still very much of a conundrum whether recasts are superior to other feedback types when grammatical features constitute the targets of correction.
3. One could argue, as Patsy Lightbown, a reviewer of this chapter, points out, that this may only be a reflection of lack of 'uptake', and not necessarily an indication of lack of learning.
4. The semantic and conceptual systems overlap but may not be identical – an insight from Odlin (2005; cf. Levinson, 1997) who distinguished between meaning transfer and conceptual transfer as follows: 'All conceptual transfer involves meaning transfer but not all meaning transfer involves conceptual transfer. In effect, conceptual transfer is a subset of meaning transfer' (Odlin, 2005: 6). In my discussion, I, however, assume that the two systems are interconnected, one (semantic) being concrete and local, and the other (conceptual) abstract and global. Thus, talking about one necessarily entails the other.
5. Kathleen Bardovi-Harlig, who also served as a reviewer for this chapter, offered a different interpretation: '[The learners] are just regularizing grammatically odd expressions'.
6. In English, it is possible to pluralise 'hair' in some pragmatic circumstances. For example, while *It made the hair on his head stand up* is a standard expression, it is also possible to say *It made the hairs on his head stand up*, where the plural form, 'hairs', refers to each hair individually.
7. Evidence suggesting a close interface between explicit and implicit knowledge is as yet non-substantial. Hence, the debate continues over the extent to which explicit knowledge contributes to the underlying linguistic competence (cf. Lightbown, 2000, this volume; R. Ellis, 2005).
8. L2 pedagogy should benefit greatly from theoretical linguistic findings of clusters of syntactic and morphological properties, but unfortunately, not many have been found. The few that are available, for example, question formation and adverb placement (White, 1991), and the correlations between the $\pm$prodrop parameter, subject inversion, and *that*-trace effects (Rizzi, 1982), have not really been put to pedagogical application in the way suggested here (cf. Ying, this volume).

Chapter 5

The Efficacy of Visual Input Enhancement in Teaching Deaf Learners of L2 English

GERALD P. BERENT and RONALD R. KELLY

This chapter reports the results of a classroom research study on the use of visual input enhancement in the teaching of grammatical form to college-level deaf students of English as a second language (L2). Deaf learners of English share many similarities with hearing learners of L2 English. In the case of deaf learners, restricted access to English input results from restricted auditory access to spoken language, which ranges from severely reduced access to no access at all, depending on the degree of hearing loss. As a result, many deaf learners' meaningful exposure to English begins only with the commencement of formal education. In the case of hearing L2 learners, restricted access to English input results from the cognitive and neurobiological factors that constrain later (i.e. L2) acquisition generally. Therefore, irrespective of the factors that contribute to restricting access to linguistic input, any demonstrated efficacy of visual input enhancement (Sharwood Smith, 1993, this volume) in enabling later learners – deaf or hearing – to notice English input supports an L2 theory (e.g. Gass, 1997) in which *noticing* is a prerequisite to the ultimate acquisition of form–meaning connections.

With respect to the visual processing and the acquisition of a first language (L1), deaf learners acquire visual–spatial languages such as American Sign Language (ASL) as effortlessly as hearing learners acquire a spoken L1. However, most deaf learners with severe and profound (as opposed to mild or moderate) hearing losses struggle, for the access reasons noted, to acquire spoken language knowledge, irrespective of the learning or use of speech (for more information on the spoken language development of deaf children see Blamey, 2003; Levitt, 1989). Deaf learners can receive compensatory spoken language input through environmental visual cues (gestures, facial expression), lip-reading, reading of text, finger-spelling, and English-based sign language, that is, the use of ASL signs following English word order and the approximation of other grammatical features of English. However, as compensatory mechanisms, these channels of input can be very limited in their effectiveness.

For example, it is virtually impossible to represent English morphology through sign (Supalla, 1991) because sign language phonology realises morphology through movement and directionality in the signing space and not through any equivalent to spoken language affixation (Fischer & van der Hulst, 2003). Reading alone cannot serve as a primary visual conduit of spoken language input because reading presupposes linguistic knowledge of the spoken language symbolised through the writing system. Furthermore, because successful reading in an L2 requires knowledge of the L2 syntax, vocabulary, and discourse structure (Eskey, 2005), it is paradoxical that reading could serve as the primary *source* of the acquisition of L2 syntax, vocabulary, and discourse structure.

Consequently, severely and profoundly deaf learners exhibit, on average, English grammatical knowledge that is measurably years behind age-equivalent hearing learners' grammatical knowledge of English (Berent, 1996; Quigley & King, 1980). In a national study of 4800 deaf students' performance on the Stanford Achievement Test, 9th edition, no cohort of students at the 80th percentile across the age range of 8–18 scored higher than 'Below Basic' or 'Basic' skills on the subtests for Language, Spelling, Reading Comprehension, and Reading Vocabulary (Traxler, 2000). It is important to note, however, that certain deaf learners attain very high or native levels of English proficiency. The college students targeted in Toscano *et al.* (2002) had English literacy levels equivalent to their hearing peers. As one might expect, the key to their success was early access to English input. All the students reported growing up in families that provided consistently rich communicative environments with sustained access to English language input through any means available. In contrast to such students, the classroom research reported in this chapter targeted deaf students who have experienced a lifelong struggle to acquire English grammatical knowledge and, for the access reasons discussed above, are effectively 'L2 learners without an L1' (Berent, 2004).

The Study

At the National Technical Institute for the Deaf (NTID), a college of the Rochester Institute of Technology, deaf students have exhibited a broad and stable range of English language proficiency over the years from as low as a 5th grade assessed reading level to a high of 12th grade and beyond (Walter, 1988). The students targeted in this study tested toward the lower end of the English proficiency range for NTID students, with an average reading level of 7.8 on the California Achievement Tests (Tiegs & Clark, 1957).

Grammar for academic writing

The setting for this classroom research study was a one-credit remedial grammar course, 'Grammar for Writing II', which is a co-requisite to the students' 'Academic Writing II' course, which focuses on English paragraph development. The grammar course met one hour per week during the 10-week academic quarter. The NTID English programme had identified nine English structures for mastery in the grammar course, which are listed in Table 5.1 along with the codes that were used in one of the input enhancement procedures and in one of the assessment procedures.

Visual input enhancement

Three specific input enhancement interventions were developed for use in this study: (1) essay coding with metalinguistic feedback,

Table 5.1 Nine English structures for the grammar course

English Structure	Code
Present tense	PRS
Past tense	PST
Present progressive	PRS/PROG
Past progressive	PST/PROG
That clause	THAT
Adjective clause	ADJC
Modal verbs	MOD
Infinitives	INF
Present perfect	PERF

(2) textual enhancement of course readings, and (3) a 'visuogloss' (visual dictogloss) procedure.

Essay coding

The essay coding procedure (Berent, 2005a, 2005b) required students to type a short essay on one of three topics related to personal experience: (1) 'My Best Friend', (2) 'My First Job', and (3) 'My Worst Day'. Students typed their essays under supervision and submitted both a paper and electronic file copy. The instructor coded each student essay by indicating where the student successfully produced each of the target structures in Table 5.1 and where the student produced target structures unsuccessfully or failed to use a target structure clearly required by the discourse. Each target structure was highlighted by the inclusion of the relevant code preceded by a ' + ' sign signalling successful structures and a ' − ' sign signalling unsuccessful structures. These codes were typed into the electronic file of the student's original essay and returned to the student in hard copy and as a coded electronic file. The following excerpt from a student essay illustrates the coding procedure. The target structures are italicised for illustration, but were not italicised in the student's coded file.

> Last year I −PST *work* first day at my city's Community College and −PST/PROG I'*m doing* landscaping job. First day in morning, my boss +PST *told* me +INF *to air blow* all on sidewalk on campus. Then I +PST *went* −INF *get* air blow in shop and −PST *start* −INF *blow* on sidewalk. In 30 minute later, my boss −PST *check* on me and −PST *make* sure +THAT −PST I'*m* all right and −PST/PROG *do* the job. I −PST *keep* blow and walk on sidewalk and finally −PST *finish* in one and half hours. Then I −PST *return* to boss's office and −PST *ask* him what −PST ___ next list +INF *to do*? He −PST *give* me list +ADJC *that* I −PST *have* +INF *to do* for day. Then I −PST *look* at paper and −PST *see* what I −PST *suppose* +INF *to do*.

Coding essays in this manner constituted visual enhancement of the student's own original output in the form of coded metalinguistic feedback. The feedback codes identified successful and unsuccessful productions, and the feedback was metalinguistic in that the codes did not constitute explicit correction of student errors. Instead, the codes were grammatical labels representing the structures targeted for instruction in the grammar course. Students were told to examine their coded essays, noting their successful (+) productions and contemplating their unsuccessful (−) productions through comparison with their successful productions and other conscious reflection. Accordingly, the coding procedure involves visual input enhancement through text coding. Only the nine target structures in Table 5.1 were enhanced via coding. No other structures received feedback coding.

Once students received their coded essays, they were required to revise their essays by retaining their successful structures and reformulating their unsuccessful structures in their revisions. However, they were instructed not to delete or alter the original coding. Their instructor provided subsequent feedback on their first revisions by indicating in ink which of the original unsuccessful productions had been successfully corrected and which had not. In the students' second revision, they were told to continue reformulating unsuccessful structures and then to remove all codes from the essay file. The total revision process occurred between the third and seventh weeks of the 10-week quarter, providing students not only time for reflection, but to learn from other course activities related to the nine target structures.

Textual enhancement

The second input enhancement intervention involved the *textual enhancement* of five course readings and homework assignments during the 10-week course. This *explicit* input enhancement was considered a supplement to the essay coding intervention that would help students to further notice input related to the target structures. Textual enhancement involved the use of a larger bold font, underlining, or italics to highlight specific structures. The following is an excerpt from a reading on 'Hollywood and Broadway' (n.d.):

> American movies and live theater **have influenced** the entire world, and this influence **has grown** stronger and stronger over the years. People in almost every country in the world **have seen** movies that were produced in Hollywood and plays that began on Broadway.

Activities involving textually enhanced readings and assignments included explicit discussion and clarification of the form and function of the enhanced structures.

Visuogloss

The dictogloss methodology (see Doughty & Williams, 1998b) was adapted for visual presentation into a visual dictogloss, or *visuogloss*. Rather than an input-flooded dictation, each visuogloss was developed as a typed paragraph flooded as naturalistically as possible with the target structure. These structures were *not* textually enhanced. The following visuogloss targets the past progressive formation:

> Sharon was walking down the sidewalk with her friends. They were all discussing their summer plans. Sharon was explaining that she and her family were planning to visit California this summer. Marcia was telling everyone about her plans to visit Europe. When they were crossing the street, they were not paying attention, and a speeding car almost hit them.

For the visuogloss exercise, students gathered in teams of three. The visuogloss paragraph was displayed on a full screen for the deaf students to read three or four times, just as a dictogloss would be dictated three or four times. When students had read the paragraph a few times, the displayed paragraph was removed, and the students discussed and clarified the text among each other within their teams. Then one team member in each group typed the paragraph as best as it could be recalled in collaboration with team members. Students' collected paragraphs were corrected, duplicated, and returned to students the following week with a brief class discussion of the target structure.

Participants

Sixty-eight deaf students enrolled in the 'Grammar for Writing II' courses participated in the classroom research project. These students made up three groups – two experimental groups and one control group. One experimental group, designated the *Input Group*, was taught using (1) the essay coding procedure and (2) the textually enhanced readings and assignments. The second experimental group, designated the *Visuogloss Group*, was taught using the same enhanced input methods (1) and (2) as the Input Group plus (3) the visuogloss procedure. The Control Group of deaf students received no visual input enhancement whatsoever. The instructors who taught the Control Group sections were blind to the experimental interventions. Although instruction to deaf students is always delivered largely through the visual modality, any visual enhancement that the control sections may have received would have been incidental and not a structured, theory-driven intervention.

Detailed background characteristics of the deaf student groups were discussed in Berent *et al.* (2007). The three student groups were roughly equivalent in average age, hearing loss, reading level, writing skill level, and overall English proficiency level. An indication of the groups' English proficiency levels is apparent in their mean scores in the 50

Table 5.2 Results for the Michigan Test of English Language Proficiency

	Michigan Test scores
Input Group ($N = 24$)	$M = 56.8$ (SD = 8.5)
Visuogloss Group ($N = 18$)	$M = 53.1$ (SD = 8.9)
Control Group ($N = 26$)	$M = 59.1$ (SD = 12.1)

range on the Michigan Test of English Language Proficiency (1977), as shown in Table 5.2. Research shows that 87% of NTID/RIT baccalaureate-level deaf graduates and 78% of associate's degree graduates have a Michigan Score of 70 or higher (Cuculick & Kelly, 2003: 283). The Michigan Test is an instrument familiar to many educators of hearing L2 English learners. A one-way analysis of variance (ANOVA) revealed no significant differences between the three participant groups' Michigan Test Scores, $F(2,57) = 1.59$, $p = 0.2139$.

Assessment measures

Direct assessment of grammatical knowledge

For assessing change over the 10-week period in students' knowledge of the nine target structures listed in Table 5.1, two measures were employed. The first measure was the very same essay coding procedure that was used to provide visual input enhancement to the Input Group and the Visuogloss Group. During the first week of the course, all students were required to type a short essay on any one of the following three topics: 'My Best Friend', 'My First Job', or 'My Worst Day'. This *First Essay* served to establish a baseline, for each student, of productive grammatical knowledge of the nine target structures. All three groups produced the First Essay, even though it was only the two experimental groups who received their coded essays as part of the instructional process. Students' scores on the First Essay provided a direct assessment of their productive grammatical knowledge and thus served as a pre-test instrument against which to compare their performance at the end of the course. Students' productive knowledge of each target structure was calculated as a percentage of the number of discourse-appropriate successful productions of that structure out of the total attempted productions (successful and unsuccessful) in the obligatory contexts requiring them. The total essay score was the percentage of all successful target productions out of all attempted target productions. The use of three different essay topics permitted students to flexibly select a topic of personal significance to them that would elicit naturalistic communication of meaningful life experiences.

During the last week of the academic quarter, students, including students in the Control Group, produced a *Last Essay* on one of the three topics that was not the topic chosen for their First Essay. It was anticipated that each student's free selection of one of three topics for the First Essay and one of their two remaining topics for the Last Essay would naturally distribute the three essay topics within and across participant groups. Such distribution would serve to neutralise any differences, between topics, in the occurrence of the target grammatical structures driven by discourse factors. The students' Final Essays were coded and scored in the same manner as the First Essays and served as a post-test measure of change in productive knowledge of the nine target structures. Difference scores were calculated based on the percentages of correct productions on the First Essay and Last Essay. Using the groups as the independent variable and the students' percentage scores on the First and Last Essays as the two dependent variables, a 3 (Group) × 2 (First Essay, Last Essay) ANOVA with repeated measures on the two dependent variables was conducted to determine the extent of improvement by group over the 10-week period.

Students' First and Last Essays were assessed relative to the successful production in obligatory contexts of a cumulative set of structures prevalent in English discourse, namely, the nine target structures in Table 5.1, which were also the instructional focus of the NTID 'Grammar for Writing II' course. It was expected that development of any of the three possible essay topics would motivate obligatory contexts for most, but not necessarily all, of those target structures. The study did not isolate individual structures for examination because of the considerable differences in discourse frequency among the nine structures and because of the possibility of learner *avoidance* of some structures.

Learner avoidance is an important consideration in the assessment of L2 grammatical knowledge. Schachter (1974) cautioned that an analysis of a learner's 'errors' in assessing L2 knowledge of isolated structures can lead to an inadequate picture of L2 knowledge. For example, in Schachter's study of L2 learners' acquisition of English relative clauses, learners whose L1s had relative clauses typologically similar (e.g. right-branching) to English relative clauses *attempted* more relative clauses in their productive essays than learners whose L1s contained non-English-like (e.g. left-branching) relative clauses. In avoiding the production of relative clauses to a considerable extent in their essays, the learners in the non-English-like relative clause group exhibited error rates that were proportionally lower than the error rates of the learners in the English-like relative clause group. The reason for this result is that, in attempting more English relative clauses, the latter group made many more incidental errors (e.g. choosing the incorrect relative pronoun), which increased their error rate. Accordingly, the error analysis provided an artificial picture of English relative clause knowledge. In the present study, the phenomenon of avoidance was irrelevant, because growth in grammatical knowledge was assessed through change over the 10-week period through pre- and post-averaging among *a set* of discourse-frequent structures that were the focus of instruction in both the experimental groups and the Control Group.

Indirect assessment of grammatical knowledge

The second assessment measure used in this study was a grammar test developed as an indirect assessment of knowledge of the nine target structures. The grammar test consisted of two parts, an 18-item grammaticality judgement task and a 9-item sentence-rewrite task. Part 1 included two sentences for each target structure, randomised, one grammatical and one ungrammatical. Students were instructed to circle the word 'yes' if they felt that a sentence was a correct English sentence and to circle the word 'no' if they felt that it was not. Table 5.3 (a) is an example of a grammatical Part 1 item containing a well-formed present progressive formation, and (b) is an example of an ungrammatical sentence containing an ill-formed present progressive formation.

For Part 2 of the grammar test, students were told that every sentence contained an error and that, in rewriting the sentence, they should correct whatever error they had identified in the sentence. The expected correctly rewritten response to the Part 2 item in Table 5.4 (a) is (b).

Table 5.3 Part 1 of grammar test

| (a) Our friends are playing cards in the living room. |
| (b) Mary is write a letter to her mother right now. |

Table 5.4 Part 2 of grammar test

| (a) Last year my counselor help me with my schedule. |
| (b) Last year my counselor helped me with my schedule. |

There were two versions of the grammar test. Students who completed pre-test version A at the beginning of the course completed post-test version B at the end of the course, and vice versa. Difference scores calculated on pre-test and post-test performance were submitted to analysis of variance to determine the extent of change over the 10-week period.

Screening of assessment measures

Research designed to assess the abilities of deaf students raises several issues. First, applicable to and consistent with all research, does the assessment procedure have content validity (i.e. is it intrinsically sound, relevant, and representative) to measure what it purports to measure (see Nunnally, 1967)? And second, specific to research findings with deaf students, how would a typical student population of hearing peers perform on the same measure(s) being used to assess their abilities? To obtain a realistic perspective, educators of deaf students almost always want to have a sense of deaf students' performance relative to their hearing peers. This is not to be confused with the concept of a *control group*, whose primary purpose is to address potential sources of invalidity and contribute to the strength and internal validity of the research design itself (see Campbell & Stanley, 1963). With the current study, the control group consists of deaf students for internal validity purposes of the research design.

In order to evaluate the content validity of the direct and indirect assessment measures to reflect students' grammatical knowledge of the target structures, hearing college student peers were utilised because they have acquired the grammatical structure of their L1 naturally through auditory input in contrast to the deaf student participants, and they provide the needed perspective to educators of deaf students. Twenty-nine hearing NTID students were recruited to complete the two measures. These students were native speakers of English enrolled in NTID's interpreter training program or in its teacher training program for future teachers of deaf students at the secondary level of education. Eleven of these students wrote short essays on their choices of one of the three topics assigned to the deaf students. These essays were coded and scored following the established procedure (Berent, 2005a). These students' overall performance revealed an accuracy level of 99.5%, that is, a level of productive grammatical knowledge reflective of native speakers of English. It was concluded, therefore, that the essay procedure possessed sufficient content validity to provide an accurate assessment of deaf learners' productive knowledge of the target structures. This procedure also supports the *face validity* of the assessment instruments used, because, as one aspect of content validity, *face validity* concerns the inspection of the final instruments to make sure that they perform as planned (Nunnally, 1967: 99).

Eighteen of the 29 hearing students completed the grammar test; half of these students completed version A and half completed version B. Their average correct scores were 95.1% on Part 1 and 92.6% on Part 2, with a total mean score of 93.8%. These non-ceiling values from native speakers raised concern that the grammar test might not serve as a valid reflection of the deaf students' grammatical knowledge. Nevertheless, because these values were greater than 90%, it was decided to include the grammar test as an indirect assessment measure (see Discussion).

Results

Essay analysis

Analysis of the First and Last Essays produced by the three deaf student groups revealed that the Input Group and the Visuogloss Group significantly improved on the nine target English structures over the 10-week period. A 3 (Group)×2 (First Essay, Last Essay) ANOVA with repeated measures on the dependent variable showed that there was overall student improvement from the First to the Last Essay, $F(1,65) = 38.80$, $p < 0.0001$. However, a significant Group × Essay interaction, $F(2,65) = 16.90$, $p < 0.0001$, revealed that it was the two experimental groups that exhibited significant improvement, whereas the Control Group did not. The interaction is illustrated in Figure 5.1.

The improvement of the experimental groups, in contrast to the Control Group, is further underscored by the percentages of students per group that experienced a positive rather than a negative change between the First and Last Essay. These percentages are represented in Figure 5.2. As illustrated in the figure, a very high percentage of students in both the Input Group (96%) and in the Visuogloss Group (78%) demonstrated greater success on the Last Essay than on the First Essay. In contrast, a greater percentage of students in the Control Group experienced a negative, rather than a positive, change between the First and Last Essay. Only 38% of the Control Group students scored higher on the Last Essay than on the First.

A second analysis was performed on the difference scores between the First and Last Essays to determine the extent of the deaf students' change over 10 weeks in their 'mastery' of the nine target structures, where mastery was defined as $\geq 80\%$ accuracy on any given structure. A liberal 80% criterion was chosen because it was felt that, for any given

The Efficacy of Visual Input Enhancement 91

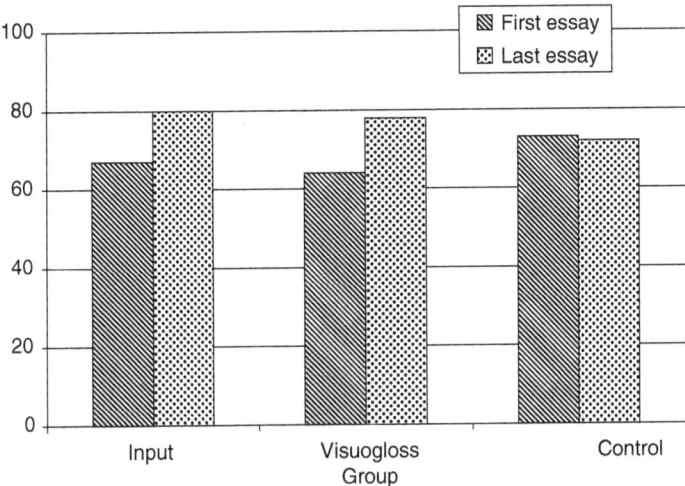

Figure 5.1 Changes in successful productions, by group, between the First and Last Essays

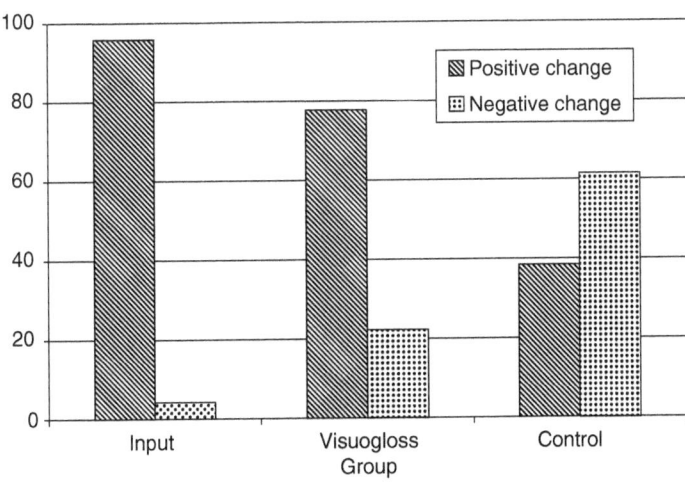

Figure 5.2 Students per group who experienced positive and negative change between the First and Last Essays

structure, the successful production of every four out of five attempted productions reflected an impressive level of grammatical knowledge for the type of deaf student participating in this study, who has struggled for years toward learning the target structures. For each group, mastery was measured as the total number of individual target structures on which any student attained a ≥80% accuracy rate. Table 5.5 shows the total instances of mastery by group on the First and Last Essays and the changes in the number of instances of mastery between essays. The percentages of students per group who experienced an increase in their number of mastered structures between essays is also noteworthy: 75% of the students in the Input Group, 44% of the students in the Visuogloss Group, and 35% of the students in the Control Group increased their number of mastered structures.

A one-way ANOVA for Group × Essay Difference Percentage Score yielded a significant difference in mastery among the three student groups, $F(2,65) = 6.38$, $p = 0.003$. Post hoc pairwise comparison of means using Fisher's Protected Least Significant Difference revealed that the Input Group differed significantly from the Control Group in change in mastery, Fisher's PLSD mean difference = 1.9, $p = 0.0007$, but that the Visuogloss Group did not differ significantly from the Control Group in this regard, Fisher's PLSD mean difference = 1.1, $p = 0.063$. The values in Table 5.5 provide insight into the results of the mastery analysis. In terms of percentages of mastered structures on the First Essay, the three participant groups are fairly equivalent. In terms of percentages of mastered structures on the Last Essay, the two experimental groups are virtually identical. Furthermore, the Input Group's increase was only 5% greater than the Visuogloss Group's increase. The striking result is the Control Group's decrease in the incidence of mastered

Table 5.5 Total instances of mastery (≥80%) of target grammatical structures by Group on the First Essay and Last Essay

	Group		
	Input	*Visuogloss*	*Control*
First Essay	56(30%)	55(34%)	84(36%)
Last Essay	98(45%)	72(44%)	68(29%)
Change	42(15%)	17(10%)	−16(−7%)

The value in parentheses next to each frequency value indicates the percentage that the value represents out of the total possible instances of mastery that could occur in that group (= group $n \times 9$ structures).

structures from 36% on the First Essay to 29% on the Last Essay. This issue is explored further in the Discussion section.

To verify that the results of the essay analysis were not biased by differences in discourse structure that might arise out of the development of three different essay topics, students' essays were examined for comparability in the occurrence of obligatory contexts for the nine target grammatical structures. As noted above, it was anticipated that students' selections from among the three topics would result in a distribution that would neutralise the effects of any discourse differences. In fact, students' topic selections did result in balanced variation both within groups and between First and Last Essay, as anticipated. Nevertheless, the distribution of the nine target structures within essays was examined by group and by topic to confirm whether differences in discourse grammatical organisation had occurred. Table 5.6 contains correlation matrices that reflect comparisons in the frequency of occurrence in students' essays of the nine target structures listed in Table 5.1.

The first part of Table 5.6 contains r-values indicating the extent to which participant groups' essays correlated in the frequency of occurrence of obligatory contexts for the nine target structures, irrespective of essay topic. The Pearson product–moment correlations were based on groups' mean production of each of the target structures in their First Essays (e.g. F-Input) and in their Last Essays (e.g. L-Input) separately. The hearing assessment screening group was also included in this analysis to see whether the hearing native speakers of English produced discourse environments similar to those produced by the deaf students in this study. The extremely high correlations between all groups, as seen in Table 5.6, are striking. These values indicate that the groups' essays were virtually identical in their established patterns of discourse grammatical structure, whether the structures were successfully produced or not. That is, the deaf students in this study, despite their relatively low level of assessed English grammatical knowledge, had a relatively high level of understanding of required syntactic and morphological environments but, to varying extents, could not accurately produce the English forms to fill those environments.

The second half of Table 5.6 directly addresses the issue of essay topic. For this analysis all participants in the experimental groups and the Control Group were re-grouped according to their essay topic, separately for the First Essay (e.g. F-First Job) and the Last Essay (e.g. L-First Job). The very high correlations between topic groups, as shown in the table, verify that all three essay topics, whether developed in the First Essay or the Last Essay, were essentially equivalent in the discourse

Table 5.6 Intercorrelations based on frequency of occurrence of target grammatical structures by participant group on the First and Last Essay and by essay topic for the First and Last Essay

Essay/Group	1	2	3	4	5	6	7
(1) Hearing	–	0.98	0.95	0.97	0.98	0.96	0.97
(2) F-Input		–	0.96	0.98	0.99	0.99	0.99
(3) F-Visuogloss			–	0.99	0.98	0.96	0.98
(4) F-Control				–	1.00	0.97	0.98
(5) L-Input					–	0.98	0.99
(6) L-Visuogloss						–	0.99
(7) L-Control							–
Essay/Topic	A	B	C	D	E	F	
(A) F-Best Friend	–	0.93	0.91	1.00	0.96	0.92	
(B) F-First Job		–	0.99	0.94	0.99	1.00	
(C) F-Worst Day			–	0.91	0.97	0.99	
(D) L-Best Friend				–	0.97	0.92	
(E) L-First Job					–	0.99	
(F) L-Worst Day						–	

F = First Essay; L = Last Essay. The values represent Pearson product–moment correlations.

grammatical environments that they elicited in students' essays. It can therefore be concluded that the results of the essay analysis discussed above and illustrated in Figures 5.1 and 5.2 reflect change over the 10-week period in students' grammatical knowledge of the target structures in Table 5.1 and were not confounded by any differences in discourse production based on essay topic or other factors.

Grammar test analysis

Analysis of group performance based on the grammar test pre-testing and post-testing did not reveal group differences. In fact, a 3 (Group) × 2 (Pre-test, Post-test) ANOVA with repeated measures on the dependent measure yielded a significant main effect for the repeated measures between Pre-test and Post-test, $F(1,65) = 12.64$, $p = 0.0007$. This main effect indicates that all groups improved over the 10 weeks, based on an overall pre-test mean score of 65% and an overall post-test mean score of 70%. To determine the contribution from each part of the test to the overall improvement, separate ANOVAs were calculated for Part 1 and Part 2. The Part 1 ANOVA indicated no significant improvement over time, $p = 0.21$ (76% → 78% correct), but the Part 2 repeated measures ANOVA yielded a significant main effect for the Pre-test/Post-test, $F(1,65) = 17.26$, $p = 0.0001$ (53% → 61% correct). Accordingly, it was Part 2 performance that contributed primarily to the overall significant improvement on the grammar test.

Discussion

Review of findings

The two student groups that received different combinations of visual input enhancement for the duration of the 10-week course showed overall significant improvement, based on a direct measure of productive grammatical knowledge, as compared to the Control Group, which received no formal visual input enhancement. Such results support the predictions of theory-based L2 teaching methodologies that are motivated by acquisition models that maintain that the noticing of L2 input within communicative contexts leads to the subsequent integration of L2 grammatical knowledge into the developing grammar (see Lightbown, this volume). The study's results also revealed that this significant improvement occurred over a relatively short, though 'longitudinal', 10-week period with only one contact-hour of instruction per week.

Direct versus indirect assessment

Although the significant results were established through the direct essay assessment procedure, the indirect grammar test assessment was not able to discriminate performance among the three student groups. There are several possible reasons for this result. First, the performance of the hearing assessment screening group was not at ceiling level, in contrast to their ceiling performance in their essay assessment. This raised the suspicion that the grammar test might not afford a valid assessment of deaf students' knowledge of the nine target structures. Secondly, there are reliability and validity issues that have been discussed in the L2 literature regarding the use of grammaticality judgement tasks, which is what Part 1 of the grammar test represented. For example, Cowan and Hatasa (1994) argued that, in order to obtain reliable learner judgements, a grammaticality judgement task should incorporate at least three exemplars of each target structure, an equal number of distractor items and, ideally, between 60 and 72 sentences (1994: 300). Part 1 of the grammar test fell far below satisfaction of such standards. It contained 18 sentences, two exemplars of each target structure (one grammatical and one ungrammatical), and no distractor items. Regarding the grammaticality judgement items themselves, in addition to their presentation outside of any discourse context, there were adverbials and other clues to the grammatical status of items aside from the target structures themselves. For example, in the item, *Joe's parents lived in Boston now*, the formation of the past tense *lived* is accurate, yet the sentence is ungrammatical in the time context established by *now*. There is no surrounding discourse to guide the judgement of such a sentence, only the intrasentential adverb *now*, which may or may not be noticed.

It was on Part 2 of the grammar test, an error recognition and a sentence rewrite task, that the participant groups collectively exhibited a significant 8% increase between the pre-test and the post-test, with no differences between groups. For the nine sentences comprising Part 2, students were told that each and every sentence contained an error. Reliability and validity issues aside, knowing that a sentence like *The students were try to buy tickets to the concert* contains an error and being required to rewrite the sentence 'correctly', students should have a reasonable likelihood of rewriting the sentence correctly by revising a sentence structure most likely to contain an error. As 'ready learners' (Han *et al.* 2005; see below), the deaf students would have at least partial knowledge of the sentence structures. By the time of post-testing, students in all groups would have had more experience with all the target structures, whether or not they received visual input enhancement during the instructional process – hence, the significant improvement by all groups on Part 2.

Another source of evidence that the grammar test might not be able to validly assess deaf students' English grammatical knowledge is suggested by previous research in another area of English assessment – writing skill development. Berent *et al.* (1996) compared deaf college students' performance on three indirect measures of writing skill with their performance on a direct measure, the Test of Written English (1986). The results of that study verified that a direct measure of deaf students' writing skills (using an elicited essay) is a more valid assessment than indirect measures of writing skill. Incidentally, that study revealed that most indirect measures of writing skill development rely heavily on the indirect assessment of English grammar because grammatical ability is presumably predictive of (*hearing* students') writing skill levels. (See also Lightbown, this volume for discussion of transfer appropriate processing.)

To summarise, the essay assessment procedure, as a direct measure, elicited productive grammatical knowledge as a naturalistic sample of communicative value (students' personal experiences), which is the kind of linguistic environment in which theory-based input enhancement is predicted to succeed. In contrast, the grammar test attempted to assess grammatical knowledge outside of any communicative context. Furthermore, its validity was questioned above on a variety of grounds, including the non-ceiling performance of the hearing assessment screening group. Therefore, we conclude that it is the results of the direct essay assessment that support the experimental hypothesis of improvement of grammatical knowledge through visual input enhancement. In contrast, the results of the indirect grammar test measure, in view of the issues noted, must be considered inaccurate on validity grounds and therefore do not support the null hypothesis of no differential improvement in grammatical knowledge.

Exploring group differences

The results of this study, as illustrated in Figure 5.1, revealed significant improvement by the Input Group and the Visuogloss Group, relative to the Control Group, in overall knowledge of the target structures listed in Table 5.1. This improvement was measured on the basis of group changes between the First and Last Essay in successful productions as a percentage of all attempted productions in the relevant obligatory discourse contexts. Figure 5.2 illustrated the change across the three groups as a function of the percentage of students per group who experienced a positive rather than a negative change between the First and Last Essays. That figure shows that 96% and 78% of the students in the Input Group and the Visuogloss Group, respectively, experienced a positive change. In stark contrast, only 38% of the students in the Control Group experienced a positive change. These results support the efficacy of visual input enhancement in promoting deaf students' growth in English grammatical knowledge.

However, the 'mastery' analysis produced some seemingly puzzling results. Change in mastery was calculated as the difference between the percentage cumulative mastery rate on the First Essay and the percentage rate on the Last Essay. The mastery analysis revealed that the Input Group's mastery of target structures increased by 15%, the Visuogloss Group by 10%, but that the Control Group's mastery rate *decreased* by 7%. At the same time, the percentages of students per group who increased in their number of mastered structures between essays were

75% (Input), 44% (Visuogloss), and 35% (Control). These figures suggest the following performance patterns:

(1) Growth in mastery of the target structures within the Input Group was greater than mastery within the other groups both in terms of the increase in overall mastery rate (15%) and in terms of the number of students who exhibited an increase in their number of mastered structures (75%).
(2) Growth in the overall mastery rate within the Visuogloss Group was positive (10%), but there were fewer students who exhibited an increase in their number of mastered structures (44%).
(3) The overall mastery rate within the Control Group decreased (-7%) between the First and Last Essay, but a 'respectable' 35% of the students exhibited an increase in their number of mastered structures.

Patterns (1) and (2) do not detract from the robustness of the overall improvement observed within the experimental groups, who received visual input enhancement in their English instruction. The minor variations in their performance patterns could be due to a variety of factors. For example, the variation could be due simply to chance, especially as the Visuogloss Group was smaller ($n = 18$) than the other two groups. Another possibility is that, in receiving one more input enhancement methodology than the Input Group, the Visuogloss Group could have been 'over-enhanced' (Han et al., 2005). That is, the three interventions could have cumulatively exceeded an ideal enhancement threshold, resulting in fewer students achieving a positive change between essays (Figure 5.2) and a lower percentage of students increasing their mastery levels (Table 5.5). Along similar lines, the employment of three visual input enhancement interventions of necessity decreased the amount of course time that could be devoted to each intervention relative to the time devoted to each of the two interventions in the Input Group. If any one of the interventions was more efficacious than another, the relative benefit to the Visuogloss Group would have been decreased. It is even possible that the efficacy of the visuogloss methodology (like the dictogloss) might be compromised by its requirement for the simultaneous processing of meaning and form rather than the sequential processing of meaning and form (VanPatten, 2004b). Despite these speculations, the present study did not control for such factors. Therefore, attention to these important issues must be left to future replication research on input enhancement.

Pattern (3) noted above with respect to the Control Group appears puzzling at first glance. With respect to the Control Group's overall performance in this study, the patterns revealed in Figures 5.1 and 5.2 are the kind of performance patterns predicted by the experimental hypothesis that visual input enhancement would lead to greater learning of a set of English grammatical structures than would be observed among students who did not receive visual input enhancement instruction. This hypothesis was supported by the groups' overall performance as assessed in the essay analysis (Figure 5.1), including the numbers of students per group who exhibited a positive change between the First and Last Essay (Figure 5.2). It is the Control Group's 7% decrease in its overall mastery rate along with the 35% of its students who exhibited an increase in their number of mastered structures that warrants an explanation.

From the theoretical perspective of a model that incorporates noticing as a prerequisite to L2 learning, it must be assumed that those students in this study who improved in their grammatical knowledge of particular structures did, in fact, notice the relevant English input. Input enhancement is argued to *facilitate* the noticing of input, not to guarantee noticing, and is not the only mechanism that effects noticing. The results of this study in fact reinforce these assumptions. The question remains, however, as to what accounts for the discrepancy between the Control Group's decrease in overall mastery rate and its increase in the percentage of students whose mastery increased. An examination of the raw data associated with the mastery analysis reveals the source of the apparent discrepancy. Although any student whose Last Essay contained at least one more mastered structure than the First Essay contained was considered to have increased in mastery, some students attained mastery in more structures than others did. Of the 35% of the Control Group students who exhibited an increase in mastered structures, 67% of that number increased mastery by only one structure; 22% increased by two structures and 11% (one student) by three structures. In the Input and Visuogloss Groups, 71% and 89%, respectively, of the students who increased in mastery increased by mastery of two or more structures. In the Input Group students increased by as many as six newly mastered structures, and in the Visuogloss Group by as many as four structures. This distribution accounts for what at first glance seemed like an oddity in the performance of the Control Group.

Research design: The valid assessment of visual input enhancement

Han (2005) and Han *et al.* (2005) undertook a comprehensive review of research on visual input enhancement over the past 15 years. In view of the conflicting results of input enhancement studies, neither the efficacy nor the inefficacy of input enhancement has ever been firmly established. In analysing the vacillating findings of this L2 research agenda, Han *et al.* determined that many of the studies that failed to demonstrate the efficacy of visual input enhancement possessed flaws in research design or other characteristics that confounded the results of those studies.

We maintain that the robust confirmatory results obtained in the present study were facilitated through our conformity to positive design characteristics independently articulated in Han *et al.* (2005). The specific characteristics they identified that are relevant to this study are shown in Table 5.7. Han *et al.* (2005) noted that many input enhancement studies were short in duration and sometimes involved a single instructional treatment. They argued that there needs to be 'a shift away from one-shot research to longitudinal research' for reliably assessing the efficacy of visual input enhancement. The present study satisfied criterion (a) in Table 5.7 in that instruction and related activities took place over a 10-week period.

Regarding (b) in Table 5.7, the deaf students who participated in this study clearly match the definition of 'ready learners', who have at least partial knowledge of the target forms. Through lifelong education in an English-language environment, these students have certainly had exposure to the target forms. They demonstrated this partial knowledge through their successful or attempted discourse-driven production of target structures on the First Essay.

As for (c) in Table 5.7, in view of the duration of this classroom research and the use of a variety of activities that focused on the target structures, the students in the experimental groups had ample opportunity to 'act upon' noticed input. In addition to exercises related to textually enhanced readings, the students' essay revision process, a process that involved two revisions of their First Essay over an extended period of time, was designed precisely to be an opportunity to act upon noticed input that had been visually enhanced through the coded metalinguistic feedback.

Table 5.7 Characteristics

(a) Longitudinal research
(b) Ready learners
(c) Opportunity to act upon noticed input
(d) Sequential processing

Regarding (d) in Table 5.7, Han *et al.* (2005) reviewed the issue of *simultaneous* versus *sequential* processing of meaning and form as determinants of the outcomes of visual input enhancement studies. Simultaneous processing involves tasks in which learners are expected, in reading a text, for example, to derive meaning and to notice form at the same time. Sequential processing involves tasks in which input is processed first for meaning and subsequently processed for form (or vice versa). Although designs that employ sequential processing have been rare in visual input enhancement studies, Han *et al.* summarized the few studies, such as VanPatten (1990) and Overstreet (1998), whose results strongly support a prerequisite for processing input first for meaning and then for form.

The essay procedure employed in the present study involved the *implicit* processing of meaning followed by the *explicit* processing of form (see also Lightbown, this volume). The procedure involved the conversion of students' own output into visually enhanced input, which was subsequently processed for form and reformulated through text revision. In producing communicative text based on personal experience, students naturally comprehended the meanings that they themselves were communicating. Thus, text comprehension was automatically satisfied through the essay procedure and was followed by activities that stimulated the processing of form. In sum, this study satisfied all the criteria in Table 5.7 that Han *et al.* (2005) identified as desiderata for the valid assessment of visual input enhancement in L2 teaching.

Enhanced output
It should be noted with respect to the essay procedure in this study that others have used students' own output for the purpose of enhancing input in the context of the *output hypothesis* (Swain, 1993). For example, Lapkin *et al.* (2002) employed the reformulation of L2 French learners' essays as one intervention in their study of English speakers' acquisition of French pronominal verbs. However, in that study the reformulation was done by native French-speaking adults, who revised students' essays 'to reflect target-language usage, while preserving the students' original meaning' (2002: 488). In the 'noticing stage' of their study, students were told to notice and discuss differences between their original essays and the native speakers' reformulations. The process of which that procedure was a component resulted in students' improvement in knowledge of the target structure. In the present study the noticing was facilitated through coding, with students being instructed to compare

their successful productions with their unsuccessful productions in the subsequent process of reformulating their original output more successfully, a somewhat different procedure. The important point is that learners' output not only serves the L2 acquisition process (Swain, 1993); it also provides a naturalistic object for exploitation in facilitating noticing and subsequent learning during L2 teaching (see also Tocalli-Beller & Swain, 2005).

Implications for deaf learners

The teaching and learning of English literacy skills

Unlike L2 learners, native speakers of English process form and meaning simultaneously because that is the quintessence of native linguistic competence. In L2 acquisition, however, VanPatten (2004b) and others have argued that L2 learners process text for meaning over form and that L2 text comprehension commonly occurs in the *absence* of knowledge of form, through contextual information, linguistic redundancy, and world knowledge (Long, 1996). The processing of text for meaning over form and/or in the absence of knowledge of form epitomises the predicament of deaf learners of English. The multiple and frequently conflicting perspectives that have driven the teaching of English literacy to deaf students, along with the pressures of long-standing political agendas in the field of deaf education (see Power & Leigh, 2000), have resulted in pedagogy that actually *promotes* the processing of meaning detached from or devoid of the processing of form.

For example, the whole-language approach has been advocated for enabling deaf students' literacy development (see Livingston, 1997). This approach involves the use of ASL for communication and instruction under the assumption that the goal of education is to convey content and that English language development is not the priority but an adjunct to educational success. Accordingly, this approach offers no opportunity for students to develop form–meaning connections in English. In their overview of research on the teaching of reading to deaf students, Schirmer and Williams (2003) cited studies that demonstrated that a focus on specific components of the reading process – phonological coding, knowledge of vocabulary or syntax or text structure, inferencing abilities, and so on – can facilitate reading. However, they maintained that these studies offer very little guidance for instructional practice. They concluded that 'the paucity of intervention studies with developing [deaf] readers provides few answers and leaves open many questions regarding best practices' (2003: 119).

Bilingual programs for deaf students

One of the most controversial instructional methodologies for teaching English literacy to deaf students involves bilingual education (see Strong, 1995) based on Cummins' (1986, 1991) model of *linguistic interdependence*. According to linguistic interdependence, there is a common underlying proficiency across all languages such that high levels of literacy in the L1 should transfer to the L2, given sufficient exposure to the L2. Bilingual–bicultural models of deaf education have maintained that linguistic interdependence will lead to successful L2 English literacy development in an environment in which L1 ASL is the primary language of instruction.

Mayer and Wells (1996) challenged the assumption that linguistic interdependence could effect the transfer of literacy in ASL, a natural sign language that has no recordable form comparable to written text, to literacy in English, a spoken language that can be written and read. It is important to emphasise that Mayer and Wells were not challenging Cummins' linguistic interdependence model or the use of ASL in educating deaf students. They were challenging the claim that 'literacy' in a signed L1 could transfer to a spoken/printed L2 under the assumptions of linguistic interdependence.

Based on the results of the present study, we would add that the problem is more fundamental than linguistic interdependence. The essence of the problem is that the evidence from this study and from other L2 research strongly supports the need to facilitate the visual noticing of L2 input *per se* within a meaningful context in which text is processed first for meaning and subsequently for form. What appears to have characterised English language and literacy education for deaf students is a disconnect between the processing of meaning and form. Deaf students have easy access to communicative (non-English) input but restricted access to target linguistic (English) input.

In summarising the arguments against linguistic interdependence as a bridge between sign language and spoken language literacy, Mayer and Akamatsu (2003) concluded that 'currently there is a much wider recognition...that deaf literacy learners will require pedagogical approaches beyond ESL methodologies and exposure to visually accessible print forms of the target language' (2003: 145). In reality, nothing could be further from the truth. This conclusion is misguided on three counts: first, it promulgates one particular theoretical proposal from the field of bilingualism as the sole representative of L2 research; secondly, it underscores the lack of familiarity within the field of deaf studies with the vast field of mainstream L2 teaching and research; and thirdly, it implies that visual access to L2 English language input is not a viable source of English language learning by deaf students. Such views underscore the vital need for researchers and educators of deaf students to develop broad familiarity and detailed knowledge of research on L2 acquisition and teaching if meaningful change is ever to occur in deaf students' English language and literacy development.

Conclusions

The classroom research reported in this chapter lends support to the efficacy of visual input enhancement in L2 teaching and learning. This study responded to the need, identified in Han (2005) and Han et al. (2005), for the valid assessment of this theory-driven L2 teaching methodology. This need followed from their analysis of previous research on visual input enhancement and their determination that the mixed reviews on the efficacy of visual input enhancement were largely attributable to flaws in research design. The present study incorporated several design characteristics that overcame weaknesses attributed to previous studies.

In addition to supporting the efficacy of visual input enhancement generally, the results of this study specifically support the efficacy of the methodology in teaching English to college-level deaf students whose early linguistic experiences situate them as L2 English learners without an L1. Through the instructional essay procedure employed in this study, deaf students were provided with visual input enhancement in the form of coded metalinguistic feedback on their own communicative output. This procedure facilitated the visual noticing of form within a context that was already processed for meaning. Accordingly, students experienced the sequential processing of meaning and form, which is the requisite L2 processing sequence supported by other research (e.g. Overstreet, 1998; Sagarra & Dussias, 2001; VanPatten, 1990, 2004b).

It was noted that most methods that have been employed in the literacy education of deaf students appear to promote the processing of meaning separately from the processing of form or in the absence of the processing of form. This is likely the reason that no single methodology has ever led to any remarkable change in the rate of deaf students' English literacy development. Within the context of an L2 theory that incorporates input *noticing* as a prerequisite to the ultimate acquisition of form−meaning connections, the results of the present study, along with other empirical research, have the potential of leading to significant advancement − perhaps a long-sought breakthrough − in the English education of deaf students. It is therefore essential that further research be conducted on the efficacy of visual input enhancement and similar input-oriented methodologies in teaching deaf students of L2 English.

Acknowledgements

We gratefully acknowledge the students who participated in the study reported in this chapter and our colleagues who participated in other aspects of this research: Stephen Aldersley, Kathryn Schmitz, Baldev Kaur Khalsa, John Panara, Susan Keenan, and Kathleen Eilers-Crandall. Other aspects of the research were reported in Berent *et al.* (2007). We also express our gratitude to ZhaoHong Han for her valuable insights and discussions over the past few years.

Chapter 6
Learner Spontaneous Attention in L2 Input Processing: An Exploratory Study

EUN SUNG PARK and ZHAOHONG HAN

Cognitive perspectives in second language (L2) acquisition research have emphasised the role of attention in learning. A plethora of empirical studies have been conducted to examine how best to facilitate learner attention so as to bring about maximum intake during input processing. Findings from such studies have, however, led to an understanding that although malleable to some extent, learner attention, by and large, takes its own course, irrespective of external intervention.

This chapter reports on part of an ongoing empirical study that investigated learner spontaneous (as opposed to instructed) attention during L2 input processing, tracing, in particular, the influence of two factors: knowledge of the target language (TL) and knowledge of the first language (L1). The chapter is organised as follows. The first section briefly provides the research background for the study. The second section presents the design of the study, followed by the third section reporting the results. Findings are then discussed in the fourth section along with research directions. The chapter concludes by highlighting the need to investigate learner spontaneous attention in second language acquisition (SLA).

Theoretical Background

Input, as Gass (1997: 1) notes, is the 'most important concept of second language acquisition'. Without it, no individual can learn a language (first, second, third, and so on). Nevertheless, it is clear to all that not all of the input to which learners are exposed is utilised for learning.

Learners process only a subset of it for intake, which, all else being equal, may constitute data for the developing system (known also as 'interlanguage'; Selinker, 1972).

Three theoretical perspectives on the nature of attention in SLA

Although there is no clear account of what portions of the input are selected for intake, there is considerable consensus among researchers that the selection process is largely regulated by the cognitive mechanism of attention. The nature of attention, however, has remained a point of controversy (see Sharwood Smith, this volume). At the centre of the debate are, notably, three theoretical accounts, proposed respectively by Schmidt (1990), Tomlin and Villa (1994), and Robinson (1995).

First, according to Schmidt (1990, 1993, 1994a, 1995, 2001), attention at the level of noticing is necessary for input to become intake. Noticing, according to this view, is a subjective state of mind induced by encounters with sensory and cognitive stimuli (i.e. input) and, critically, linked to awareness. According to Allport (1988), awareness in SLA may be evident in learners' (1) cognitive and behavioral changes, (2) verbalisation of their subjective experience, and/or (3) ability to describe a linguistic rule, pattern, or feature.

In contrast to Schmidt's view, Tomlin and Villa (1994) argue against an isomorphic relationship between attention and awareness. Drawing on the work of Posner and Petersen (1990), they suggest instead that attention be viewed as a cognitive system made up of three separate yet interrelated networks or functions: alertness (i.e. general readiness to deal with incoming stimuli), orientation (i.e. attentional resources directed to some stimuli at the exclusion of others), and detection (i.e. cognitive registration of particular stimuli). The three alleged facets of attention, arguably, implicate a linear gradient of cognitive engagement, with one potentially facilitating the next. Although all three functions are of import to SLA, detection is the most taxing of cognitive resources and yet crucial for acquisition, insofar as it constitutes the threshold necessary for converting input into intake. Tomlin and Villa further liken detection to Schmidt's notion of noticing, but only with the caveat that detection does not entail awareness.

Building on, or rather, reconciling Schmidt's and Tomlin and Villa's accounts, Robinson (1995) proposes that it is detection plus rehearsal in short-term memory that converts input into intake. This view implies that the onset of attention to input may be devoid of awareness, but if detection is followed by mental rehearsal, awareness (and intake, for that matter) will result.

Two sources of attention

The three perspectives, all contingent on interpretations of the cognitive psychology literature, have more or less shaped the current general conception of the role of attention in SLA. However, hitherto, limited empirical research has been undertaken to test their validity. As Simard and Wong (2001) rightly point out, testing the generalisability of psychology studies to SLA is important, and 'until we have more studies that address this generalizability issue, we cannot hope to make any substantial claims regarding the role of attention and awareness in SLA' (2001: 120).

There is, however, one clear exception to the lack of interest in validation research. Since the mid-1990s, Leow has conducted a series of studies (e.g. Leow, 1997a, 2000; Leow & Morgan-Short, 2004), which used learners' concurrent protocols to document (1) the presence of awareness in attention during L2 input processing and (2) a correlation between noticing, awareness, and intake (cf. Rosa & O'Neill, 1999). Leow's research largely confirmed Schmidt's hypothesis. It is nevertheless worth mentioning that Leow (1998) also made an attempt to test Tomlin and Villa's (1994) model, with results showing, *inter alia*, that detection, as Tomlin and Villa have argued, can indeed occur independently of alertness and orientation (see, however, Simard & Wong's critique, 2001, and Leow's rebuttal, 2002). As yet, Robinson's model has received little empirical investigation. Clearly, there is on the whole a critical empirical void here waiting to be filled.

The overall dearth of validation research notwithstanding, the role of attention has already been extensively appealed to as an *explanans* for success or failure in SLA. More specifically, driven by the conviction (1) that learner attention is malleable, and (2) that through manipulating learner attention, learner intake increases, and moreover, guided by Schmidt's and Tomlin and Villa's models, researchers have set out to develop and test an array of psycholinguistic proposals in laboratory and naturalistic classroom settings. A prominent strand of this research is that of 'focus on form' (Doughty & Williams, 1998a; see also Han, this volume) whose central mission is about manipulating learner attention in order to facilitate learner noticing, and hence intake, of certain aspects of the TL. Owing to its SLA research and pedagogical appeal, the focus on form paradigm has generated a flurry of studies over the past two and a half decades, painting a rather intricate picture of the relationship between external intervention and learner intake.

By way of illustration, the studies on input enhancement, a focus-on-form proposal put forth by Sharwood Smith (1991, 1993, this volume) that aims at enhancing the salience of the target language input for L2 learners, have led to incongruent findings. For example, research on typographic enhancement has shown:

(1) Textual enhancement promotes noticing of target L2 form and has an effect on learners' subsequent output (Jourdenais *et al.*, 1995: 208; see also Berent & Kelly, this volume).
(2) Input enhancement failed to show measurable gains in learning despite the documented positive impact of enhancement on the noticing of the target form items in the input (Izumi, 2002: 542).
(3) Results revealed a significant main effect for text length on readers' comprehension but not on intake, no significant main effect for input enhancement on either comprehension or intake, and no significant interaction (Leow, 1997b: 151).

Collectively, these findings point to the indeterminate effects of the external approach to drawing learner attention to input, raising concerns over its efficacy and leading researchers to search for factors that may modulate its efficacy (for a review, see Han, 2005; Han *et al.*, 2005). Leow (1993: 342), for one, suspected that it is 'the learner's existing language system [current IL] that defines what in the input is taken in and not any external manipulation of the input' (cf. Lightbown, 2000; Philp, 2003; Sharwood Smith, 1986; for first language acquisition, see Nelson, 1987; Saxton, 1997).

In a similar vein, other researchers (e.g. Gass *et al.*, 2003; Izumi, 2002; Izumi *et al.*, 1999; Kim & Han, 2007; Mackey *et al.*, 2000; Pienemann, 1985; Sorace, 1993; Spada & Lightbown, 1993, 1999; Williams & Evans, 1998) have argued that, while divertible, learner attention is, in large part, driven by their own perceptions about what is worth attending to, irrespective of the external intervention (as provided by the researcher or the teacher). In other words, learners appear to have their naturally preferred targets to delegate attention to.

This so-called default processing bias entails, according to VanPatten's Input Processing theory (VanPatten, 1996, 2004b), an overarching tendency to channel focal attention to meaning-laden elements (e.g. content words) in the input to the exclusion of meaningless elements (e.g. grammatical morphemes) (cf. Clahsen & Felser, 2006). One immediate corollary is that the processing of meaningless elements often fails to occur, or occurs only after the learner is able to process the meaningful elements with ease and automaticity (cf. Sagarra, this volume). Related empirical research largely confirmed VanPatten's characterisation (e.g. VanPatten, 2004b; see also Berent & Kelly, this volume).

Thus, in contrast to the earlier understanding that learner attention is solely malleable through an outside source, a more current conception is that there is a potential competition between two sources of attention, one being learner-external and the other learner-internal, and moreover, that when the two are at odds, any external manipulation of learner attention will fail to achieve its purported outcome (Doughty, 2001; Han, 2001; Sharwood Smith, 1991; Terrell, 1991). From a theoretical and a pedagogical stance, then, this understanding underpins the necessity to empirically research learner-generated attention and its awareness correlate, noticing (Schmidt, 1990).

One avenue through which to develop some insights into the phenomenon is to pursue a rudimentary question: What is it in the input that induces learner attention? According to some researchers (e.g. DeKeyser, 1998, 2005; Doughty, 2003; Gass & Selinker, 2001; Long, 2000), there is a causal link between attention and salience, a physical attribute of input; that is, the more salient the input is, the more attention it will garner, and hence more noticing. In this light, what focus-on-form researchers have sought to do is – essentially – make the target features in the input salient. By the same token, what prompts learner spontaneous attention has to be some internally perceived salience in relation to certain features in the input. There are thus likely to be two types of salience corresponding to the two types of attention discussed above.

Two types of salience

Such conception is, indeed, that which undergirds the input enhancement proposal. Sharwood Smith (1991, 1993; cf. Terrell, 1991) contends that salience can be externally generated (as engineered by a teacher or researcher; hereafter 'external salience') as well as internally generated (as naturally born from the learner; hereafter 'internal salience'). The internal salience may, in his view, override the impact of the external salience, if the two are out of synch. It further follows that instruction should seek to capitalise on the internal salience and create harmony between the external and the internal (cf. Corder, 1967; Han, this volume; Sagarra, this volume).

Empirical research on input enhancement, as mentioned, has produced mixed findings on its efficacy. Nonetheless, it has confirmed Sharwood Smith's foresight about internal salience: Evidence has been found in this line of research of learners attending to, and subsequently noticing, items that were unenhanced (e.g. Park, 2004). Similar evidence, albeit random, has showed up in other areas of the focus on form research such as attention, corrective feedback, role of output, and structural effects (e.g. Gass *et al.*, 2003; Han, 2001, 2002; Izumi & Bigelow, 2000; Williams & Evans, 1998). In the meantime, theoretical speculations continue to surface with regard to what drives internal salience (e.g. Corder, 1981; Doughty, 2003; Robinson, 2003; Sorace, 2005), to which we now turn.

What drives internal salience?

Several factors have been implicated with varying explicitness in the SLA literature as contributing to internal salience. The frequently suggested ones are input frequency (N. Ellis, 2002, 2005), input novelty (N. Ellis, 2005); comprehension failure (White, 1987); learners' current interlanguage knowledge (e.g. Carroll, 1999; N. Ellis, 2005; Gass, 1997; Harley, 1994; Leow, 1997; Lightbown, 2000; Philp, 2003; Pienemann & Johnston, 1987; Sharwood Smith, 1986; VanPatten, 1996; White, 1987), learners' processing bias for meaning over form (e.g. Clahsen & Felser, 2006; VanPatten, 1996, 2004b), learners' training experience (e.g. Han, 2004c; Han & Selinker, 1999), learner differences (e.g. Izumi *et al.*, 1999; Park, 2004), and last but not least, learners' L1 (e.g. Carroll, 2005; DeKeyser, 2005; N. Ellis, 2005, 2006a; Han, 2004c; Lightbown, this volume; Schachter, 1996; Sorace, 1993, 2005; VanPatten *et al.*, 2004; Ying, 2003).

Reviewing the past research on instructed SLA, Lightbown (2000) notes that 'Even when forms are frequently present in classroom input, learners may filter them out because of characteristics of their L1 or their current interlanguage' (2000: 451). Similarly, Philp (2003) concludes from her empirical investigation of learner uptake following interactional feedback that learners are biased to the input by their current interlanguage knowledge as well as by their natural orientation for meaning. White (1987: 97) also asserts that 'the learner's current grammar ... acts as a filter on the input... That is, the learner rejects input which cannot be interpreted in terms of his or her current knowledge, or modifies it so that it can be dealt with'. It must be pointed out, however, that all these insights are either retrospective or products of inferences made from studies that were designed to examine other SLA issues, and in consequence, that despite its obvious importance to SLA theorising and second language pedagogy, few studies have directly dealt with learner-created attention and salience. As Carroll (2005: 81) aptly notes, 'most research dealing with "input" provided descriptions of what people say to learners, not what learners can perceive and represent'.

The skewed landscape is gradually changing, however, with the recent emergence of several empirical studies, conducted in different settings, that directly examined how learners process auditory and/or visual input (e.g. Carroll, 2005; Han & Peverly, 2007; Rast, 2003; Rast & Dommergues, 2003; Sagarra, this volume). One study is of particular relevance to the present study. Han and Peverly (2007) conducted a study in which they attempted to validate VanPatten's Input Processing Principle One ('Meaning Primacy') and its corollaries. Unlike VanPatten and his associates who employed learners who had achieved some proficiency in the L2 as participants in their studies on input processing (e.g. VanPatten, 1990), Han and Peverly's study involved complete beginners, who, by definition, had zero knowledge of the target language, Norwegian. Twelve participants, equally divided into two groups (i.e. the experimental and the contrast group), received two exposures to a reading passage of 125 words, and depending on the group they were in, were administered a written-recall task either following the first or the second exposure. In addition, they completed a fill-in-the-blank task and an exit questionnaire. The resulting data yielded disconfirming evidence for VanPatten's prediction. Specifically, the learners adopted a form-oriented, rather than meaning-oriented, approach to processing the input. The former was operationalised, in line with VanPatten's (2004b: 8–11) input processing principles 1a–e, as an approach whereby learners rely on meaningful and non-meaningful forms, *indiscriminately* and irrespective of their communicative redundancy, and the latter as one whereby learners *selectively* rely on meaningful forms. Based on their findings, Han and Peverly (2007: 17) argued that

> When positing principles of input processing, there is a need to differentiate between learners who have and who have not developed intermediate grammars of the target language, and that input that is linguistically incomprehensible as well as devoid of extra-linguistic clues induces form-based processing.

Further, the researchers postulated two hypotheses for future research:

(1) Learners who have acquired some knowledge of the target language will adopt a meaning-based approach to input processing.
(2) Learners who have no existing knowledge of the target language will adopt a form-based approach.

Motivated, in part, by these hypotheses, the present study explored learner spontaneous attention with beginning learners of Korean as the target language, and examined the differences that arose as a result of the learners having no knowledge about the target language initially and then later on, being equipped with some knowledge. Furthermore, by controlling for participants' L1, the study looked into the impact of the L1, one of the main alleged factors, on learner-generated attention and internal salience.

L1 as a contributing factor to internal salience

Learners' experience with, and knowledge of, their L1 may contribute to their perception of what is salient in the L2 input, and hence what is attended to and noticed. This understanding comes from numerous studies on crosslinguistic influence on various aspects of L2 acquisition (passim the SLA literature), and in particular, from the theoretical and empirical studies that either discussed or demonstrated any of the following:

(1) How learners' L1 grammatical knowledge guides their processing of an L2 grammar (e.g. Bialystok, 1994; Carroll, 2005; Han, 2001; Hopp, 2005; Schachter, 1996; Sorace, 1993; Wode, 1981);
(2) How human processing mechanisms change as a result of primary language acquisition (e.g. Doughty, 2003; MacWhinney, 2006);
(3) How L1 experiential and conceptual knowledge may affect the processing of an L2 grammar (Cadierno & Lund, 2004; N. Ellis, 2006a; Han, 2004c, this volume; Kellerman, 1995; Odlin, 2005; Slobin, 1993, 1996);
(4) How L1 literacy training experience may impact on L2 input processing (Gass & Selinker, 2001; Lin, 1998).

Carroll (2005) investigated the initial input processing of, and sensitivity to cues to, French gender in 88 Anglophone adults. The input consisted of highly patterned auditory sequences of [DetþN]French + translation equivalent English forms which embodied phonological, morphosyntactic, or semantic cues. Three tasks were administered to measure acquisition, and the results showed that the participants' processing of the stimuli was largely biased by their L1 knowledge. Carroll therefore concluded that, as has been previously hypothesised by many, the initial state is marked by the transfer of L1 grammatical knowledge and/or the transfer of L1-based processing procedures.

Although Carroll's study focused on input processing of planned and highly structured auditory input, the present study dealt with the processing of natural written input in beginning learners of Korean whose L1 was either Japanese or English. Japanese is generally considered typologically close to Korean, and English typologically distant. A central characteristic of Japanese but not of English is that, like Korean, Japanese is a SOV language, which follows the typological characteristics of a verb-final language (e.g. left-branching and head-final) and abounds in particles or suffixes (e.g. subject markers, object markers, locative markers) that carry a heavy morphosyntactic load. The rationale for having two contrasting L1s is self-evident – it would allow transfer effects to be isolated, as it would any common tendencies.

Research questions

In the present study, we sought to explore the effects on learner spontaneous attention of two variables, viz., knowledge of the TL and knowledge of the L1, addressing specifically the following questions:

(1) What features of the L2 input do novice learners notice when exposed to the TL input for the very first time?
(2) What features of the L2 input do they notice after they have been taught some linguistic items of the TL?
(3) Do learners with different L1 backgrounds exhibit differential attentional behaviour, and if so, to what extent is it related to their existing knowledge of the L2?

We operationalised noticing as learners' externalised observation of or comment on features of the input text (cf. Bowles, 2003).

The Study

Participants

A total of 60 adults – 30 native speakers of Japanese and 30 native speakers of English – participated in the study. They had been sampled on the basis that they were born, brought up, and educated in their respective L1 environments. None of the participants had had any prior exposure to Korean, the chosen target language for the present study. All of them had at least an undergraduate degree, and more than half of them had either attended or were attending a graduate school. All of the participants in both L1 groups had studied at least one additional language. The Japanese participants had studied English as an L2 in junior high and high schools where it was taught as a mandatory subject. The mean length of English instruction received was 8.2 years (range: 5–11 years; SD: 1.69). In addition, 21 participants had had experience learning a third language (L3) as well. Their L3 included French, Spanish, German, and Chinese. The mean length of L3 instruction was 2.3 years (range: 1–5 years; SD: 1.11). As for the English group, all of them had also studied an L2 (French, Spanish, German, or Russian) with a mean of 5.23 years of instruction. In addition, 17 of them had studied an L3 (French, Spanish, German, Russian, Latin, Hebrew, or Hatian Creole) with a mean of 3.41 years of instruction.

Procedure

Two experimental conditions were created for all participants. Condition 1 involved exposing the participants in the zero-knowledge state to a Korean text. Condition 2, on the other hand, exposed the same participants to a comparable text but after they had been taught six words that were to appear in the input text (see Table 6.1).[1] Under both conditions, participants met individually with one of the researchers. They first filled out a background questionnaire, and were then provided a one-page text. While reading it, they were asked to perform two tasks:

(1) Input marking, that is, underlining anything that stood out for them;
(2) Asking questions, that is, writing down any questions pertaining to the text on a piece of paper.

The tasks were intended to tap, from different angles, into the content of participants' attention during input processing and were completed in their L1, each task lasting about 10 minutes.

Input text

Two input texts were devised respectively for Conditions 1 and 2, by reference to a popular textbook used in U.S. universities, *Integrated Korean: Beginning 1* (Cho et al., 2001). For Condition 1, a text entitled 'Columbia University' was developed, which contained 11 sentences (63 words[2] excluding the title, 130 syllable blocks altogether). For Condition 2, a comparable text was created; it was entitled 'My Younger Sibling' and likewise consisted of 11 sentences (65 words excluding the title, 130 syllable blocks). Both texts (see Appendix) featured the words and

Table 6.1 Six pre-taught items for Condition 2

Linguistic item	Meaning
동생 [dongseng][3] (noun)	'younger sibling'
이름 [ireum] (noun)	'name'
이다 [ida] (copular verb)	'to be'
전공하다 [jeongonghada] (verb)	'to major'
은/는 [eun/neun] (topic marker)[4]	
에서 [eseo] (post-positional suffix)	'at', 'in'

grammatical structures that typically appear in the first four weeks of an introductory Korean course. Their naturalness was verified by two native speakers of Korean. Additionally, a Korean language expert who had taught the textbook was consulted to ensure that the texts created for the study were comparable with regard to the type of vocabulary and level of grammar.

Analyses and results

Here we report the analyses and results from the first two tasks, viz., input marking and asking questions, the two content-orientated measures.

Our first research question asked: What features do novice learners notice when exposed to the TL input for the very first time? The answer to this question must be sought from the participants under Condition 1. The relevant data are therefore (1) the items that the participants marked in the input text (Task 1), and (2) their spontaneous questions (Task 2). First, with regard to input marking, our analysis of the data began with identifying and categorising all the items that had been marked (circled or underlined) by at least one participant. One point was added to the category each time the input item(s) corresponding to a particular category was marked by a participant. The points were then summed and converted into percentages for each group and for each category. In other words, the percentages represent the learners that marked the particular item. A summary of the results with respect to the categories identified by both groups is presented in Table 6.2.

There are several things to note from Table 6.2. First, the verb ending *da* was the most noticed item for both groups, followed by *Columbia*, *daehakgyo*, and *sikdang*, all of which made recurring appearances (ranged 3 to 6) in the input text. Secondly, English speakers noticed the nominal suffixes *neun*, *e*, and *do* more frequently than did Japanese speakers (40% vs 13%). Third, English speakers noticed the periods and commas more frequently than did Japanese speakers (50% vs 17%). Fourth, Japanese speakers picked out certain graphemic elements from some of the characters (e.g. ㅇ,ㅅ,ㅈ,ㅁ) more than did English speakers (47% vs 10%). Lastly, five Japanese speakers (17%) circled or underlined one or more isolated syllables (그,스,아,가) and also wrote next to the marked item a Japanese character that they seemed to have associated with the item in focus (e.g. 가 = 外).

In summary, all participants, irrespective of their L1, tended to notice items that were salient by virtue of their recurring pattern, as seen in the case of the verb ending, *da*, which consistently appeared at the end

Table 6.2 Items marked by groups under Condition 1

Items marked		Japanese	English
다 [da]	Verb-ending, frequently occurring	50%	67%
콜럼비아 [Columbia]	'Columbia'	37%	50%
대학교 [daehakgyo]	'University'	43%	40%
식당 [sikdang]	'Restaurant'	33%	23%
는,에,도 [neun,e,do]	Nominal suffixes	13%	40%
이 [i]	Frequently occurring syllable; also a nominal suffix	17%	33%
Punctuation marks		17%	50%
ㅇ,ㅅ,ㄹ,ㅈ,ㅁ, ㅐ, ㅣ	Alphabets making up a syllable block)	47%	10%
존은 [jon-eun]	'John' + topic marker	30%	20%
먹는다 [meokneunda]	'Eat'	20%	10%
다닌다 [daninda]	'Attend,' 'go to' (school)	10%	17%
있 [it]	Frequently occurring syllable	10%	17%
비빔밥 [bibimbap]	Name of a Korean dish	17%	3%
이,아,에 [i], [a], [e]	Frequently occurring syllables, all containing an empty consonant[5]	13%	13%
그,스,아,가 [geu], [seu], [a], [ga]	Random syllables	17%	0%
많 [man]	Syllable, appeared twice	7%	0%
학 [hak]	Frequently occurring syllable	0%	13%

of each sentence, and/or their physical attributes such as frequency and shape. Nevertheless, the two groups exhibited a differential preference for particular items. This scenario is to a large extent corroborated by the participants' spontaneous questions on Task 2.

Our analyses of the learner-generated questions on Task 2 proceeded with reviewing all the questions and identifying emergent categories based on their content, first for each learner and then for each group.

For instance, the question of 'Does Korean have gender?' resulted in the category of 'gender'. Each question earned 1 point, the sum score for each category for each group being then computed into a percentage. On average, each participant asked 5 questions. In total, the L1-Japanese group asked 135 questions (mean: 4.5; range: 3–6; SD: 1.61), and the L1-English group 197 questions (mean: 6.57; range: 4–8; SD: 1.57). Table 6.3 provides an item-based summary of the results for both groups under Condition 1.

As shown in Table 6.3, overall, both groups asked about the orthography of the TL (e.g. character formation, use of alphabets), the verb

Table 6.3 Learner-generated questions under Condition 1

Question categories	Japanese	English	Sample questions
Text content	40%	43%	'What is the text about?'
다 [da], the verb ending	37%	40%	'Why does each sentence end with the character 다?'
What each 'character' represents?	23%	47%	'Does one character represent a word or a thought or idea or something else?'
Character formation	27%	47%	'How are the characters created – i.e. parts put together?'
Direction of reading	7%	43%	'In which direction is the language read?'
Alphabet	37%	33%	'How many letters are there in the Korean language?'
Random grammar	30%	30%	'What words do you need to have a sentence? (SVO)? Is there a strict word order?'
Punctuation	17%	33%	'Are Korean punctuation marks the same as in English?'
Type of text	10%	33%	'Is this a story, song, essay?'
Title	13%	30%	'What is the title of this writing?'
Spaces	17%	27%	'Do the spaces between the groups of characters indicate a pause?'

Continued

Table 6.3 (*Continued*)

Question categories	Japanese	English	Sample questions
Meaning of a certain word	17%	23%	'What does 대학교 mean? It repeats throughout the sample.'
Word boundary	10%	23%	'What does each segment mean?'
Pronunciation	13%	20%	'If one can add on to the characters, how does that affect pronunciation?'
ㅇ (empty consonant)	13%	20%	'Do circular marks (ㅇ) indicate vowels?'
Suffixes, particles	10%	7%	'Does it have a "connecting word" like in Japanese?'
Consonant/vowel	3%	17%	'How many vowels are there in Korean?'
Polite forms	7%	0%	'Does Korean use polite forms like Japanese?'
The use of Kanji, Hiragana, Katakana	40%	0%	'Japanese consists of the combinations of Kanji and Hiragana. What about Korean?'
Capitalisation	0%	17%	'Are there capital and lower case letters?'
Gender	0%	7%	'Does Korean have feminine and masculine forms?'

ending *da*, particles, punctuation, empty consonant ('ㅇ'), grammar (e.g. word order, placement of adjectives), as well as the content of the text (e.g. *What does the text say?*). The two groups, however, differed in the following aspects:

(1) Only the Japanese participants asked if Korean used *Kanji* in their writing system.
(2) Only the Japanese participants asked if there were any respectful (polite) forms used in the text.
(3) Only the English participants asked if capitalisation is used in Korean.
(4) Only the English participants asked if gender is marked in Korean.
(5) Predominantly more English participants (43% vs 7%) asked about the direction in which the text is read, that is, whether the text is

read from left to right or right to left, an interesting behaviour in itself, given the presence of punctuation marks in the text.
(6) More English participants (47% vs 23%) asked about what each character represents (e.g. idea or concept?) and how a character is formed (47% vs 27%).
(7) Participants in both language groups noticed the punctuations used in the text. English participants seemed happy to notice that Korean uses the same punctuation as in English, while Japanese participants seemed rather amused that Korean uses 'Western-style' punctuation, because Japanese employs a different set of punctuation marks.
(8) More English participants asked if the text was a story, poem or an article (30% vs 13%). They also made more reference to the title as well as the format of the text, focusing on the overall structure of the writing as well as the significance of the text.

Thus, similarly to the results for the first task, the participants' spontaneous questions revealed some common tendencies as well as L1-specific biases. Some of the questions stemmed from common-sense knowledge of language, namely that any given language consists of words and sentences strung together via syntactic rules, and employs punctuation marks to mark sentence boundaries. Other questions, such as those regarding the use of *Kanji*, articles, capitalisation, and polite forms, were clearly a function of insights drawn from the two groups' respective L1s.

Turning to our second research question, what features do the learners notice after they have been taught some linguistic items that are to appear in the second input text? The relevant data for this question are the participants' performance on Tasks 1 and 2 under Condition 2. Following the same analytical procedures as for Condition 1, the results from input marking (Task 1), summarised in Table 6.4, indicated that more than 90% of the participants across the two groups marked all or most of the pre-taught items. Overall, both groups exhibited similar noticing patterns in terms of what they marked in the input. However, there were some noticeable intergroup differences and changes from Condition 1 to Condition 2. For one, Japanese participants made more markings in the text than their English counterparts, which was not the case for Condition 1, where the L1-English speakers marked more in the input. Another notable change is that the Japanese generated more questions under Condition 2 than Condition 1, whereas the opposite was true for the English group. In addition, some specific words seemed to have attracted the attention of one group, but not that

Table 6.4 Input marking under Condition 2

Items marked		Japanese	English
이다 [ida]*	'To be'	100%	100%
은/는 [eun/neun]*	'Topic marker'	100%	97%
전공하다 [jeongonghada]*	'To major in'	97%	100%
이름 [ireum]*	'Name'	100%	93%
동생 [dongseng]*	'Younger sibling'	97%	97%
에서 [eseo]*	'Postpositional marker'	93%	90%
레이첼 [raeichael]	'Rachel'	80%	67%
다이안 [daian]	'Diane'	53%	40%
내 [nae]	'My'	43%	37%
고향 [gohyang]	'Hometown'	27%	40%
대학교 [daehakgyo]	'University'	37%	20%
존 [jon]	'John'	17%	33%
경제학을/영문학을 [kyongjaehak-eul, yeongmunhak-eul]	'Economics' + object marker 'English literature' + object marker	30%	3%
있 [it]		13%	27%
학원 [hakweon]	'Academic institute'	27%	13%
지금 [jigeum]	'Now, currently'	17%	20%
뉴욕 [nyuywok]	'New York'	13%	13%
삼학년 [samhangnyun]	'Third-year student'	13%	10%
다 [da]	Verb ending	13%	3%
자 [ja]		13%	0%

*Indicates a pre-taught item.

of the other group. A case in point is that the majority of the Japanese group noticed the words 경제학을 ('Economics'+을 [object marker] and/or 영문학을 ('English literature'+을 [object marker]), both of which were placed immediately before the verb 'to major' (one of the pre-taught items); they either underlined or circled it. Several of the Japanese participants also tried to translate it, by glossing its meaning. By contrast, this item was marked by only one English participant.

Another input item noticed exclusively by the Japanese participants (17%) was the syllable 자 [ja], which appeared in the input text just once, as a second syllable of 남자 ('male'). This syllable was marked by four Japanese participants, with three of them writing [watashi] or 'I' next to the item. These learners seemed to have associated this syllable with the Japanese character for 'I'. Such idiosyncratic noticing is more clear-cut on Task 2.

A total of 304 questions were generated for Task 2 under Condition 2: 145 questions from the Japanese group, and 159 from the English group. At first glance, it appears that the English group asked more questions, but when compared to Condition 1, it turns out that the Japanese participants asked 10.7% more questions under Condition 2 than Condition 1. One the other hand, the number of questions generated by the English group decreased by 19.3% from Condition 1 to 2, as shown in Table 6.5.

A closer inspection on the questions generated on Task 2, which are summarised in Table 6.6, revealed that the English participants asked predominantly about the word order, gender, subject/topic marker, verb position, and tense. In addition, they also generated questions that were not asked by the Japanese group such as questions on word boundaries, use of article, plural marker, and use of pronoun. By contrast, the Japanese

Table 6.5 Descriptive statistics of spontaneous questions across conditions

	Condition 1	*Condition 2*
Japanese group		
Mean	4.50	4.83
Median	4	5
Standard deviation	1.61	1.62
Range	3–6	3–8
Total number of questions	135	145 (increased by 10.7%)
English group		
Mean	6.57	5.30
Median	6	5
Standard deviation	1.57	1.49
Range	4–8	3–8
Total number of questions	197	159 (decreased by 19.3%)

Table 6.6 Learner-generated questions under Condition 2

Question categories	Japanese	English	Sample questions
Text content	53%	40%	'Does the passage talk about where the sibling is a student?'
Meaning of a word	57%	33%	'레이첼 – is this a person's name?'
Word order	23%	53%	'What is the word order in a typical Korean sentence?'
Other suffixes	30%	33%	'Do you also have characters that can be used to identify the object?'
Meaning of 내	37%	13%	'What is 내? Is it "my"?'
Tense	10%	37%	'Does 다 indicate a verb or the present tense?'
Topic marker	7%	23%	'Why does the subject get marked by a symbol and not word order?'
Verb at the end	7%	20%	'Does a verb always end a sentence?'
Gender	3%	20%	'How is gender represented through Korean language?'
Subject	13%	17%	'How many subjects can appear in the same sentence? In some sentences, I don't see the subject. Can you omit the subject if you've mentioned it before?'
Preposition	10%	10%	'Are all (or most) Korean prepositions added to the word? Does preposition always come after noun?'
Use of pronoun	3%	7%	'Are pronouns such as "he", "she", and "it" expressly written or are they part of the verb form?'

Continued

Table 6.6 (*Continued*)

Question categories	Japanese	English	Sample questions
Respectful form	10%	0%	'Which part of the writing is the respectful form?'
Word groupings	0%	10%	'How do you know to break up words/space between?'
Use of article	0%	7%	'Are there articles written in Korean or are they simply implied?'
Possessives	0%	7%	'How do you denote possession?'
Plural marker	0%	3%	'Does the text reflect any plural words?'

participants asked mainly about the content of the text, meanings of recurring words like 'university', or 'Rachel', including the meaning of a specific word, 내 ('my'), which appeared in the title and which was also the very first word in the text. Figure 6.1 shows the rates of the impromptu questions asked by the Japanese versus the English group.

Turning now to our third research question: Do learners with different L1 backgrounds exhibit differential noticing behaviour, and if so, to what extent is it related to their existing knowledge of the L2? The above-reported results from Condition 2 already shed some light on the question inasmuch as they showed that Japanese speakers asked more meaning or content-related questions as opposed to English speakers who asked more form-related questions. This pattern received additional support from a follow-up analysis of all the questions participants asked under Condition 1 and Condition 2. Specifically, the analysis identified four types of questions: (1) form-orientated, (2) meaning-orientated, (3) orthography/format-related, and (4) other. A rubric based on these types was then created to guide the analysis of the same data by one of the researchers twice to ensure intrarater reliability, and by a second rater, a fluent speaker of Japanese and English who also had a working knowledge of Korean. The interrater agreement rate was 92%. Table 6.7 provides examples for the question types, and Table 6.8 shows the distribution of questions by type.

Table 6.8 shows that under Condition 1, the two groups exhibited much similarity with regard to the types of questions asked. Both groups

Learner Spontaneous Attention in L2 Input Processing

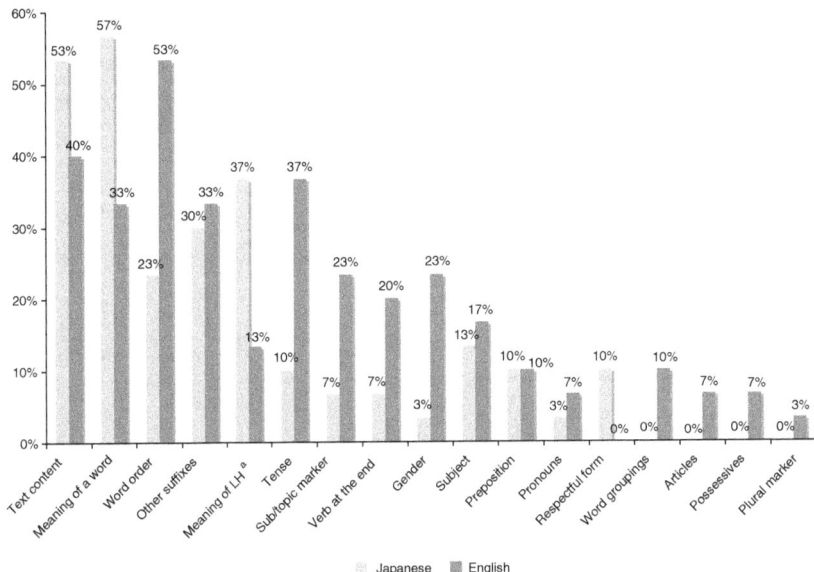

Figure 6.1 Learner-generated questions under Condition 2

Table 6.7 Four question types

Question type	Examples from learner-generated questions
Content/meaning-orientated questions	'What is the story about?' 'Is the sister coming to the U.S. to study?' 'Is 레이첼 the name of the sibling?' 'What does 다이안 mean?'
Form-orientated questions	'Is the word order SOV?' 'Are the adjectives attached or separate words?' 'Why do some sentences have subject markers and others do not?'
Orthography/format-related questions	'Is there the equivalent of script as well as printing?' 'Is there a reason for the shapes of the characters?' 'Does Korean character work similar to English alphabet?'
'Other' questions	'Is memorising the characters best way to learn?' 'What level Korean is this?' 'How do you express numbers?'

Table 6.8 Distribution of questions under Conditions 1 and 2

Question types	Japanese participants		English participants	
	Condition 1	Condition 2	Condition 1	Condition 2
Meaning-orientated	20 (15%)	70 (48%)	25 (13%)	41 (26%)
Form-orientated	35 (26%)	51 (35%)	57 (29%)	86 (54%)
Orthography/format	77 (57%)	16 (11%)	101 (51%)	22 (14%)
Other questions	3 (2%)	8 (6%)	14 (7%)	10 (6%)
Total	135 (100%)	145 (100%)	197 (100%)	159 (100%)

asked more form-orientated than meaning-orientated questions, although with an interesting difference. The split between the two types of questions is greater for the English group (16%) than for the Japanese group (11%), with the former asking a higher number of form-orientated questions (3% more) than the latter, and vice versa for the meaning-orientated questions (2% less). This pattern of split was striking under Condition 2 (28% for the English and 13% for the Japanese) where the English group asked 19% more form-based questions and 22% fewer meaning-based questions than did the Japanese group, suggesting that the English group had a greater inclination for form when processing input as opposed to the Japanese group, who appeared to have a greater tendency to process input for meaning. Differences between the two groups are not significant on chi-square tests for Condition 1, but are significant for Condition 2 ($\chi^2 = 16.547$; $p = 0.000$, for meaning-orientated questions; $\chi^2 = 10.961$, $p < 0.001$ for form-orientated questions). Figure 6.2 illustrates the similarities and differences between the groups.

Discussion

Summing up the results of the study, the two L1 groups behaved differently, more so under Condition 2 than Condition 1. Under Condition 1, while both groups adopted what may be considered a form-orientated approach to input processing, being attracted to items that were frequent in the input text (cf. N. Ellis, 2006a), they differed in terms of the additional items they noticed. For example, the L1-English group noticed several nominal suffixes, whereas the L1-Japanese group

Learner Spontaneous Attention in L2 Input Processing 127

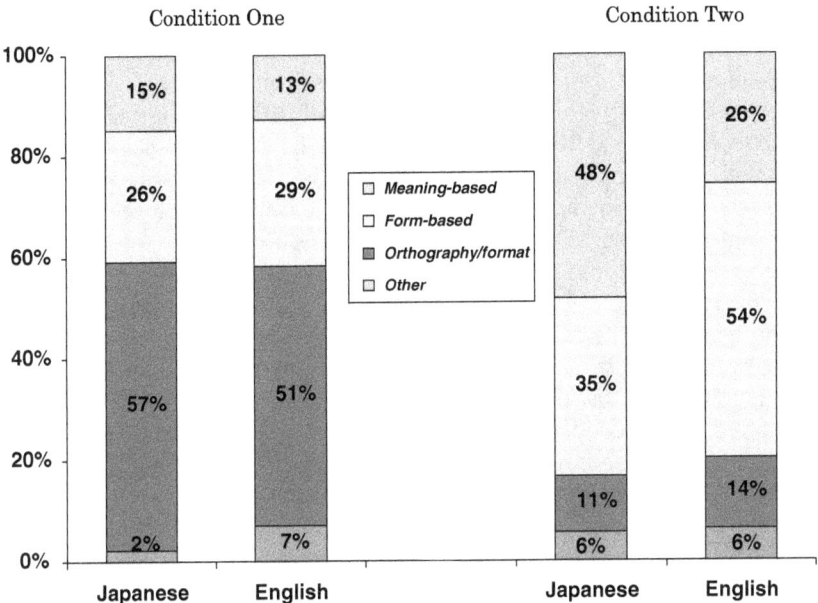

Figure 6.2 Distribution of question types across the two conditions

noticed some graphemic elements (which they associated with Japanese *Kanji* characters). This difference may be interpreted in terms of the typological characteristics of English versus Japanese and their respective distance from Korean. Of particular relevance is the fact that English, unlike Korean, uses the Roman alphabet for its writing system and is primarily a syntax-based language where the morphosyntactic rules are rigid. In contrast, Japanese is similar to Korean in that it utilises a non-Roman alphabet for its writing system and is primarily a pragmatically orientated language whose syntax is not as rigid as that of English (for a detailed contrastive analysis, see Park, 2007). The unique features of each language appear to have predisposed their speakers to notice some items in the L2 input to the exclusion of others.

Under Condition 2, having been pre-taught six items from the input text, the participants showed similar as well as different behaviours during input processing. The latter is most evident on Task 2, where the groups exhibited two distinct orientations when asking questions, with the L1-English group asking more questions on form and the L1-Japanese group asking more on the meaning.

Overall, these results provide confirming evidence that L1 does affect L2 input processing, as researchers have claimed, particularly in the early stage of learning. Furthermore, results from Condition 2 point to an interaction between such influence and the typological distance between the L1 and the L2. That is, if the L1 is typologically distant from the L2, the input-processing approach tends to be form-orientated; however, if the L1 is typologically close to the L2, it tends to be meaning-orientated. This interpretation amounts to suggesting that the greater the typological distance, the greater the learning difficulty (cf. Schachter, 1996).

The results of the present study contradict VanPatten's (1996, 2004b) Input Processing Principle One ('Meaning Primacy'), inasmuch as they showed (1) that the default approach for input processing is form-orientated as opposed to meaning-orientated, and (2) that learners' use of a meaning-based approach is non-automatic, mitigated by their current knowledge of the L2 and the typological similarity (or lack thereof) of their L1 to the L2.

The present study provides modest support for the two hypotheses advanced by Han and Peverly (2007). It may be recalled that their first hypothesis was that for complete beginners, the default approach to L2 input processing is form-based (cf. Lee et al., 1997). The participants in the Han and Peverly study, constrained by absence of knowledge of the target language, had no recourse but to focus on forms in the input text. Similarly, the participants in the current study, when in Condition 1, sought to identify formal features in processing the input text. However, the form-orientated approach changed, in the case of the Japanese group but not of the English group, as a result of increasing knowledge of the target language. Thus, the study provides only partial support for Han and Peverly's second hypothesis, that L2 learners who have developed intermediary grammars are likely to adopt a meaning-based approach to processing input. Even so, it bears pointing out that the participants in the current study were only pre-taught a few linguistic items, and for as little instruction as they received, they should not be expected to develop even a minimum (let alone intermediary) grammar. For this reason, the partial support we are claiming here for Han and Peverly's second hypothesis needs to be interpreted with caution.

In view of the findings from the present study, we can suggest a few directions for future research to take. One direction would be to further verify the hypothesis that the initial approach to input processing is form-orientated. It would also be interesting to identify the amount of current knowledge needed to make the attentional switch from form to meaning. Another potentially productive direction would be to verify a tentative finding from our study concerning the existence of transfer-inspired idiosyncrasies alongside common tendencies in L2 input processing, by involving more L1 groups than we have included in this study. The goal of this line of research should be to reach a consistent and generalisable understanding of which input features are susceptible to L1-based processing, thereby leading to interlearner differences, and which ones are not. Last but not least, it would be worthwhile to expend efforts on developing sensitive measures of learner spontaneous noticing. Results from the two tasks we used preliminarily suggest that Task 2 is more sensitive than Task 1, in that the former was better than the latter at revealing intergroup differences, a key concern of our study. In addition, Task 2 allowed us to trace not only the content of, but also the 'path' taken *en route* to, noticing, that is, how the learners approached the task of processing the input. One obvious difference between the two tasks is that Task 1 does not demand verbal output from the participants, but Task 2 does. It may be that Task 2 (asking questions) prompted the learners to look more closely at the input text than Task 1 (marking items in the input), which resulted in a more fine-grained attention to features that variously stood out for them.

Conclusions

Existing research on the role of attention in SLA has, for the most part, centred on how learner attention may be manipulated for the purpose of enhancing it, and hence enhancing acquisition (see Berent & Kelly, this volume; Han, this volume). Findings from this line of research have been conflicting, rendering, thus, a highly limited understanding of such questions as (1) what strategy would be effective in drawing learner attention to certain features in the input, (2) when a given strategy would be effective, or even (3) whether or not a given strategy is at all necessary. It is becoming increasingly clear that further research focusing on external manipulation of learner attention will continue to fall short of desired outcomes unless some understanding is in place on how learner attention works by itself. Recent L2 literature has begun to see empirical attempts to investigate the latter, the present study being one of them.

Results from our analyses of the data gathered via two measures of learners' spontaneous attention during input processing under two different conditions (i.e. ±current IL knowledge) reveal both shared and idiosyncratic processing tendencies as a function of a common perceptual capability and of the influence of the L1. However, this picture is only suggestive, due to our insufficient control over the selection of participants for the study. The simple fact that the participants came with prior learning experience in one or more second languages may have 'contaminated' the data by introducing confounding variables, posing a threat to the role claimed for the L1 in input processing. As one reviewer rightly pointed out, all members of the Japanese group had studied English, which is also the L1 of the English group. Hence, 'what the Japanese group attended to would likely be influenced not only by their L1 but also by their L2 English orientation and the attentional/noticing processes that had been used in their prior SLA experience'. Although this possibility is in and of itself an empirical question, we concur that it is important to circumvent it in future research. A related problem is that the participants in the study were all instructed learners. Instruction may have had an impact on their input-processing strategies. In sum, future research seeking an understanding of the relationship between learner spontaneous attention and the influence of the L1 should strive for a more rigorous sample.

The present study, nevertheless, serves to underscore the importance of the research on learner spontaneous attention, insofar as it directly addresses the issue of what learners themselves can do. A sound understanding thereof is critical to advancing the field as it continues to search for strategies that may facilitate the process and outcome of SLA. As Corder once remarked:

> We shall never improve our ability to create ... favorable conditions [for learning] until we learn more about the way a learner learns and what his built-in syllabus is. When we do know this, we may begin to be more critical of our cherished notions. We may be able to allow the learner's innate strategies to dictate our practice and determine our syllabus; we may learn to adapt ourselves to his needs rather than impose upon him our preconceptions of how he ought to learn, what he ought to learn and when he ought to learn. (Corder, 1967: 169)

Acknowledgements

This study is supported by a Spencer Research Training Grant to Eun Sung Park for her doctoral research. We gratefully thank Jerry Berent and Patsy Lightbown for their insightful comments and helpful suggestions on an earlier version of this chapter.

Appendix
Input text 1

콜럼비아 대학교

존은 학생이다. 콜럼비아 대학교에 다닌다. 대학교 삼학년이다. 콜럼비아 대학교는 뉴욕에 있다. 캠퍼스가 아주 크고 도서관도 많다. 제일 큰 도서관은 버틀러 도서관이다. 대학교 근처에 식당이 많다. 식당 종류가 아주 다양하다. 미국 식당, 한국 식당, 그리고 일본 식당도 있다. 존은 주로 한국 식당에서 점심을 먹는다. 비빔밥을 먹는다.

Columbia University

John is a student. He goes to Columbia University. He is a junior in college. Columbia University is in New York. The campus is big with many libraries. The biggest library is Butler library. There are many restaurants near the university. There are various kinds of restaurants. There is an American restaurant, a Korean restaurant and a Japanese restaurant. John usually eats at the Korean restaurant. He eats Bibimbap.

Input text 2

내 동생

내 동생 이름은 레이첼이다. 레이첼은 대학교 삼학년이다. 경제학을 전공한다. 고향은 시애틀이지만 지금은 뉴욕에서 산다. 레이첼은 친구가 많다. 제일 친한 친구는 다이안이다. 다이안은 일본 사람이다. 뉴욕에 있는 학원에서 일본어를 가르친다. 동생은 남자 친구도 있다. 이름은 존이다. 존은 뉴욕 대학교에서 영문학을 전공한다.

My younger sibling

My younger sibling's name is Rachel. Rachel is a junior in college. She majors in Economics. She is from Seattle but currently lives in New York. Rachel has many friends. Her closest friend is Diane. Diane is Japanese. She teaches Japanese at an academic institute in New York. My younger sibling also has a boyfriend. His name is John. John majors in English literature at New York University.

Notes

1. The six chosen words are typically taught in the first month of an Introductory Korean class. As shown in Table 6.1, the six items included one action verb, one copula (to be), two nouns, a topic marker, and a preposition.
2. The words were counted in accordance with School Grammar of South Korea.
3. The Revised Romanization of Korean, rather than the Yale System (typically used for linguistic analysis), is used in this study.
4. In the two texts used in the study, the topic marker also consistently marks the subject of each sentence.
5. This category differs from the fifth category '이' in that in the latter, the participant specifically marked just this particular item without marking or making reference to 아 or 에, which is very similar in shape. However, there were some cases in which the participants marked '이,아' or '이,에' as a pair, as indicated by arrows, lines joining the two items, or by the question written in the margin of the text, 'What is the difference between the two?' Such markings were categorised under '이,아,에'.

Chapter 7
Working Memory and L2 Processing of Redundant Grammatical Forms

NURIA SAGARRA

Psycholinguistic accounts of language acquisition coincide on the major role that attention plays in converting input to intake (Gass, 1997). According to Long (1991) and Swain (1998), attention to form helps learners notice the gaps that exist in their interlanguage grammar and can facilitate intake derivation. However, attention to form should be accompanied by attention to meaning, and form–meaning connections require great mental effort. Because the cognitive resources needed to respond to this demand are limited (Just & Carpenter, 1992), learners have to select which aspects of the input they will process (Gass *et al.*, 2003).

VanPatten (1996, 2004b) has shown that learners tend to process features of the language that carry more meaning (e.g. content words) before those that are less meaningful (e.g. grammatical forms) (see also Clahsen & Felser, 2006). VanPatten (2004b) also notes that, when processing meaningful forms, learners prefer to process non-redundant over redundant elements (see also Lee, 1999, 2002; Lee *et al.*, 1997; Leeser, 2004; Musumeci, 1989; Rossomondo, 2003). Han and Peverly (2007) (see also Park & Han, this volume) expand VanPatten's input processing theory, arguing that, whereas learners with previous L2 knowledge prefer to process non-redundant forms first, those with no existing L2 knowledge attend to grammatical forms independently of their communicative redundancy.

Despite the substantial body of literature devoted to investigating whether L2 learners are able to attend to redundant grammatical forms, most studies have examined this question employing off-line techniques and, thus, can only provide circumstantial evidence about L2 processing. In order to explore what happens during real-time processing, studies need to adopt on-line techniques that measure attention as processing unfolds. In 2001, Sagarra and Dussias began to cover this lacuna by using eye movement records to examine attention to redundant grammatical forms in intermediate L2 learners. The present study employs another on-line technique, a non-cumulative self-paced moving window task, in order to continue this much needed line of research with learners at a lower proficiency level, and to advance our understanding of the relationship between working memory and L2 processing. This is important because working memory constrains the processing of redundant grammatical forms (VanPatten, 1996, 2004b).

Working Memory and L2 Processing

Baddeley (2003: 189) defines working memory as 'the temporary storage and manipulation of information that is assumed to be necessary for a wide range of complex cognitive activities'. The amount of activation needed to support processing or storage is limited and varies from person to person (Just & Carpenter, 1992). Whenever such capacity becomes insufficient to maintain the level of activation necessary to perform a specific task, processing will slow down and/or storage will decrease. Thus, people with larger working memory capacity will process linguistic information more quickly and effectively than those with smaller working memory capacity.

Learning another language as an adult imposes an additional processing load on cognitive resources, because it requires more computation and activation (Hasegawa *et al.*, 2002). Therefore, working memory explains a great deal of variability in adult L2 processing with regard to lexical and syntactic processing (Miyake & Friedman, 1998; Vos *et al.*, 2001), lexical access (Kroll *et al.*, 2002), comprehension (Geva & Ryan, 1993; Harrington & Sawyer, 1992), and noticing of recasts (see Sagarra, 2007, for a review).

Processing of Redundant Grammatical Forms

Given that working memory capacity is limited, VanPatten (1996, 2004b) suggests that learners will focus first on the parts of the input that are semantically richer, such as content words (nouns, verbs, adverbs, or chunks of language processed as content words) (see also Bardovi-Harlig, 1992; Klein & Rieck, 1982, cited in Klein, 1986; Mangubhai, 1991). Thus, 'inflections on verbs and nouns may be *skipped over or only partially processed* and then dumped from working memory as the processing resources in working memory are exhausted by the efforts required to process lexical items' (VanPatten, 2004b: 8, emphasis added). This implies that learners will tend to use the adverb to assign tense in sentences like *yesterday I played the guitar*, rather than the verb inflection *-ed*, because the inflection is redundant. The processing of redundant verb morphology has been investigated with a vast array of techniques.

Musumeci (1989), for example, examined how beginning learners of Italian, French and Spanish assigned tense to sentences they heard with verb morphology only, verb morphology and temporal adverbs, verb morphology and gestures, or verb morphology together with temporal adverbs and gestures. Results from a multiple-choice tense identification test showed that adverbs were the determining factor in tense assignment. Lee *et al.* (1997) explored the same question at the discourse level by asking learners of Spanish to listen to a passage with preterite regular verbs in the third person singular, with or without temporal adverbs. Findings from a multiple-choice tense identification test revealed that first-semester learners, with fewer than 60 contact hours, did not detect temporal information from the adverbs or the verbs, but that third- and fifth-semester learners exposed to lexical cues improved in the reconstruction of the propositional content of the passage. These findings suggest that learners need to have previous knowledge of the target structure to take the utmost benefit of content words and attend to these words over redundant grammatical forms (see also Han & Peverly, 2007; Park & Han, this volume).

Given that input mode affects processing (Leeser, 2004; Leow, 1995; Wong, 2001), further evidence was warranted to determine whether results in the oral mode (Lee *et al.*, 1997; Musumeci, 1989) would also be obtained in the written mode. Lee (1999) asked second- and fourth-semester learners of Spanish to read and recall a passage with or without past temporal adverbs, and to read the passage again one week later while thinking aloud. Results from learner verbalisations revealed that learners who read the passage without adverbs identified preterite verb inflections without probing, whereas those who read the passage with adverbs heavily relied on these temporal cues to make temporal references. He also noted that the low comprehenders' engagement in a wider variety of cognitive and linguistic behaviours prevented them from attending to form.

The studies presented so far investigate attention to redundant grammatical forms by classroom learners with existing knowledge of the target language. However, some researchers posit that external interventions typical of classroom contexts can modulate learner attention (Berent & Kelly, this volume; Doughty, 2003; VanPatten, 1996, 2004b; Wong 2004b;

but see Gass *et al.*, 2003, and references therein, for a review of studies supporting that attention is exclusively learner-driven). If attention to input is malleable by means of an outside source, then it is important to determine how learners naturally attend to the input to make pedagogical interventions more effective (Park & Han, this volume). To address this question, a series of studies have examined the incidental acquisition of grammatical forms.

For example, Lee (2002) investigated the effect of frequency of target forms and presence of temporal adverbs on L2 comprehension and processing of a new morphological form (the Spanish synthetic future tense). He asked second-semester learners of Spanish to read one of six versions of a passage. Three versions included a title and a temporal adverb at the beginning of each paragraph with 6, 10, or 16 future tense forms, and the other three versions only contained 6, 10, or 16 future tense forms. He found that passages with temporal adverbs yielded greater recall of target verbs, but the presence or absence of temporal adverbs did not affect learners' performance on a multiple-choice tense identification test, a form recognition test, or a form production test.

Lee's (2002) unexpected results that verbs rather than adverbs facilitate recognition of tense in beginning learners can be explained in different ways. One explanation is that learners with no preexisting L2 knowledge may rely on meaningful and non-meaningful forms indiscriminately (Han & Peverly, 2007; Park & Han, this volume). Han and Peverly exposed beginning learners of Norwegian (i.e. with zero prior knowledge of the TL) to a TL passage. Results from a recall and a fill-in-the-blank task revealed that learners adopted a form-orientated approach. In a similar study with beginning learners of Korean, Park and Han reported that the form-based approach adopted by complete beginners became a meaning-based approach once learners had acquired an intermediate knowledge of L2 grammar. Rossomondo (2003), however, proposes another explanation for Lee's findings, namely, that temporal adverbs in Lee's study may not have been sufficient to produce significant differences. To test this hypothesis, she examined the incidental acquisition of the Spanish synthetic future tense with first-semester learners of Spanish who read a passage with 13 target forms, with or without a title and temporal adverbs. Findings from multiple-choice and cloze passage tasks showed that the presence of temporal adverbs facilitated comprehension without obstructing processing in silent reading and think-aloud protocols.

The studies presented in this section show that learners with existing knowledge of the target language prefer to process meaning over form and content words before redundant verb morphology. However, these studies have the drawback of employing off-line measures (recalls, comprehension tasks, multiple-choice tense identification tests) that can only speak to what happens *after* processing, and hence can only draw *post facto* conclusions about what occurs *during* processing. Although the act of thinking aloud may seem on-line in the sense that data are collected as learners read a text, it still depicts an incomplete picture of processing. Furthermore, think-aloud protocols are limited to what learners consciously believe that they are processing and fall short in assessing unconscious processing. Demonstrations of dissociations between conscious and unconscious perceptual processes date back to the 19th century (see Cleeremans, 2001, 2005, for a review), and extend from Freud to recent neuroimaging studies (Stanislas & Changeux, 2004). Furthermore, for connectionist models of information processing, knowledge is implicit to the point that it cannot be separated from the mechanisms that subserve processing. The fact that selective attention can occur without awareness (Robinson, 1995; Tomlin & Villa, 1994) only emphasises the pressing need to conduct studies on attention to redundant grammatical forms by employing techniques sensitive to conscious and unconscious real-time processing. On-line techniques assess processing as it unfolds and include moving window, eye movement records, and event-related brain potentials.

The Study

Despite the urgent need to use on-line techniques, only Sagarra and Dussias (2001) have investigated the processing of L2 redundant morphological forms with an on-line technique: eye movement records (see Rayner, 1998, for a discussion about the relationship between this technique and implicit information processing). Eye movements of intermediate learners of Spanish were recorded as they read sentences with past temporal adverbs that agreed in tense with preterite verbs, and disagreed in tense with present verbs. Results from gaze duration time on the critical verbs indicated that learners spent more time processing verb morphology that disagreed in tense with preceding temporal adverbs, suggesting that they were able to process redundant grammatical forms. Thus, these results differ from the results of the studies described in the first part of this chapter, which suggest that learners with existing knowledge of the target language prefer to assign tense by means of adverbs rather than verb morphology. The discrepancy in the findings calls for further research to separate the effects of proficiency level and means of measurement. The present study addresses this issue.

In particular, the goal of this empirical study is to examine whether third-semester learners of Spanish process redundant verbal morphology encountered in visual stimuli, and whether working memory constrains their ability to do so. To address these questions, this study employed a non-cumulative self-paced reading moving window paradigm to measure real-time processing. A non-cumulative moving window technique was chosen to avoid the regressions to the adverb possible in eyetracking studies because regressions ease the cognitive load and can alter reading times on the critical verb as well as working memory's degree of predictability. In addition, the present study included a greater sample (156 vs 32 participants) and a larger number of comprehension questions (100% vs 20% of the trials) than Sagarra and Dussias (2001). These methodological procedures were adopted to better address the following research questions:

(1) Do third-semester learners process redundant L2 grammatical forms?
(2) Is there a relationship between working memory and learners' ability to process redundant L2 grammatical forms?

Method

Participants

In total, 156 adult native English speakers, 85 females and 71 males, participated in the study in exchange for extra credit. They were enrolled in a third-semester Spanish course at a major American university. The course followed the guidelines of processing instruction, an input-based communicative language teaching methodology with focus on form (VanPatten, 1996). Participants completed a language background questionnaire, and data from those with previous or current exposure to Spanish or another Romance language outside the course were removed from the study. To be included in the study, participants also had to complete all tasks, show the same proficiency level in a Spanish placement test, score 100% on two recognition tests, and answer comprehension questions on a moving window test with greater accuracy than could be achieved by chance. Finally, they had to be between 18 and 40 years old, because working memory declines with age (Park *et al.*, 2003) and processing speed starts to slow down when people reach their mid-40s.

Target structure

The target form consisted of Spanish transitive regular verbs in the present and past preterite tenses. Spanish present verbs in third person singular are formed by adding the suffix *-a* to the stem of conjugational class I verbs (infinitive ending in *-ar*) (e.g. *hablar* – *habla* 'to talk – (s)he talks'), and *-e* to the stem of conjugational class II and III verbs (infinitive ending in *-er* or *-ir*) (e.g. *comer* – *come* 'to eat – (s)he eats'). Spanish past preterite verbs in third person singular, on the other hand, are formed by adding *-ó* to the stem of class I verbs (e.g. *hablar* – *habló* 'to talk – (s)he talked'), and *-ió* to the stem of class II and III verbs (e.g. *comer* – *comió* 'to eat – (s)he ate'). There were 16 target verbs: 4 *-ar* present verbs, 4 *-er/-ir* present verbs, 4 *-ar* preterite verbs and 4 *-er/-ir* preterite verbs. Target verbs were controlled for length (2 syllables long) and frequency. Verb frequency was determined by the content covered in the Spanish course (the book contained lexical lists at the end of each chapter). Although participants were enrolled in different sections, all sections followed the same syllabus and completed the same homework.

Materials

Screening tasks

Three screening tasks were administered in addition to the language background questionnaire: a language proficiency task, a verb recognition task, and a tense recognition task. For the language proficiency task, learners completed multiple-choice questions about Spanish grammar, vocabulary, and reading. The verb recognition task required learners to match a list of Spanish verbs to a list of English verbs. Finally, the tense recognition task asked learners to read Spanish regular verbs and identify whether they referred to an action in the past or in the present. The verb and tense tasks served to ensure that learners knew the meaning and form of the target verbs in order to avoid latencies in the reading times due to unfamiliarity with the experimental stimuli.

Moving window task

Participants were randomly presented with one of eight 140-sentence sets. Each set contained 4 practice trials, 16 experimental sentences (half with adverb–verb tense agreement and half with adverb–verb tense disagreement), 48 sentences with temporal adverbs (half with adverb–verb tense agreement and half with adverb–verb tense disagreement), and 72 filler sentences. Sentences were randomised using a Latin square to avoid having experimental sentences appear close to each other. All sentences were controlled for length, lexical frequency, and vocabulary adequate to the learners' level of proficiency in Spanish. The order of presentation was counterbalanced so that each of the 16 target verbs appeared once in the preterite (adverb–verb tense agreement condition) and once in the present (adverb–verb tense disagreement condition) in different sentences. Because intake derivation is based on form–meaning connections, a yes–no comprehension question appeared at the end of each sentence to ensure that learners were processing the text for meaning. Half of the questions required a 'yes' answer, and the other half a 'no' answer. Experimental sentences followed the structure of Adverb–NP1 (subject)–VP–NP2 (object)–PP1–PP2 and were divided into two conditions:

Adverb–verb tense agreement

(1) *Ayer el estudiante miró una película de terror en el cine.*
'Yesterday the student watched a horror movie at the cinema.'

Adverb–verb tense disagreement

(2) **Ayer el estudiante mira una película de terror en el cine.*
'*Yesterday the student watches a horror film at the cinema.'

The choice of the Spanish preterite–present contrast with regular verbs in the third person singular was motivated by several factors. First, Spanish is a pro-drop language where subject pronouns can be elided once the context has been established. Thus, L2 learners of a pro-drop language, especially those whose L1 is non-pro-drop like English, often overuse personal pronouns (Belletti *et al.*, 2005) and tend to rely on lexical items before verbal morphology (VanPatten, 2004b). This means that information encoded in Spanish verbal morphology (tense, person, number) easily goes unnoticed by L2 learners. Second, Spanish preterite and present verbs in the third person singular have the same length, a necessary condition to ensure that latencies in the verbs are caused by morphological differences between the two verbs rather than length differences. Third, sentences like (2) are incorrect because of pragmatic violations, but are both grammatically possible (historical present tense) and syntactically congruent.

Reading span task

The reading span task was used to measure working memory and was conducted in the participants' L1 (English), because most research suggests that working memory is language independent (Osaka & Osaka, 1992; Osaka *et al.*, 1993), and because the learners' low L2 proficiency level would affect the outcome of the test. Participants were asked to read 80 sentences on a computer screen, one by one, make plausibility judgements and remember the last word of sentences within a set. Sentences were taken from Waters *et al.*'s (1987) and Waters and Caplan's (1996) version of the reading span task, and were grouped into sets from two to six sentences. Half of the sentences were semantically plausible and the other half were semantically implausible. Implausible sentences were formed by inverting the animacy of the subject and the object (e.g. *It was the cavity that extracted the dentist*).

Procedure

Participants completed the screening tasks and the moving window and reading span tasks in four sessions. Session 1 was conducted in a computer laboratory and included a reading span task. Session 2 was carried out in class and included a language background questionnaire and the grammar and vocabulary sections of the language proficiency task. Session 3 took place in a computer laboratory, where participants completed the moving window task and the verb and tense recognition tasks. Finally, participants completed the reading part of the language proficiency task in class during Session 4. A detailed explanation of the procedure for the moving window task and the reading span task is provided next.

Moving window task

The task consisted of a non-cumulative reading moving window technique (Just *et al.*, 1982) that required participants to read two-line sentences on a computer monitor, word by word. Words appeared in their corresponding position within the sentence, and when a word was displayed, the remaining words of the sentence were indicated by an underscore symbol, as displayed in Figure 7.1. For each sentence, participants were asked to look at a 500-ms fixation sign (+), press the space bar to make the first word appear, read the first word silently, press the space bar to make the second word appear and the first one disappear, read the second word silently, and repeat this procedure to display the remaining words within the sentence. After reading a sentence, participants pressed the space bar to make a comprehension question appear, and indicated their answer to the question by pressing a 'yes' or a 'no' button. Questions were focused on the meaning of the sentence to avoid biasing the results by directing the learners' attention to redundant verb morphology. For example, the question for sentences (1) and (2) was *¿La película era una comedia?* 'Was the movie a comedy?'

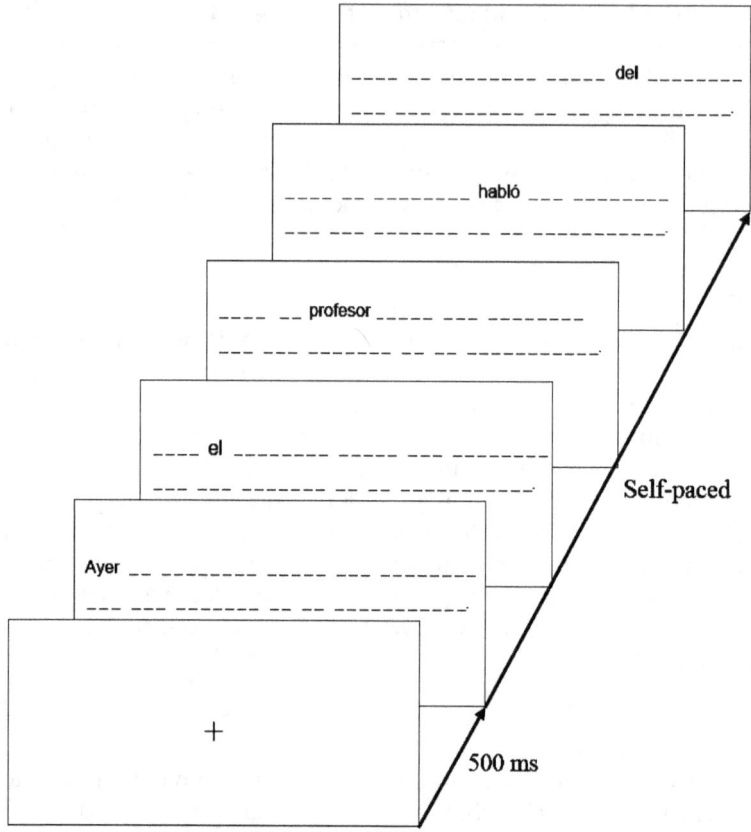

Figure 7.1 An example of a trial for the reading moving window task

Reading span task

For each sentence, participants pressed a button to initiate the trial, looked at a 500-ms fixation sign (+), read the sentence silently, pressed a 'yes' or a 'no' button to indicate whether the sentence was semantically plausible, and repeated the cycle as many times as there were sentences in the set (see Figure 7.2). At the end of the set, the word 'recall' appeared on the screen and participants wrote down the final word of each sentence within that set.

L2 Processing of Redundant Grammatical Forms 143

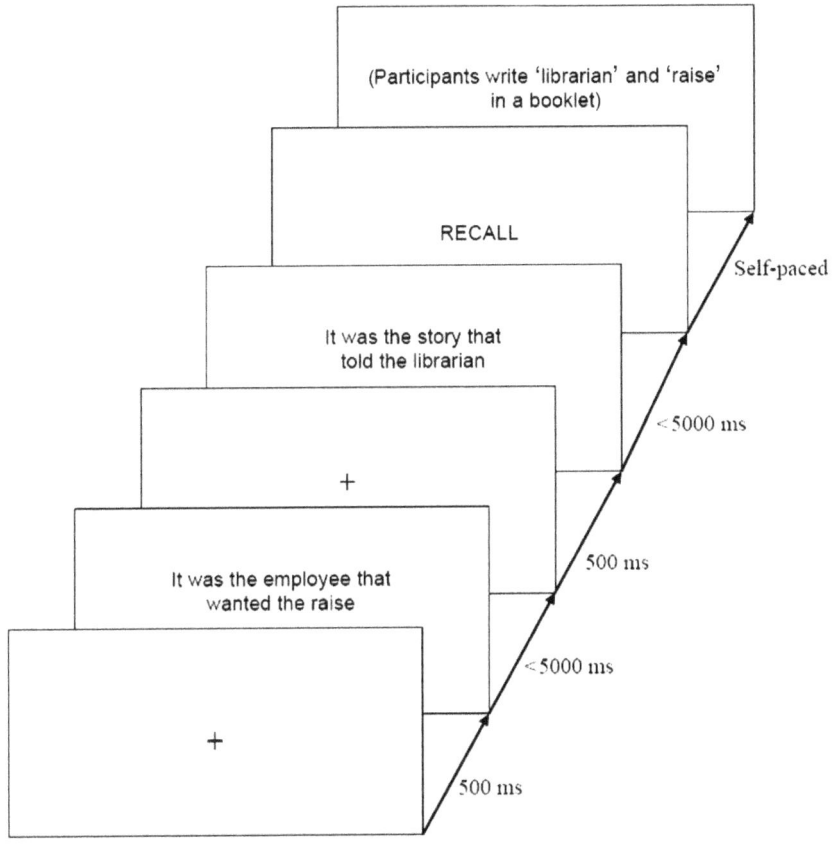

Figure 7.2 An example of a trial for the reading span task

Scoring

Scoring of the moving window task was based on two scores. The first score consisted of the time spent between the appearance of a target verb and the press of the space bar. Reading times below 200 ms and above 2000 ms were excluded, following standard procedure in reading moving window experiments. The second score measured the accuracy in the comprehension questions by assigning 1 point to correct responses and 0 points to incorrect responses. Reading times were only included for sentences with correct responses to the comprehension questions, and students needed to respond to the comprehension questions correctly above the 50% chance mark.

Scoring of the sentences of the reading span task depended on several factors. To obtain 1 point on a sentence, learners needed to be accurate in making the plausibility judgement and recalling the last word. In addition, learners had to make plausibility judgements faster than 5000 ms so as not to jeopardize the complexity of the task, but slower than 300 ms in order to have enough time to process it (Rayner & Pollatsek, 1989; note that college students process single words at between 225 and 400 ms). The mean reading times for plausible and implausible sentences were calculated separately.

Results

Mean reading times on the correct verbs (624.51) and incorrect verbs (628.27) of the moving window task were similar, and there were no latencies preceding or following the target verbs (see Figure 7.3). The mean reading span was 44.35 out of the maximum possible score 80, and the mean reading times for plausible and implausible sentences were 3327 ms and 3398 ms, respectively.

To address the research questions of the study, a one-way repeated measures ANCOVA was performed on the mean reading times of the target verbs, with working memory entered as a covariate. The results

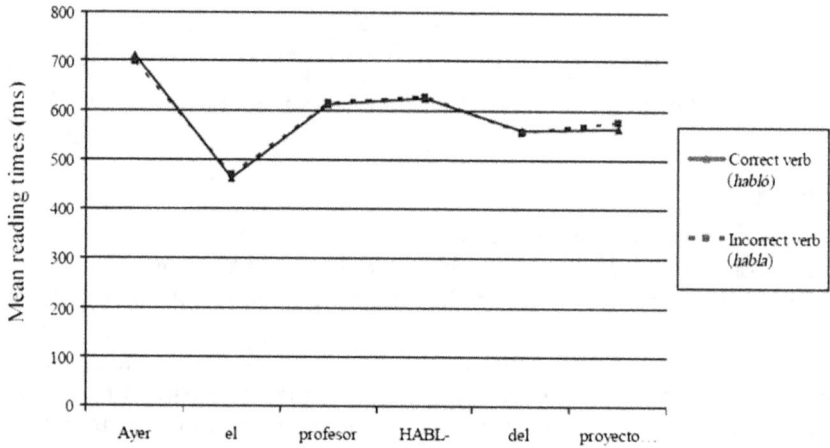

Figure 7.3 Mean reading times at words preceding and following the target verb

confirmed a non-significant main effect for tense agreement ($F(1) = 0.089$, $p > 0.05$), indicating that learners spent the same amount of time reading preterite verbs that agreed with a preceding past temporal adverb as they did reading present verbs that disagreed with a previous past temporal adverb. However, the findings revealed a significant main effect for working memory ($F(1) = 16.709$, $p < 0.01$) and a significant interaction between working memory and agreement ($F(1) = 196.051$, $p < 0.01$). This means that the non-significant effect found for tense agreement was caused by low span learners, and that high span learners could process incorrect tense agreement more often than low span learners. In sum, these results suggest that individual differences in working memory capacity constrain low-proficiency L2 learners' ability to process redundant morphological cues when forced to attend to the overall meaning of the sentence at the same time (comprehension questions).

Discussion and Conclusions

The results of the present study indicate that third-semester learners spent the same amount of time reading preterite and present verbs preceded by a past temporal adverb, suggesting that they were not able to process redundant grammatical forms. These findings are in line with previous studies that employed off-line measures (Lee, 1999, 2002; Lee et al., 1997; Musumeci, 1989) with learners of a similar proficiency level. However, the findings of the present study contrast with those reported by Sagarra and Dussias (2001), who found that intermediate L2 learners are able to process redundant grammatical forms, based on eye movement records.

This discrepancy can be attributed to differences in the learners' proficiency levels (seventh- and eighth-semester learners with study abroad experience in Sagarra & Dussias, 2001, vs third-semester learners in the present study). This hypothesis is consonant with previous studies reporting an effect of proficiency level on attention to grammatical forms (Han & Peverly, 2007; Park & Han, this volume). According to these studies, learners with no existing knowledge of the target language pay attention to meaningful and less meaningful features of the input indiscriminately and independently of their communicative redundancy, whereas those with basic L2 knowledge tend to skip or only partially process redundant grammatical forms. The findings of Sagarra and Dussias (2001) suggest that learners with higher proficiency who can process meaningful elements with ease and automaticity are able to devote their cognitive resources to processing redundant grammatical forms.

The present study also shows that learners with existing L2 knowledge who have higher working memory capacity can better process meaningful and redundant grammatical forms simultaneously. These findings make a significant contribution to VanPatten's model of input processing (1996, 2004b). VanPatten (2004b: 11) posits that 'for learners to process either redundant meaningful grammatical forms or non-meaningful forms, the processing of overall sentential meaning must not drain available processing resources'. He attributes the availability of resources to proficiency level, word familiarity, and learners' ability to access lexical information already incorporated into their developing system (i.e. stored in long-term memory). Although he mentions the role of working memory in the noticing of forms, he does not identify working memory as a factor responsible for availability of attentional resources. Because working memory determines how well and how fast learners process and store linguistic information, it plays a central role in determining availability of attentional resources and should be included in future studies.

Future research should also control for the distance between the adverb and the verb (Sagarra *et al.*, 2005). The greater the distance between the verb and the adverb, the longer the learner will need to hold the tense information from the adverb in memory and the less cognitive resources will be available to process redundant morphology. It would also be interesting to investigate the relationship between working memory, distance, and processing of unknown morphological forms. The present study informs us about what affects the *strengthening* of form–meaning connections, but does not speak to the formation of form–meaning mappings. Researchers should also bear in mind the characteristics of the materials (type of form, perceptual salience) and the learners (presence of a monolingual control group, L2 proficiency level). For example, the results of the present study are restricted to verb morphology made redundant by the presence of previous temporal adverbs. Research shows that not all grammatical forms are equally amenable to instruction (DeKeyser, 1995, 2005; Han, 2004c) or correction (R. Ellis, 2007). However, the extent to which perceptual salience of morphological forms affects processing as measured by on-line measures remains an open subject. For example, the written accent in the preterite verbs of the present study (*habló* '(s)he talked') could make verb morphology more salient and increase mean reading times on these verbs to the extent of making the difference between present and preterite verbs non-significant. Thus, when possible, it is preferable to compare morphological forms of equal perceptual salience.

With regard to learner characteristics, data from a monolingual control group would help determine the magnitude of mean reading times and accuracy rate on comprehension questions. In addition, the discrepancy between the findings of studies with intermediate learners (Sagarra & Dussias, 2001) and those with beginning learners raises the question of whether proficiency level plays a role in the processing of redundant grammatical forms. A study with on-line techniques that combines various proficiency levels would shed light on the debate about whether attention to grammatical forms increases (McLaughlin, 1990) or decreases (Sagarra, 2001) with greater L2 level of proficiency.

The research and results discussed in this chapter have the following pedagogical implications. First, lexical cues could be used during learners' initial creation of form–meaning connections in order to enhance comprehension (Rossomondo, 2003). Second, teachers could implement compensatory practices to help reduce the learners' cognitive load and thus release their cognitive resources to attend to grammatical forms. These compensatory devices include minimum distance between the lexical and the morphological cue (Sagarra *et al.*, 2005), use of familiar forms (Lee, 2002) and topics (Leeser, 2004), simplification of the input (see Sagarra, 2002, for a review) and the tasks (Robinson, 2001), input enhancement (see Wong, 2004a, for a review), and use of written before oral input (Wong, 2001). These compensatory devices may potentially maximise the possibilities that learners process redundant grammatical forms.

In conclusion, the present study suggests that low-proficiency learners with basic L2 knowledge do not process redundant grammatical forms unless they have high working memory capacity. These findings are based on an on-line technique (moving window paradigm), and they demonstrate the need to investigate L2 processing using real-time measures in addition to off-line measures, because off-line measures provide no information about implicit processing. Indeed, the use of real-time measures is critical if we hope to advance our understanding of the implicit, as well as explicit, cognitive mechanisms that affect L2 processing, so as to contribute to the improvement of pedagogical practices. Fortunately, the number of studies that use on-line measures to assess the conscious and unconscious nature of processing is increasing, and the present empirical study is another step forward in this direction.

Chapter 8
L2 Learners' Interpretation of Operator-Variable Binding in VP Ellipsis

HONG GUANG YING

In current Universal Grammar (UG) theory, operator-variable binding plays a critical role (Safir, 2004). The study reported in this chapter investigates whether the binding relation between an operator and a variable is part of the innate language faculty consistent with the claims of UG. I will examine VP-ellipsis structures. The operator-variable binding in VP ellipsis is interesting in that it gives rise to ambiguity of antecedence that does not exist in the absence of ellipsis. It allows 'sloppy reading' (Example 1 below) in which the reflexive *himself* in the elided VP co-refers with *Bill* and 'strict reading' (Example 2 below) in which the pronoun *him* in the elided VP co-refers with *John* (Fiengo & May, 1994).

(1) John$_i$ defended himself$_i$ and Bill$_j$ did [defend himself$_j$] too.
(2) John$_i$ defended himself$_i$ and Bill$_j$ did [defend him$_i$] too.

Following Huang (1987, 1994), I claim that both sloppy and strict readings involve variable binding, that is, the reflexives in both these structures reflect variable binding without either an overt WH[1] operator or quantifier.

Chinese shows similar binding possibilities as English. However, Chinese differs from English in that Chinese VP-ellipsis structures can include a lexical verb (Example 3) or the verb *shi* 'be' (Example 4).

(3) Zhangsan tian-yi-xia   taziji-de   bing-bang,   Lisi ye tian-yi-xia.
     Zhangsan lick-1-time   himself-s   ice-bar,   Lisi also lick-1-time.
     'Zhangsan licks his ice-bar and Lisi does too.'

148

(4) Zhangsan tian-yi-xia taziji-de bing-bang,   Lisi ye [$_{IP}$ *shi* [$_{VP}$ [$_{NP}$ e]]].
    Zhangsan lick-1-time himself-s ice-bar,   Lisi also   be
    'Zhangsan licks his ice-bar and Lisi does too.'

The verb *shi* lacks the semantic content of a lexical verb. This contrast in Chinese between a lexical verb and *shi* 'be' does not exist in VP-ellipsis structures in English (Foley *et al.*, 1997). Chinese thus allows a test that would have been impossible in English: we can test whether lexical representations in Chinese will affect English learners' representation of UG constraints regarding the ambiguity of these structures.

Previous Analyses: Semantic Versus Syntactic

It is relatively uncontroversial that reflexives have a sloppy reading, on the assumption that they function obligatorily as bound variables. However, there has been disagreement in the linguistic literature on the status of a strict reading. Work by Dalrymple, Shieber, and Pereira (Dalrymple *et al.*, 1991; Shieber *et al.*, 1996) represents the semantic approach. Dalrymple *et al.* (1991) proposed that the availability of a strict reading of a reflexive depends on the semantic property of individual verbs. They distinguished between verbs such as *lock* and *defend*, stating that no matter what the structure is, the verb *defend* allows a strict reading, but not the verb *lock*.

(5) Bill defended himself against the accusation, and John did too.
(6) John locked himself in the bathroom when bad news arrived, but Bill would never do so.

They explained that *defend* gets both sloppy and strict readings because it does not intrinsically impose a requirement of co-reference between its subject and object. On the other hand, *lock* does not allow a strict reading because it imposes a requirement of co-reference between its subject and object. However, as Hestvik (1995) pointed out, the semantic properties of lexical items do not determine whether reflexives allow a strict reading. Compare (6) with (7):

(7) John locked himself in the bathroom before Bill could.

Evidently, a strict reading is possible in (7), suggesting that an account based on the semantic property of verbs does not work (Hestvik, 1995).

Kitagawa (1991) approached the problem of strict reflexives by reconstructing reflexives as pronouns at LF (Logical Form, the level of representation wherein sentences are assigned a representation of meaning). She suggested that a feature [+ anaphor] on the reflexive can be suppressed in the copying of the antecedent VP into the elided VP. This is illustrated in (8), where LF of (8a) is (8b) with the reflexive reconstructed as the pronoun:

(8)(a) John$_i$ likes himself$_i$, and Bill does too.
 (b) John$_i$ likes [+a] himself$_i$, and Bill likes [−a] him$_i$ too.

Fiengo and May (1994) developed Kitagawa's suggestion and proposed a structural account under the term 'vehicle change'. They stated that the strict reading of reflexives involves a change to the pronoun from the reflexive, although at the level of LF the empty VP is replaced with material as a function of a dependency on the VP in the preceding clause. That is, a reflexive, when copied from the first to the second clause, is allowed to change to a pronoun. Thus, vehicle change allows the strict reading by reconstructing the reflexive as a pronoun, which, as set by Principle B of Binding Theory, cannot be locally bound. This explains why the reflexive in the overt VP (8a) can be reconstructed as the pronoun in the elided VP (8b), referring back to the nonlocal subject NP *John*.

To sum up, Dalrymple *et al.* (1991) proposed that the strict reading of reflexives derive from the semantic property of individual verbs, but their semantic account was deemed unsatisfactory. The property of verbs does not determine the strict reading of reflexives in VP-ellipsis (Hestvik, 1995). In contrast, Fiengo and May (1994), based on Kitagawa (1991), proposed a structural account under the name of 'vehicle change'. The structural account suggests that the strict reading of reflexives derives from 'vehicle change', which allows reflexives in the elided VP to be interpreted as pronouns at LF.

Neither account addresses how readers would interpret variable binding in VP-ellipsis. In other words, neither account tells us how readers would interpret this strict–sloppy ambiguity.

Prior L2 Research in Reflexive Binding

Previous second language (L2) research in reflexive binding studied linguistic constraints such as Binding Theory (Chomsky, 1981, 1986), the movement at LF approach (Cole & Sung, 1994), the relativised SUBJECT approach (Progovac, 1992, 1993), constraints that operate at LF (Chomsky, 1993, 1995), and the Internal Subject Hypothesis (Koopman & Sportiche, 1991). Recent L2 studies on reflexive binding examined L2 learners' interpretation of a cluster of properties of UG such as a link between monomorphemic reflexives and long-distance subject orientation.

Thomas (1995) investigated whether L2 learners of Japanese know that morphologically simplex anaphor *zibun* has the property of subject orientation. Her experiments included 58 learners of Japanese as a foreign language, 34 in a low-proficiency group and 24 in a high-proficiency group. Subjects were tested with a truth–value judgement task involving stories and pictures. The results showed that most of her subjects at a high proficiency level who bind *zibun* long distance reject object antecedents, an empirical finding consistent with the predications of the movement at LF approach. However, the lower-proficiency learners failed to bind reflexives long distance. Thus, the issue of subject-orientation could not be investigated for these learners, and these data are less readily accounted for from the perspective of movement at LF.

Yip and Tang (1998) investigated the interpretation of English reflexives by Cantonese-speaking learners of English. They employed a sentence judgement task to probe the learners' knowledge of binding. They found that learners initially identified English reflexives with the monomorphemic reflexives in their native language, and that, as learners became more advanced, they were able to treat the binding properties of the L2 as an independent system consistent with UG.

Bennett and Progovac (1998) expanded on Bennett's (1994) investigation of the interpretation of English reflexives by Serbo-Croatian learners of English. They used a picture-identification task and a multiple-choice questionnaire to investigate whether Serbo-Croatian speakers learning L2 English apply the +AGR parameter setting and initially transfer the L1 X^o reflexive anaphor type to the interlanguage grammar and whether Serbo-Croatian speakers learning L2 English who retain the +AGR/X^o reflexive configuration will be able to compute new binding domains in the interlanguage grammar. The study yielded evidence of transfer of the L1 X^o anaphor setting to their interlanguage grammar. They treated English XP reflexives on a par with X^o reflexives in their native language in sentences lacking an AGR in the local domain, namely, sentences with reflexives in complex noun phrases. But the study also showed the evidence that reflexive binding in an L2 is constrained by UG. When a binding domain resulting from the interaction of an X^o reflexive and an AGR parameter setting is not instantiated in the L1, L2 learners set the domain in the light of UG constraints.

MacLaughlin (1998) conducted experiments on the acquisition of English reflexives by native speakers of Chinese and Japanese. She used a sentence judgement task to investigate UG constraints and L1 induced language mapping. Her results indicate that, although transfer is an important factor in L2 development, L2 learners advance beyond the constraints imposed by their native languages. That is, L2 learners can acquire a system of reflexive binding that is not found in the native language (nor in the target language), but one that is nevertheless constrained by UG.

Not until recently did L2 researchers pay attention to reconstruction, a syntactic phenomenon that has attracted a great deal of attention in current linguistic research (e.g. Barss, 1986, 1988, 1993, 1994, 2001; Chomsky, 1993, 1995; Cinque, 1982; Culicover, 1997; Haegeman, 1994; Heycock, 1995; Huang, 1993; Lasnik, 1999, 2001; Reuland & Everaert, 2001; Roberts, 1997; Takano, 1995). Reconstruction refers to sentences with a reflexive inside a moved NP (9) or sentences with a reflexive inside a moved predicate (10).

(9) $John_i$ wonders which pictures of $himself_{i/j}$ $Bill_j$ likes.
(10) How proud of $herself_{*i/j}$ does $Mary_i$ think that $Nancy_j$ is?

Reconstruction is interesting in that the reflexive inside a moved NP can be bound by either the lower or higher subject. It is also relevant to the syntactic constraint of the Internal Subject Hypothesis in that the reflexive inside a moved predicate can only be bound by the lower subject.

Ying (1999) used a sentence judgement task to investigate how English-speaking learners of Chinese interpret reconstruction in Chinese, namely, sentences with *ziji* 'self' inside a moved noun phrase (NP) or predicate. The results indicate that English-speaking learners of Chinese resorted to options of UG (the morphological constraint of monomorphemic reflexives and the syntactic constraint of the Internal Subject Hypothesis) when they interpreted reconstruction in Chinese. However, the study also presented evidence of L1-induced language mapping for non-movement sentences (e.g. $John_i$ said that $Bill_j$ likes pictures of $himself_{*i/j}$). The English-speaking learners of Chinese identified the wider parameter setting of *ziji* in Chinese with the narrower setting of reflexives in English.

Ying (2000, 2003) used a timed judgement task to study how Chinese-speaking learners of English interpret reconstruction in English. The results suggest that the Internal Subject Hypothesis (ISH) constrained their interpretation of reflexives inside a moved predicate. The Chinese L2 learners bound the reflexive in predicate fronted sentences locally. However, the experiment also presented evidence of L1-induced mapping effects for non-movement sentences. The Chinese-speaking learners of English mapped the long-distance property of *ziji* onto English reflexives while interpreting such sentences.

To the best of my knowledge, none of the published studies on reflexive binding in second language research has examined variable binding in VP-ellipsis.[2] This study intends to bridge the gap.

The Study

Subjects

The subjects were 22 intermediate and 15 advanced English-speaking learners of Chinese (the experimental groups), and 20 native speakers of Chinese (the control group). The English-speaking learners of Chinese were students at a large institution in Shanghai, China. The intermediate English-speaking learners of Chinese were enrolled in intermediate Chinese learning classes and the advanced English-speaking learners of Chinese were enrolled in advanced Chinese composition classes or graduate classes. They met each day studying Chinese for four hours. None of the participants reported that they had been to other Chinese-speaking regions or countries. The native speakers of Chinese were students at a large institution in the United States.

Materials and design

The experimental materials were 17 Chinese VP-ellipsis structures that include a lexical verb and 17 VP-ellipsis sentences that involve the verb *shi* 'be'. In addition, 64 fillers were included in the list. The fillers included statements that do not involve VP-ellipsis. The sentences were presented in random order for interpretation. Each sentence appeared in the form of a statement and was followed by four choices, each proposing a potential antecedent for the reflexive in VP-ellipsis, as illustrated in (11).

(11) GF tian-yi-xia   taziji-de bing-bang, NT ye tian-yi-xia.[3]
    The underlined part means

   (a) NT tian-yi-xian NT de bing-bang   Agree   Disagree
   (b) NT tian-yi-xian GF de bing-bang   Agree   Disagree

This design, similar to Lakshmanan and Teranishi's (1994) sentence judgement task, has potentially four ways in which subjects could respond to sentences like (11):

(a) They could agree with statement 1 and disagree with statement 2. (This would be coded as local response only.)

(b) They could disagree with statement 1 and agree with statement 2. (This would be coded as nonlocal only.)
(c) They could disagree with both statement 1 and statement 2. (This would be coded as either local or nonlocal, that is, the sentence is ambiguous.)
(d) They could agree with both statements. (This would be coded as neither local or nonlocal; that is, the reflexive is not bound in the sentence.)

Procedure

Before the experiments, the English-speaking learners of Chinese were asked to complete a language history survey. Table 8.1 summarises the relevant background information for the English-speaking learners of Chinese. The survey indicates that none of the subjects had had explicit instruction on variable binding.

After the survey, the students participated in the experiment. They were given an example before the experiment:

(12) GF tian-yi-xiataziji-de bing-bang, <u>NT ye shi</u>.
 <u>The underlined part</u> means

  (a) NT tian-yi-xian NT de bing-bang   Agree   Disagree
  (b) NT tian-yi-xian GF de bing-bang   Agree   Disagree

The students were asked to consider each statement and indicate whether they agreed or disagreed with the statement by circling the relevant option. The instruction also specified that agreement or disagreement with one option did not necessarily exclude agreement or disagreement with

Table 8.1 Background information for subject pool by group

	Intermediate L2 learners	Advanced L2 Learners
Total (n)	22	15
Mean Age (SD)	22.7 (2.3)	27.4 (3.66)
Mean number of years studying Chinese as L2 (SD)	4.1 (0.7)	7.3 (1.3)
Mean age at first Exposure to Chinese (SD)	20.2 (1.3)	19.3 (1.4)

the second statement. The reverse was true, too. In other words, they were instructed to think about each statement separately.

Predictions

Williams (1977), Sag (1976), Reinhart (1986), Fiengo and May (1994) and Safir (2004) claim that the operator-variable binding, an essential component at the level of LF, is part of Universal Grammar (UG). This claim implies that the capacity for operator-variable binding is innate, and therefore is not learned as part of specific language grammar. Although the Chinese VP-ellipsis sentence involving the verb *shi* 'be' does not exist in English, this structure closely parallels the English VP-ellipsis structure. Thus, I predict that if both the *shi* 'be' structure and the lexical verb structure truly involve operator-variable binding, there should be little difference in L2 learners' representation of the ambiguity in these structures. In other words, I predict that knowledge of operator-variable binding exists independently of language-specific knowledge about lexical variables, namely, the verb types in question.

Results

Table 8.2 shows the result as percentages of acceptance of either the higher or lower subject binding for the VP-ellipsis sentences with a lexical verb. Turning first to the native speaker group, there is a high rate of acceptance of either the lower or higher subject (86.59%), indicating that either long-distance or local binding of the reflexive anaphora in VP ellipsis is possible for native speakers. Similarly, there is a high rate of acceptance of either the lower or higher subject by English-speaking learners of Chinese, although the advanced learners did so to a greater extent

Table 8.2 Performance on the 17 VP-ellipsis sentences with a lexical verb by English-speaking learners of Chinese and native speakers of Chinese

	E-Group 1 (intermediate) (n = 22) lexical	E-Group 2 (advanced) (n = 15) lexical	Chinese Group (native speakers) (n = 20) lexical
Lower subject	18.4%	15.3%	11.8%
Higher subject	4.8%	2.4%	1.7%
Either	76.7%	82.3%	86.5%
Neither	0	0	0

Table 8.3 Performance on the 17 VP-ellipsis sentences with the verb *shi* 'be' by English-speaking learners of Chinese and native speakers of Chinese

	E-Group 1 (intermediate) (n = 22) shi	E-Group 2 (advanced) (n = 15) shi	Chinese Group (native speakers) (n = 20) shi
Lower subject	16.6%	12.1%	8.7%
Higher subject	3.5%	1.7%	2.1%
Either	79.9%	86.2%	89.2%
Neither	0	0	0

than the intermediate learners, suggesting that either binding is also possible for L2 learners. Analysis of variance (ANOVA) shows that the differences of either binding between the intermediate and advanced English-speaking learners of Chinese were statistically significant, $F(1, 35) = 3.04, p < 0.05$.

Table 8.3 shows the result as percentages of acceptance of either the higher or lower subject binding for VP-ellipsis sentences with the verb *shi* 'be'. There is a high rate of acceptance of either the lower or higher subject (89.2% for native speakers of Chinese, 86.2% for advanced L2 learners and 79.9% for intermediate L2 learners), indicating that either long-distance or local binding of the reflexive anaphora in VP ellipsis is possible for both native and non-native speakers, despite the fact the differences of either binding between the intermediate and advanced English-speaking learners of Chinese were statistically significant, $F(1,35) = 3.14, p < 0.05$.

Discussion and Conclusions

The results of the experiment confirm the prediction that knowledge of cross-linguistic lexical variables can be dissociated from knowledge of abstract operator-variable relations. The L2 learners' representation of the ambiguity in Chinese VP-ellipsis structures does not appear to be affected by the lexical variables in Chinese. The intermediate and advanced English-speaking learners of Chinese both bound the reflexive anaphora in VP-elliptical structures with the lexical verb and the verb *shi* 'be' to either the lower or higher subject (Tables 7.2 and 7.3), indicating that their representation of ambiguity in these Chinese structures appears to be independent of their knowledge of lexical variables in Chinese.

There is a question of whether the results of this experiment simply derive from the L2 learners' transfer of their knowledge of ambiguity in the VP-elliptical structures in English. Although the question of language transfer cannot be ruled out (Juffs, 2005), it appears to be unlikely. L2 researchers working on the source of language transfer (Müller & Hulk, 2001; White, 2001) proposed that language transfer occurs in a *unidirectional* fashion. Learners are more likely to transfer a wide setting from their L1 (say, Chinese) to the target language with a narrow setting or parameter (say, English). If this is the case, then it is unlikely that the representation of ambiguity of these Chinese structures by English-speaking learners of Chinese occurred because of language transfer. Rather, their representations of ambiguity in these structures in Chinese appear to have derived from UG constraints on the binding possibilities of these structures.[4]

An examination of the results indicates that the finding did not come about because all L2 learners responded to a few of the test stimuli with a response indicating the lower or higher subject. Rather, whereas most of the L2 learners responded to the test stimuli with the lower or higher subject, some of the L2 learners responded to the stimuli mostly with the lower subject. Two intermediate students bound the reflexive anaphora in VP ellipsis to the lower subject 62.5%. It is true that these intermediate students' deviations from the general tendency may indicate a straightforward difference among subjects, but the fact that most of the L2 learners did not have such an interpretation indicates that UG constrained their representation of such structures.

In summary, the experiment reported in this study presented evidence that the L2 learners' representation of ambiguity of antecedence of reflexive anaphora in the VP-elliptical structures in Chinese appears to have derived from options of UG independent of their knowledge of lexical variables in that language.

Potential implications for instructed learning

The relevance of UG to language teaching is controversial. Some researchers (e.g. Cook, 1990) argue that because UG is concerned with principles and parameters that constitute the innate human capacity for language acquisition, not with peripheral aspects of grammar that are dealt with in language classrooms, it is very unlikely that UG could constitute the basis for language teaching. Other researchers (e.g. Hilles, 1986; White, 1995) suggest that teaching one property in a cluster of properties associated with a parameter (e.g. 'dummy' place holders in English) might serve as a 'trigger' for the rapid learning of the rest of those properties (e.g. the fact that English, a non-PRO-drop language, cannot leave subject position unoccupied). Still other researchers argue that in the case of an identical parameter setting of L1 and L2, as in the case of the PRO-drop parameter in Spanish and Italian, it is not necessary to teach it, because 'the learning of either of these languages by speakers of the other involves no resetting of the PRO-drop parameter' (Rutherford & Sharwood-Smith, 1989: 112).

The experimental evidence from this study indicates that the lexical contrast in Chinese between a lexical verb and the verb *shi* 'be' does not appear to affect English learners' representations of UG constraints regarding the ambiguity of these structures. Thus, little teaching intervention seems to be needed for features of variable binding in VP Ellipsis: L2 learners appeared to possess such knowledge, despite the differences of their proficiency levels in the target language (TL). However, Ying (2003) suggests that teaching may be effective when it draws L2 learners' attention to the cross-linguistic properties of reflexives such as *ziji* 'self' in Chinese and *himself* in English, where L1-induced language mapping typically occurs. R. Ellis (1994a, 2001a, 2001b, 2002) assumes that explicit knowledge enables instructed learners to overcome at least some negative transfer effects, possibly by sensitising them to the differences between the target and native language forms (see also Lightbown, this volume). The experimental results by White *et al.* (1996) indicate that explicit instruction on the properties of *zibun* 'self' in Japanese was effective in causing half of the subjects to acquire long-distance binding in Japanese. Thus, form-focused instruction (Doughty, 2001, 2003; Doughty & Williams, 1998a; R. Ellis, 2001a, 2001b, 2002; Leow, 2001; Long, 1991; Long & Robinson, 1998; Lyster, 2001; Lyster & Ranta, 1997; Williams, 2001) on cross-linguistic properties of *ziji* 'self' and *himself* may help to sensitise L2 learners to these formal properties and help them 'delearn' the mapping problem.[5] Further, depending on learning goals, time limitations, and other constraints that formal language instruction may be subject to, teachers may wish to prioritise on vocabulary learning, comprehension strategies, and communicative skills (Clahsen & Felser, 2006).

Acknowledgements

I would like to thank Dr ZhaoHong Han, two anonymous reviewers, and the audience at the 2005 SLRF meeting for their comments and advice. Any weaknesses that remain are my own.

Notes
1. Examples of WH-phrases are *Who* and *Which*.

2. Because the phenomenon in question is a syntactic one, I did not review earlier L2 lexical studies. Interested readers may wish to read Kroll and Dussias (2004) and Kroll and Sunderman (2003) for an overview of lexical studies, and Shah and Baum (2006) and Trofimovich (2005) for recent lexical studies. For recent studies on filler-gap dependencies, please refer to Clahsen and Felser (2006), Juffs (2005), Marinis et al. (2005), and Williams et al. (2001). For recent studies on reduced relative and main verb ambiguity, see Juffs (2006).
3. Transliteration of (11):
GF tian-yi-xia taziji   de   bing-bang, NT   ye   tian-yi-xia.
GF licked   himself's   popsicle,   NT   also licked
'GF licked his popsicle, and so did NT'.
4. An anonymous reviewer suggested that the participants' experience with the target language (TL) input may have contributed to their representation of ambiguity in these structures in Chinese, given that the participants were all instructed learners. Although this cannot be entirely ruled out, it is unlikely that their classroom experience with the TL input would tell them that the Chinese structures in question were ambiguous. An examination of the Chinese textbooks indicates that there are no examples of variable bindings in VP ellipsis. Thus, it appears to be more convincing to argue for the UG constraints.
5. This study only included *taziji* 'him/herself' in Chinese. Thus, it did not directly address the mapping problem. A study that includes both *taziji* 'him/herself' and *ziji* 'self' is being carried out.

Chapter 9
Metasyntactic Ability in L2: An Investigation of Task Demand

DAPHNÉE SIMARD and VÉRONIQUE FORTIER

French, the official language of the province of Quebec, is spoken by over 80% of the children (Institut de la statistique du Québec, 2005) and all new arrivals are educated in French-language schools. Although a very high percentage of children in French-language schools have two French-speaking parents, in Montreal growing numbers of *allophone* children, speakers of languages other than French or English, are entering the French school system. As Armand *et al.* (2004: 438) state, 'In Quebec, as is the case in most countries, schools in large urban centers are characterized by a wide ethnocultural, religious and linguistic diversity'.

In 2004–2005, only 53% of the students in the French school board of Montreal had French as a first language (Commission scolaire de Montréal, 2005). Unfortunately, studies show that allophone children experience difficulties in written French all the way up to the postsecondary level (Ministère de l'Éducation du Québec, 1996). It is thus urgent that French-language schools come to grips with the education of non-native speakers in their mainstream programmes. In order to fulfil this need, a large-scale research programme was planned.

The study reported in this chapter is part of a larger research programme investigating the language development of French among allophone children in the Quebec school system, and represents the first step towards creating a description of their language development with the aim of developing programmes designed to help them perform better in school. More specifically, this chapter reports on the results obtained from three metalinguistic tasks devised to examine the metasyntactic ability of elementary school allophone children.

Metalinguistic Ability Among Children

The notion of *metalinguistic ability*, defined as a learner's capacity to use his knowledge about language (Gombert, 1992), has been the object of many recent studies (e.g. Armand, 2005). In first and second language development, the metalinguistic ability that allows learners to use abstract and decontextualised language is an important asset in successful learning of reading and writing (Armand, 2000, 2005; Gagné, 2003; Gombert, 1992).

A child's metalinguistic ability may be related to any language aspect such as syntax and phonology (e.g. metasyntactic or metaphonological ability) (Gombert, 1992; Tunmer *et al.*, 1988). *Metaphonological ability*, the capacity to identify and intentionally manipulate the phonological components in linguistic units (Gombert, 1992), is by far the most commonly examined aspect of metalinguistic ability (Bowey, 1986; Smith-Lock, 1995). It is thought by many researchers to predict reading competence in L1, in turn predicting success in school (Bialystok, 2001a). However, researchers such as Gaux and Gombert (1999a) have underscored the limitation of phonological processing in L1. According to them, 'some children fail to understand sentences in a text, in particular one processing a complex syntactic structure, even when they manage to decode all the words it contains' (1999a: 169). The difficulties experienced by these children are likely to lie at the metasyntactic level that is associated with word recognition and reading comprehension (Gaux & Gombert, 1999a).

Metasyntactic ability refers to an individual's capacity to reflect on and intentionally manipulate the syntactic structure of sentences (Gombert, 1992) such as words, grammatical classes, and rules governing their combinations (Gaux & Gombert, 1997). Recent empirical studies underline the relationship between metasyntactic ability and reading competence in L1 (e.g. Armand, 2000; Blackmore & Pratt, 1997; Nation & Snowling, 2000; Tunmer, 1990; Tunmer *et al.*, 1988). However, the picture is not as clear when examining the relationship between metasyntactic ability and L2 reading. Although authors such as Armand (2000) and Chiappe and Siegel (1999) found no relation between metasyntactic ability in L2 and any aspect of reading in L2, other researchers, such as Lefrançois and Armand (2003), observed a relation between metasyntactic ability and the beginning stages of learning to read in L2. Moreover, as Lipka *et al.* (2005) mention, 'syntactic awareness tasks have also been found to differentiate between English native speaking students and English language learners' (2005: 44). Thus, it is important to examine closely the metasyntactic tasks among L2 learners. Given that to date only a few studies have examined the relationship between metasyntactic ability in L2 and reading competence in L2 (Armand, 2005), more studies are needed to fully understand the role of metasyntactic ability in L2 development.

Assessment of Metasyntactic Ability

One of the challenges related to the study of metasyntactic ability is its assessment. It is thus no surprise that the tasks used to measure metasyntactic ability are at the centre of a debate (e.g. Birdsong, 1989; Bryant et al., 1997; Demont, 1994; de Villiers & de Villiers, 1972; Gaux & Gombert, 1999b). Researchers, such as Bialystok (2001a) and Gaux and Gombert (1999a, 1999b), argue that many of the tasks used to assess metasyntactic ability do not allow for the observation of metalinguistic ability.

Metasyntactic tasks usually focus on error imitation, judgement, correction, localisation, explanation, error replication, and completion (Correa, 2004; Gaux & Gombert, 1999b). The *error imitation task* consists of asking learners to repeat orally correct and incorrect sentences while respecting the ungrammaticality of the incorrect sentences (Bowey, 1986; Demont, 1994). The incidental correction of ungrammatical sentences is believed to reveal an instance where the participants unconsciously apply a grammatical rule (Gaux & Gombert, 1999a, 1999b). The *judgement task* requires learners to decide whether the sentences provided are grammatically correct or incorrect (Bialystok, 2001a; Demont, 1994; de Villiers & de Villiers, 1974). The judgement task is not known to reflect metasyntactic ability, because participants often rely on semantic rather than grammatical cues to judge the sentences (Birdsong, 1989; Bowey, 1986). Bialystok (2001a) differentiates between judgement tasks made up of semantic sentences and those made up of asemantic sentences saying that 'in standard judgement tasks, subjects must decide whether or not there are grammatical violations in sentences. If the sentence also contains incorrect semantic information, then it is difficult for young children to ignore these errors and attend only to well-formedness criteria' (Bialystok, 2001a: 174). The *correction task* consists of providing the correct form of a syntactic feature in an ungrammatical sentence (Bowey, 1986; Demont, 1994; de Villiers & de Villiers, 1974). The correction task is often used as a complement to the judgement task in order to make sure that the participants actually pay attention to syntax (Gaux & Gombert, 1999b). However, Gaux and Gombert (1999a, 1999b) and Gombert (1990) believe that the correction task does not allow for the assessment of metasyntactic ability, because it is possible for the participants to manage this task at a subconscious level. In this respect, Bowey (1986) showed that children spontaneously correct ungrammatical sentences. The *localisation task* requires learners to identify an error in a sentence (Smith-Lock & Rubin, 1993). Although this task confirms whether or not the participants are able to locate the error, it does not provide an indication as to whether or not the participants paid attention to the nature of the syntactic violation (Gaux & Gombert, 1999b). In the *explanation task*, the participants are asked to provide an explanation of why they think a sentence is ungrammatical (Hakes, 1980; Smith-Lock & Rubin, 1993). However, the fact that the participants cannot explain a grammatical rule does not mean they cannot apply it (Sorace, 1985). In fact, formal explanations of grammatical rules are infrequent in children's verbalisation (Gaux & Gombert, 1999b; Hakes, 1980). The *completion task* is claimed to assess metasyntactic ability by measuring the participant's ability to complete a series of sentences with the most appropriate words they can think of (Tunmer et al., 1987). In such contexts, it is extremely difficult to identify the factors that guided the participants when completing the sentences. For example, we cannot determine whether syntactic and/or semantic information was used (Gaux & Gombert, 1999b). Furthermore, the answers provided by the participants also greatly depend on their lexical knowledge (Gaux & Gombert, 1999b). In the *error replication task*, participants are asked to reproduce, in a correct sentence, an error that is presented to them in an incorrect sentence (Gombert et al., 1994). In other words, children have to locate the error in the incorrect sentence and produce the same type of error in the corresponding correct sentence. For instance, the participants in Gaux and Gombert (1999a) had to replicate the inversion presented in the incorrect model sentence (e.g. Lion the is finishing his meal) in the correct sentence (e.g. The spectator is reserving his meal). This task, according to Gaux and Gombert (1999b), assures that the participants know the nature of the ungrammaticality in the sentence by requiring them to explicitly analyse language and intentionally reproduce an error without resorting to an explanation (i.e. verbalisation).

The studies that investigated metasyntactic ability in L1 and in L2 generally resorted to more than one task but did not evaluate whether or not these tasks were actually accessing the metalinguistic level of the participants' language competence (Galambos & Goldin-Meadow, 1990; Ricciardelli, 1993; Willows & Bouchard Ryan, 1986). To our knowledge, the only study that specifically compared the tasks in order to determine whether they allowed for the measurement of children's metasyntactic ability was done by Gaux and Gombert (1999b).

In their study, Gaux and Gombert (1999b) compared the scores obtained from 83 pre-adolescent native speakers of French on different metasyntactic tasks: the imitation of error, localisation of error, judgement, correction, and error replication tasks. They hypothesised, on the basis of the level of intentional analysis needed to complete each task, that the judgement task would be easier than the correction one, which would in turn be easier than the localisation and replication tasks (Gaux & Gombert, 1999b: 53). The results obtained from the replication task were compared with the results obtained from the other tasks. The results revealed that the participants behaved differently on the replication task when compared to the other metasyntactic tasks. More specifically, the results obtained from the participants on the different metasyntactic tasks used in the study led the authors to assert that only the replication task required the use of metasyntactic ability. They concluded that 'their results confirm that the demands of the repetition, judgement, correction, and identification of morphosyntactic ungrammaticality tasks do not allow for a valid assessment of explicit syntactic knowledge in the sense that processes other than intentional morphosyntactic reasoning facilitate the execution of these tasks ... [C]onversely, the replication task is shown to be a pertinent paradigm for the evaluation of an individual's ability to intentionally focus attention on syntactic structure.'[1] Despite the assertion they make about metasyntactic tasks, Gaux and Gombert (1999b) fail to provide an appropriate theoretical explanation for the results obtained in their study.

Bialystok's framework (Bialystok, 1988, 1993, 2001a, 2001b; Bialystok & Ryan, 1985a, 1985b, 1985c) offers a possible theoretical explanation for the results Gaux and Gombert (1999a) obtained in their study.

Analysis of Metasyntactic Tasks

Bialystok's framework allows for the classification of metalinguistic tasks according to two aspects of language processing: (1) analysis of linguistic knowledge and (2) control of linguistic processing (Bialystok, 2001b: 132). At the level of analysis, the framework presents a distinction between explicit and implicit knowledge. *Implicit knowledge* guides production but cannot be the object of investigation, whereas *explicit knowledge* is independent of meaning and available for inspection. According to Bialystok (2001a), one of the aspects of the development of language capacity is to turn implicit knowledge into explicit knowledge, rendering it analysable. In other words, as second language learners develop their linguistic skills in the target language, they become progressively more capable of intentionally reflecting on the syntactic structure of that language. At the level of control, we find the ability to direct attention to relevant information and to integrate it in real time (Bialystok, 1990). In this sense, language learners increasingly develop control of their ability to perform metalinguistic analyses. The development of control calls for experiences other than analysis and proceeds differently (Bialystok & Ryan, 1985b). According to the authors, the focusing and retrieval mechanism that characterises control processes develop separately from the analysed representations of knowledge. They add that 'The common association of these two, however, is a reflection of the contingency that in most tasks requiring advanced proficiency, high levels of both control and knowledge are implicated' (Bialystok & Ryan, 1985b: 216).

These processes are set out as 'orthogonal axes which define a Cartesian space indicating their degree of involvement in each quadrant' (Bialystok, 2001b: 14). The x-axis corresponds to the analysis of linguistic knowledge, whereas the y-axis corresponds to the control of linguistic processing. As stated by Bialystok, 'The placement of metalinguistic tasks in this matrix takes increasing levels of analysis and control required for the solution to specific tasks to be indicated by higher values along the x and y axes respectively' (Bialystok, 1993: 228). In this respect, within Bialystok's framework, the judgement task containing only semantic sentences and the identification of error tasks requires a low level of analysis and a low level of control, whereas the judgement tasks in which the sentences are asemantic require a high level of control and a low level of analysis. The correction task, on the other hand, requires a low level of control and a high level of analysis (Bialystok, 2001a).

According to Bialystok, if the studies investigating metalinguistic ability obtain different results on different tasks, as is the case, for instance, with Gaux and Gombert (1999a, 1999b), it is because the tasks used call, in many cases, for different levels of control of attentional processes and different types of analysis of linguistic knowledge (Bialystok, 2001a). On the other hand, for Gaux and Gombert (1999b), tasks are simply regarded as either metalinguistic or not. They concluded, in their study, that the repetition, judgement, correction and localisation tasks did not require the use of metalinguistic ability. Based on Gaux and Gombert's (1999b) conclusions, these tasks would be placed in the lower left quadrant within Bialystok's framework, a quadrant representing low levels of both analysis of linguistic knowledge and control of linguistic resources. However, in Bialystok's framework (Bialystok, 2001a, 2001b), the correction task, demanding high analysis and low control, is placed in the lower right quadrant. The replication of error requires, according to Gaux and Gombert (1999a), the use of the most explicit knowledge. Consequently, it would be placed in the upper right quadrant of the framework, representing high levels of both analysis of linguistic knowledge and control of linguistic resources.

Research Question and Hypothesis

Several factors contributed to the emergence of the present research question. Foremost, as mentioned above, the differential effects of the metasyntactic tasks commonly used in studies were only examined in L1 by Gaux and Gombert (1999b). Thus, there is a need to explore this issue more closely in L2. Additionally, Gaux and Gombert (1999b) provided no theoretical explanation for the results they obtained. We suggest Bialystok's framework offers a possible explanation. Therefore, based on the assumption that metasyntactic tasks located in different quadrants within Bialystok's framework, each quadrant corresponding to different levels of control and analysis, should call for different results, we formulate the following research question:

Do elementary school learners obtain statistically different scores on three L2 metasyntactic tasks calling for different levels of analysis and control according to Bialystok's framework?

We hypothesise that the participants in our study will obtain better scores on the semantic items of the judgement task (located in the lower left quadrant within Bialystok's framework) than on the asemantic items of the judgement task (located in the upper left quadrant within Bialystok's framework), better scores on the semantic and asemantic items of the judgement task than on the correction task (located in the lower right quadrant within Bialystok's framework), and finally better scores on the correction task than on the replication of error task (located in the upper right quadrant within Bialystok's framework).

The Study

In order to verify the hypothesis stated above, a cross-sectional experimental design was set out. Children, ranging from ages 9 to 12, completed, during one class period, three tasks devised to gather information regarding their metasyntactic ability.

Participants

A total of 31 elementary school allophone children, from low to average socio-economic status (SES), participated in the study (Table 9.1). They

Table 9.1 Distribution of the participants in the two age groups

Age groups	Average age	Gender	
		M	F
9 to 10.5 years ($n = 15$)	10 years	11	4
10.6 to12 years ($n = 16$)	11 years 8 months	9	7

came from two different classes, one grade 3 and 4 multilevel class ($n = 15$) and one grade 5 and 6 multilevel class ($n = 16$) from the same school. The number of boys ($n = 20$) was almost double the number of girls ($n = 11$). The group formed by the students of the grade 3 and 4 multilevel class (ages 9 to 10.5) consisted of 9 boys and 7 girls, with an average age of 10. The second group, formed by the students of the grade 5 and 6 multilevel class (ages 10.6 to 12 years old), consisted of 11 boys and 4 girls with an average age of 11 years and 8 months.

Measurement instruments

Two types of data were collected, metasyntactic ability data and background information. Each type of measurement instrument is described in what follows.

Measurement of metasyntactic ability

In this section, we present the syntactic features that were used to create the metasyntactic tasks followed by a description of the types of tasks we used to measure the metasyntactic ability of the participants in the study.

Syntactic features

The metalinguistic ability data were collected by means of three tasks, all three targeting the same linguistic items known to be difficult in French: comparison (Bautier-Castaign, 1977), question formation (Plunkett, 1999), and placement of clitic pronouns (Kaiser, 1994). Briefly, a comparison is normally formed by framing the adjective with *plus ... que* (e.g. *plus gentil que* 'nicer than') or *moins ... que* (e.g. *moins gentil que* 'less nice than'), or, in the case of a superlative, *le plus* (e.g. *le plus gentil* 'the nicest') or *le moins* precedes the adjective (e.g. *le moins gentil* 'the less nice'). The formation of a comparison changes when using the adjectives *bon* (e.g. meilleur que 'better than' and *le meilleur* 'the best') and *mauvais* (e.g. *pire que* 'worse than' and *le pire* 'the worst'), which causes further difficulties. Questions in French are another source of difficulty for second language learners. They can be formed in different ways, either by adding *est-ce que* to the beginning of the sentence (e.g. *Il est gentil. Est-ce qu'il est gentil?* 'He is nice. Is he nice?'), or by inversion of the subject (e.g. *Il est gentil. Est-il gentil?* 'He is nice. Is he nice?'). The inversion becomes more complex when the subject is a proper name (e.g. *Paul est gentil. Paul est-il gentil?* 'Paul is nice. Is Paul nice?'). Finally, the placement of the clitic pronoun has proven itself to be yet another obstacle for learners of French as a second language. It is either placed between the subject pronoun and the verb (e.g. *Je le prends*. 'I take it.'), or in the case of a verb followed by an infinitive, it is placed between both verbs (e.g. *Je veux le prendre*. 'I want to take it.') (Riegel et al., 2004).

Metasyntactic tasks

In response to the difficulties associated with the syntactic features presented above, three tasks were designed to require different levels of attentional control and language analysis according to Bialystok's framework (2001a). The tasks selected were the judgement of acceptability task, the correction task, and the replication task.

Following the Lefrançois and Armand (2003) study, the *judgement of acceptability task* consisted of 18 items representing a combination of semantic (S) /asemantic (s) and grammatical (G)/ungrammatical (g) sentences. Of the 18 items, there were 6 related to the placement of the clitic pronoun (1SG; 2sg; 2Sg; 1sG), 6 linked to question formation (2SG; 2sg; 2sG), and 6 measuring the participant's ability to form the comparison (1SG; 2sG; 2sg; 1Sg). The sentences were read to the students through an audio recording. Following each utterance, the students had to indicate on their test sheet whether or not each sentence contained a grammatical error by checking one of three columns: No error, With error, I don't know. For instance, the following item on question formation *'Quel âge a la tasse de café de ton enseignante'* (How old is your teacher's coffee mug?) had to be checked *No error*, because it was grammatical, although the meaning did not make sense. The semantic items in the judgement task were thought to require low levels of attentional control and low levels of linguistic analysis, whereas the asemantic items, as is the case with the previous example concerning the age of the teacher's coffee mug, were thought to require a low level of linguistic analysis and a relatively high level of attentional control according to Bialystok's framework (2001b).

The *correction task* contained 18 asemantic and ungrammatical sentences as was used in Demont and Gombert (1996). Gaux and Gombert (1999b) state that the correction task on semantic sentences might not access the children's metalinguistic ability. That is the reason why we chose to only include asemantic sentences in our correction task. Each item contained only one error. Six of the items presented an error that was related to comparison, six other items presented an error regarding the placement of the clitic pronoun and the remaining six presented an error in question formation. An example of an item on the placement of the clitic pronoun was '*Le piano dit lui de ne pas manger de gateau*' (The piano him tells not to eat cake). It had to be corrected as '*Le piano lui dit de ne pas manger de gâteau*' (The piano tells him not to eat cake). The students had to rewrite the sentence correcting the grammatical mistake leaving the meaning unchanged (Demont & Gombert, 1996). Two versions of the correction task were prepared to control for ordering effects in the presentation of the items. According to Bialystok's framework, this task requires a high level of linguistic analysis and a low level of attentional control (Bialystok, 2001a).

Similar to the Gaux and Gombert (1999a, 1999b) study, for the *error replication task* the children were presented with specific types of errors and asked to replicate these errors in correct sentences. Each item contained only one error either related to the clitic pronoun placement ($n = 3$), the comparison ($n = 2$), or question formation ($n = 3$). An example of an item featuring the comparison follows:

(1) *Phrase avec l'erreur: Mes chats sont les plus pires chasseurs du quartier.* (Sentence with error: My cats are the most worst hunters of the neighbourhood.)
(2) *Phrase correcte: Samuel et Juliette sont les meilleurs amis du monde.* (Correct sentence: Samuel and Juliette are the best friends in the world.)

The students had to reproduce in the correct sentence (2) the same error that was found in the sentence with an error (1). For example, *Samuel et Juliette sont les plus meilleurs amis du monde* (Samuel and Juliette are the most best friends in the world). According to Gaux and Gombert (1999a, 1999b), the replication task is the only way to test a deliberate reflection on syntax. Thus, this task would, according to Bialystok's framework, be placed in the upper right quadrant.

Background information

In order to obtain background information, a questionnaire was administered. This questionnaire contained three questions regarding the language environment of the child: language(s) spoken at home, mother's first language, and father's first language. The questionnaire was completed by the children's parents or guardian.

Procedure

The 31 ($n = 31$) elementary school students that participated in the study were tested during regular school hours. All data were collected in the participants' regular classrooms by research assistants during two consecutive days in May 2005. The participants were informed that these tests were not being used for evaluative purposes and that all responses provided valuable research information, whether they were 'right' or 'wrong'.

The judgement of acceptability task was given to all students ($n = 31$). Three examples, presented on the students' copy as well as on an overhead projector, were given orally to the students prior to the presentation of the audio recording of the sentences in the actual task. The second task (correction) was given to all students ($n = 31$) in two versions in order to control for ordering effects in the presentation of the items. Half of the participants received one version; the other half received the other version. Once again, three examples were written on the students' copy and done by the research assistants on the board with the students. The third task (replication) was given only to students aged 10.6 to 12 ($n = 16$). Three examples of the error replication task were done on the board with the students.

Coding and analysis

One point was given for each correct answer on the three metasyntactic tasks. The dependent variable in this study corresponds to the scores obtained from the participants on each metasyntactic task, whereas the independent variable corresponds to the participants' age. We submitted our data to analysis of variance (ANOVA) in order to identify possible age and task effects (Hatch & Lazaraton, 1991). In order to identify possible differences between the results on the various metasyntactic tasks, we also ran paired t-tests on the means obtained from each age group (Toothtaker, 1991).

Results

Our research question was: Do elementary school learners obtain statistically different scores on L2 metasyntactic tasks calling for different levels of analysis and control according to Bialystok's framework? In order to answer our research question, we compared the results obtained from the participants on the three tasks.

Table 9.2 Means and standard deviations for participants aged 9–10.5

	M	SD
Task 1 asemantic	6.67	2.19
Task 1 semantic	7.25	2.07
Task 1	6.93	1.91
Task 2	6.52	1.51

Note: Maximum score = 10; n = 15

First, we present the descriptive and inferential statistics for the three tasks according to the two age groups. Table 9.2 presents the means (M) of correct responses obtained from the participants ages 9 to 10.5 and the standard deviation (SD) for the two metasyntactic tasks the participants completed: Tasks 1 and 2.

The mean obtained on the semantic items of Task 1 is slightly better than the mean obtained on the asemantic items of Task 1, and the mean obtained on Task 2 is slightly lower than all the other means obtained from participants ages 9 to 10.5. However, paired t-tests revealed no statistical difference between the means obtained from the participants ages 9 to 10.5 on the two tasks.

Table 9.3 presents the means of correct responses obtained from the participants ages 10.6 to 12 and the standard deviation for the three metasyntactic tasks. Again, the mean obtained on the semantic items of Task 1 is slightly better than the mean obtained on the asemantic items of Task 1, and the mean obtained on Task 2 is slightly lower than the means obtained from the participants ages 10.6 to 12 on Task 1 (semantic items, asemantic items, and all items together). In order to verify if there were any significant differences between the scores obtained on

Table 9.3 Means and standard deviations for participants age 10.6–12

	M	SD
Task 1 asemantic	7.19	2.01
Task 1 semantic	7.66	1.57
Task 1	7.40	1.61
Task 2	6.60	2.73
Task 3	3.59	3.47

Note: Maximum score = 10; n = 16

Table 9.4 Paired *t*-tests between the means obtained on each task for the participants ages 10.6 to 12

	t	*p*
Task 1 asemantic − Task 1 semantic	−1.07	0.30
Task 1 asemantic − Task 2	0.97	0.34
Task 1 semantic − Task 2	1.49	0.16
Task 1 − Task 2	1.29	0.22
T1 asemantic − Task 3	4.97	0.00
T1 semantic − Task 3	4.33	0.00
Task 1 − Task 3	4.78	0.00
Task 2 − Task 3	4.72	0.00

Note: $n = 16$

each task, comparisons using a paired *t*-test were done. Recall that only participants ages 10.6 to 12 did Task 3. Table 9.4 shows the results obtained for the paired *t*-test.

In Table 9.4, the analysis revealed significant differences between Task 3 and all the other tasks. No significant difference was observed between Task 1 and Task 2. In order to see if there were differences according to the age groups and tasks, we submitted the means obtained from each age group on each metasyntactic task to an ANOVA. The results showed no effect of age for either of the tasks. Because there was no effect of age, we analysed the scores that all the participants obtained on Tasks 1 and 2 altogether. Recall that Task 3 was done only by the participants ages 10.6 to 12. Table 9.5 shows the means of correct responses obtained on Tasks 1 and 2 for all the participants.

Table 9.5 Means and standard deviations on Task 1 and Task 2 for all participants

	M	*SD*
Task 1 asemantic	6.93	2.08
Task 1 semantic	5.97	1.45
Task 1	12.90	3.14
Task 2	11.80	3.93

Note: Maximum score, Task 1 asemantic = 10, Task 1 semantic = 8, Task 1 = 18, and Task 2 = 18; $n = 31$

Finally, we compared the results two-by-two in order to determine if significant differences existed between the scores obtained on each task (Tasks 1 and 2). The paired t-tests revealed a significant difference between Task 1 semantic and Task 2 (t (30) = 1.92; p = 0.03) and no significant difference between Task 1 asemantic and Task 2 and between Task 1 asemantic and Task 1 semantic.

Discussion

The research question examined in this study was: Do elementary school learners obtain statistically different scores on L2 metasyntactic tasks calling for different levels of analysis and control according to Bialystok's framework? We devised three tasks that would, according to Bialystok's framework (e.g. Bialystok, 2001a, 2001b), call for different levels of control of attentional processes and language analysis. We used a judgement task with semantic and asemantic items, a correction task composed of asemantic items, and an error replication task. We had hypothesised that the scores obtained from the participants would be higher for Task 1 semantic (judgement task) than for Task 1 asemantic, higher for Task 1 semantic and asemantic than for Task 2 (correction task) and higher for Task 2 than for Task 3 (error replication task).

This hypothesis is partly supported by the results we obtained. Although significant differences were observed between the scores obtained on the semantic items of Task 1 and those obtained on Task 2 for all the participants (t (30) = 1.92; p = 0.03) and between the scores obtained on Task 3 and the scores obtained on all the other tasks for the participants ages 10.6 to 12 ($p < 0.01$ in all cases), no statistical difference was observed between the scores obtained on the asemantic items of Task 1 and the semantic items of Task 1 and between the scores obtained on Task 1 (all items together) and those obtained on Task 2 for all participants.

As anticipated, the semantic items of the judgement task were statistically easier than the correction task and the correction task was easier than the error replication task. This indicates that the judgement with semantic items, the correction and the error replication tasks require different levels of control and analysis, giving support to Bialystok's framework for metalinguistic tasks (2001a, 2001b). The fact that no statistical difference could be observed between Task 1 (asemantic) and the correction task is probably related to the asemanticity of the items in both tasks. Our results run partly counter to Gaux and Gombert's statement (1999b), according to which, the judgement and correction tasks were equivalent in terms of degrees of explicitness of language. In our study, the semantic items of the judgement task lead to significantly different scores than the correction task. In this respect, Demont and Gombert (1996: 321) state that 'the correction of asemantic and agrammatical sentences was the most difficult task among the various syntactic tasks'. Considering the results obtained, we believe it is better to consider metalinguistic tasks along a two-fold continuum, as is the case in Bialystok's framework, instead of a binary representation (metalinguistic or not) as is suggested by Gaux and Gombert (1999b). It should, however, be noted that there was a ceiling effect in all tasks except in the error replication task of Gaux and Gombert's (1999b) study. This probably led the authors to formulate their conclusion. Also, their participants were age 12.3 on average and the authors only used semantic items in their tasks.

When considering our results, it should be kept in mind that the relatively small number of participants can act as a limitation when conducting the analyses. Also, the modality of the tasks' stimulus conditions might have influenced the results (Murphy, 1997). Therefore, an interesting avenue to explore in future research would be the comparison between oral and written metasyntactic tasks. Aside from the issues more specifically related to our tasks, other factors that possibly influenced our results should be considered. For example, our participants came from low to average SES environments. Previous studies found an interaction between the SES of the participants and the results obtained on metasyntactic tasks (e.g. Warren-Leuckerber & Warren Cater, 1988). Children coming from lower SES environments tend to score lower on metasyntactic tasks than children from higher SES environments. It would certainly be interesting to use our tasks among participants coming from different SES environments. In addition, we could not measure the level of bilingualism of our participants because of the numerous first languages they spoke. As demonstrated in Carlisle *et al.* (1999), there is an effect of metalinguistic ability and the level of bilingualism attained in the languages spoken by the children. In future studies, the linguistic background of the children should be controlled by examining one linguistic group at a time.

Conclusions

The present study sought to verify if three metasyntactic tasks calling for different levels of attentional control and linguistic analysis, according to Bialystok's framework, would lead to significantly different scores. These tasks were the acceptability judgement (with semantic and asemantic items), the correction task, and the replication task. The results from the data analysis show that students performed differently on the metasyntactic tasks. More specifically, the results show that the replication task was significantly more difficult than the other two tasks, and that the correction task was significantly more difficult than the semantic items of the judgement task.

Note

1. Our translation of : ≪ ces résultats confirment que les épreuves classiques de répétition, jugement, correction et localisation d'agrammaticalités morphosyntaxiques ne permettent pas de tester avec certitude une connaissance syntaxique explicite dans la mesure ou d'autres procédés qu'une réflexion intentionnelle sur la morphosyntaxe permettent de réaliser ces tâches... la réplication se révèle en revanche être un paradigme pertinent pour évaluer la capacité à réfléchir ou à porter intentionnellement son intention sur la syntaxe ≫, pp. 69–70.

Chapter 10
Prosody Acquisition by Japanese Learners

TOMOKO SHIBATA and RICHARD R. HURTIG

Introduction

Achieving native speaker fluency is a goal for many foreign language learners; nevertheless it is the one that is rarely achieved. The ability to be understood by native speakers requires not only mastery of grammar and vocabulary, but also the more subtle prosodic rules that influence the final output production. A poorer mastery of prosody leads at worst to a failure to be understood and at best to what is recognised as a foreign accent. Therefore, it is crucial to investigate the development of prosody in foreign language learners as a function of other measures of language proficiency. This chapter presents the results of research on Japanese prosody acquisition that examined the productive and perceptual abilities of learners who were studying Japanese as a second language.

Theoretical Background

It is a generally held belief that even very advanced second language learners, who can manipulate grammar and vocabulary very well, have moments when native speakers do not understand them because of their foreign accents. In some unfortunate circumstances, such foreign accents may cause social and/or interpersonal problems. For instance, in the workplace, a foreign accent might result in the loss of job opportunities (Sato, 1991). Moreover, a foreign accent can cause unintentional interpersonal problems in a non-native speaker's social life. Pickering (2001) reported that international teaching assistants were perceived as unsympathetic and uninvolved by their students because of their inappropriate prosodic patterns.

Accented speech also hinders understanding by listeners. Munro and Derwing (1995) examined foreign-accented speech in English produced by native speakers of Mandarin who were proficient enough to enter a university. The researchers showed that their subjects' speech intelligibility was lower when the speech was perceived to be accented. Munro (1998) further studied the effect of foreign-accentedness under natural noise listening conditions (cafeteria noise). The results indicate that the intelligibility was very low for speech produced by Mandarin speakers with cafeteria noise, but intelligibility stayed high for speech produced by English speakers presented at the same noise level.

Foreign accent can be caused by various kinds of pronunciation errors. Segmental errors, such as inaccurate production of a consonant and/or a vowel, are easy to notice. Non-segmental prosodic errors have also been identified as having a crucial influence on foreign accent. Phonologists have claimed that prosody is a very important factor for accented speech in a second language (L2), because prosody constructs a rhythmic frame of speech, which is language-specific and thus cross-linguistically easily misproduced (Beckman, 1996).

Linguistically, 'prosody' is a general term for the metrical features of speech; stress, accent, intonation, and rhythm are usually considered to be prosodic features (Chun, 2002; Major, 2001, for more general definitions of prosody). Theories of prosody (i.e. non-featural theories of prosodic structure) have claimed that prosody has its own hierarchical structure (Beckman, 1996; Clements & Keyser, 1983; Hayes, 1989; Selkirk, 1982, 1984).

The elements in the hierarchy vary among the theoretical frameworks, but the majority of them include morae,[1] syllables, prosodic words, phonological phrases, intonational phrases, and utterances (Beckman, 1996; Pierrehumbert & Beckman, 1988; Wheeldon, 2000; see also the sample prosody hierarchy in Figure 10.1). The boundary of prosodic elements does not always match the boundary of syntactic elements. For instance, when 'beer is' is spoken in fast speech, it could be uttered as [beeriz], which is considered to be one prosodic word, whereas syntactically, 'beer' and 'is' are separate words.

The feature and function of each element are language-specific. For example, in English, which is considered to be a syllable-counting language, the syllable is the rhythmic unit, and the alternation of strong and weak syllables constructs the foot structure, which creates the rhythm of English. On the other hand, in Japanese, which is classified as a mora-counting language, the mora is the unit that creates the rhythm of Japanese (Kubozono, 1998; Figure 10.1).

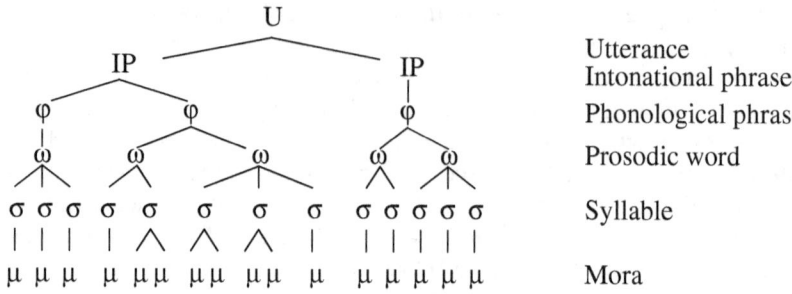

a ne-no a ka i se'e ta a -wa do ko de su ka?
'Where is my sister's red sweater?'

Figure 10.1 Prosody Hierarchy (adapted from Pierrehumbert, Janet B. & Beckman, Mary E., *Japanese Tone Structure*, Figure 1.7 © 1988 Massachusetts Institute of Technology, by permission of The MIT Press)

Such language specificity could influence foreign language prosody production. For instance, Anderson-Hsieh and her colleagues (1992) examined oral English productions by non-native speakers of English and asked native speakers of English to judge the overall intelligibility and acceptability of the pronunciation on a seven-point scale. They found that prosody had the most influence on the perceived foreign accentedness of pronunciation (Anderson-Hsieh *et al.*, 1992). Munro (1995) conducted an experiment in which native judges of English listened to non-native speakers' oral productions that had been passed through a low-pass filter that eliminated most of the segmental information. The native judges could detect foreign accent from the non-segmental information, such as speaking rates, intonation patterns, and timing.

Sato (1995) also reported that Japanese prosody had more influence on pronunciation judgements than did segmental factors. In his experiments, he collected oral data from Chinese, Korean, and Japanese informants, and created a variety of test items by changing the prosodic features (pitch height, duration, and intensity) using an acoustic synthesiser. Native judges listened to the synthesised test items and the original oral productions, and rated the accentedness of the items on a seven-point scale. Sato found that prosodic factors, especially pitch height, had the most influence on the accentedness judgement, and the segmental factors did not have as much influence on the judgements.

In first language (L1) speech processing models, prosody is considered to carry an important role for both the production and perception of natural speech. The model proposed by Levelt (1989) assumes that a

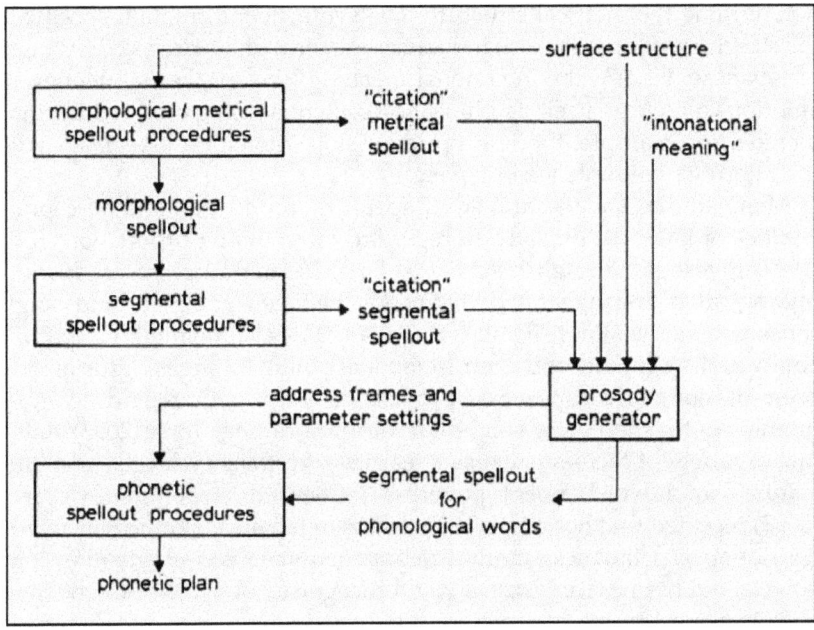

Figure 10.2 Prosody Generator (from Levelt, Willem J.M., *Speaking: From Intention to Articulation*, Figure 10.1, ©1989 Massachusetts Institute of Technology, by permission of The MIT Press)

prosodic constituent is constructed by integrating four kinds of information; segmental information, metrical information, syntactic information, and intentional meaning (see Figure 10.2). Levelt claims that a speaker has to possess appropriate production and perceptual abilities in order to produce native-like speech (for more detailed information about the speech processing model, Levelt, 1989, 1999; Levelt *et al.*, 1999; Levelt & Wheeldon, 1994).

This model has been applied to L2 speech processing including Japanese (de Bot, 1992; Iwasaki, 2000; Izumi, 2003). When applying the model to Japanese, the segmental information includes not only quality of consonant and vowel, but also the special morae, such as the long vowel, moraic nasal consonant, and geminate consonant. The metrical information is stress placement in English, but in Japanese, it is the rhythm of speech which is created by producing appropriate mora duration. English stress influences not only the duration of the stressed segment, but also the pitch height of the segment (Ladefoged, 2001). Japanese word accent, which manifests itself as pitch height, is also relevant to determining the metrical structure. The syntactic information specific to the structure of Japanese also influences the form of the prosodic structure of Japanese. Finally, the intentional meaning (the speaker's intention or emotion) manifests itself as phrasal or sentential intonation, which may include, for example, the appropriate rising intonation associated with the interrogative sentence in Japanese.

Many studies have examined L2 speakers' production and perceptual abilities of Japanese prosody. In regard to mora timing production, Toda (1997) investigated English speakers' Japanese mora timing production, finding an over-exaggerated distinction between geminate and single consonants in her English subjects. Toda (2003) also pointed out that the ability to discriminate and contrast Japanese mora timing is a crucial indicator of non-native speakers' proficiency level with regard to mora timing. As for the perceptual ability of mora timing, Toda (2003) stated that a variety of factors (such as a learner's proficiency level, segmental features, and word accent patterns) influenced perception. Ueyama (2003) reported that her advanced learners of Japanese showed an awareness of special Japanese morae such as geminate consonants and long vowels, but her novice learners could recognise only 50% of them.

With regard to the production of intonation, Ayusawa and Taniguchi (1991) found that inaccurate Japanese prosody production was mainly caused by L1 transfer. As far as the relationship between proficiency level and L2 prosody is concerned, it is not conclusive that proficiency level and accuracy of word accent production is consistently correlated (Ayusawa, 2003). Furthermore, development of prosody perceptual ability seems to be different among learners and not directly correlated with their proficiency levels (Ayusawa, 2003).

The majority of researchers have examined one or two prosodic features in their studies. Those studies give us a partial view of L2 prosody acquisition. Because L2 learners' errors could be multilayered, that is, one speaker could have different problems producing and perceiving particular prosodic features, a study that examines L2 speakers productive and perceptual abilities as a whole is needed.

In this study, we examined L2 Japanese speakers whose L1 is English in terms of their production and perceptual abilities for four kinds of information; the ability to distinguish short and long vowel (segmental information), the ability to produce/perceive mora length and word accent (metrical information), the ability to produce/perceive prosody for semantically and syntactically ambiguous sentences (syntactic information), and the ability to produce/perceive sentence-final intonation for an interrogative sentence (intentional meaning). We used controlled experimental tasks to elicit the target data from the subjects, and we analysed the data acoustically to determine the fundamental frequency and the duration of each segment.

Besides examining the production and perceptual abilities as reflected in the experimentally elicited data, it is also necessary to examine overall accentedness in naturally produced speech. The overall accentedness has been evaluated using impressionistic methods, such as asking judges to evaluate the speech on some form of scale (Anderson-Hsieh, 1992; Munro & Derwing, 1995, 2001; Sato, 1995). The intent of this study is to capture the state of prosody acquisition more accurately by combining such an impressionistic evaluation of accent in naturalistic speech samples with acoustic measurements in the experimentally elicited production data.

Method

Subject

A total of 23 college students of Japanese (JLs) from two U.S. universities were recruited to participate. All of them were English speakers. In order to measure their proficiency level, the JL subjects took a standardised Japanese proficiency test: Level 3, the grammar and listening sections (The Japan Foundation, 1996). Table 10.1 presents the mean test scores of the 23 subjects. Seven subjects were determined to be of an advanced level of language proficiency (ADV), nine subjects were of an intermediate level (INT), and the novice group comprised seven subjects (NOV).[2] As a control, ten native speakers (NSs) of Japanese who speak the Tokyo dialect also participated.

Data collection and analysis

We used a picture description task to elicit naturalistic oral samples from which excerpts were used for the native judgement task. Using computer-controlled tasks, we gathered data of the speakers' production and perceptual abilities. The production data were analysed acoustically.

Table 10.1 Result of proficiency test (average)

Group	Total (%)	Grammar (%)	Listening (%)
ADV	92.13	90.86	93.41
INT	77.30	69.56	85.04
NOV	32.52	33.71	31.32

ADV, advanced; INT, intermediate; NOV, novice.

Naturalistic narrative data

We collected the spontaneous narrative data from JLs. The JLs were instructed to describe a picture (e.g. the people, the location, and the activity in the picture)[3] in Japanese for one minute. The JLs were not given time to prepare before their descriptions were recorded. The narrative utterances were recorded directly to a computer using Sound Recorder (PCM 44.100 kHz, 16 Bit, Stereo) and saved as WAV sound files. From the narrative data, a 30-second portion that contained enough prosodic information was selected for use in the native judgement task. As a control, three NSs' narratives were also collected.[4]

Native judgement

The excerpts produced by the JLs and the control NSs were evaluated by 14 judges (eight NSs who participated in the experimental tasks and an additional six NSs[5]) in terms of the comprehensibility and accentedness of the excerpts. For the comprehensibility judgements, a 9-point scale was used, where 1 was extremely easy to understand, and 9 was impossible to understand (adapted from Munro & Derwing, 1995). The judges were told to choose the rating based on the overall clearness of the speech, in terms of how easily they could form an image of the picture from the narrative.

Foreign accent was also rated on a 9-point scale, where $1 =$ no foreign accent (native pronunciation), and $9 =$ heavily accented. The foreign accent judgements were also obtained for five subcategories, (1) pronunciation of vowels/consonants (e.g. Did the speaker produce English-like /r/ or /t/?), (2) word accent (e.g. Did the speaker put English-like stress on the word instead of correct Japanese word accent?), (3) rhythm (e.g. Did the speaker use an English-like strong-weak rhythm?), (4) segmentation (e.g. Where did the speaker put pauses?), and (5) intonation (e.g. Did the speaker use appropriate sentential intonation?).

Prior to doing the native judgement task, the researcher provided the judges with a detailed explanation of each category using concrete examples (e.g. mimicking foreign-accented pronunciation) and answering any questions about the evaluative criteria. Prior to judging the narrative excerpts, the judges had the opportunity to become accustomed to the task by listening and rating some sample excerpts.[6]

Experimental data: Production Task 1

Production Task 1 was designed to evaluate the speakers' ability to manipulate mora timing and word accent (the task examined the speakers' ability to integrate segmental information and metrical information into their prosody). Both NSs and JLs participated. The stimuli consisted of 2- and 4-mora words with various accent patterns, and some of the stimuli contained special mora types (long vowels, moraic nasals).[7] The subjects produced the word with a particle *'ga'* attached at the end of the word, such as *hon ga* ('a book') and *gakusee ga* ('a student').

It had been claimed that Japanese is a mora-timed language, for which recurring morae create an isochronic (equal timing) rhythm (Abercrombie, 1967; Pike, 1945; both cited in Beckman, 1992; and Kitahara, 1999). Nevertheless, the studies also have found that mora duration becomes non-isochronic due to various factors, such as compensational lengthening, devoicing of vowels, and inherent characteristics of segments (Toda, 2003; Warner & Arai, 2001). Other researchers have postulated that the NSs' underlying representation of mora timing might be isochronic (Warner & Arai, 2001).

In order to observe how the speaker can manage mora timing, we asked the speaker to say each phrase at different speech rates, a normal speech rate, and a slow speech rate. It was expected that the speaker might produce a citation form of mora timing at slow speech. That is, morae become more isochronic at a slow speech rate than at a normal speech rate, because under such circumstances, the speaker would focus on adjusting to the speech rate, and thus the mora timing would not be as influenced by other factors (e.g. compensational lengthening). Furthermore, Munro and Derwing (1998) found that speech rate affects native judges' comprehension of L2 speech. These researchers conducted experiments in which JLs read aloud a narrative passage twice, once at normal speed and once at slow speed. They found that slow speech was rated lower than normal speech due to the creation of more segmental and accent errors and 'difficulty following the thread of what a speaker is saying' (Munro & Derwing, 1998, p. 178). As this study indicates, the ability to produce appropriate mora duration at different speech rates should be one of the indicators of mora timing acquisition.

The participants participated in a trial session prior to the actual data collection session. The stimulus, a picture of the target word + *ga*, was presented on the computer screen. During the trial session, the participants were instructed to say the word + *ga* as normally as possible the first time and to say the same phrase as slow as they could the second time. When the speed was not slow enough (i.e. when the speech rate was not distinguishable from the first utterance), they were told to slow down more. After the trial session, the JLs were asked to look at the vocabulary list in order to confirm that they know all of the vocabulary (all JLs indicated that all the vocabulary items were familiar to them). The oral productions were recorded directly to a computer using Sound Recorder

(PCM 44.100 kHz, 16 Bit, Stereo) and saved as WAV sound files. The oral productions in Production Task 1 were acoustically analysed in terms of the mora duration and fundamental frequencies (F0) with Multi-Speech Signal Analysis (Kay Elemetrics Corp.). In this chapter, we present the results of mora duration for long vowels and nasal consonants in 4-mora words, and the results of word accent for 2-mora words (for a discussion of the remaining analyses, Shibata, 2005).

Experimental data: Production Task 2

Prosody provides very important cues to mark some syntactic structures, such as the distinction of Japanese branching structures. Phrases that contain identical words in both left- and right-branching structures are syntactically and semantically ambiguous, and only prosody can disambiguate the two (Kubozono, 1998; Venditti, 1994).

Production Task 2 examined the speaker's ability to produce prosodic cues to mark syntactic structures (left- and right-branching structures). Only the JLs participated in this task. We created semantically ambiguous branching sentences, which consisted of the same words in the left- and right-branching structures. Figure 10.3 presents the syntactic structures of the target sentence, *akai kuruma no shiito*. This sentence can be translated as 'a red car's seat' in the left-branching structure, and 'a red car-seat' in the right-branching structure.

Figure 10.4 shows the sample intonation contours produced by a NS. This particular NS produced a unified intonation contour for 'akai kuruma' in the left-branching structure and for 'kuruma no shiito' in the right-branching structure, which properly signalled that these segments were one prosodic phrase. He also put a noticeable pause at the major phrasal boundary in the right-branching structure (see the arrow placed between 'akai' and 'kuruma' in Figure 10.4(b)), which also helps

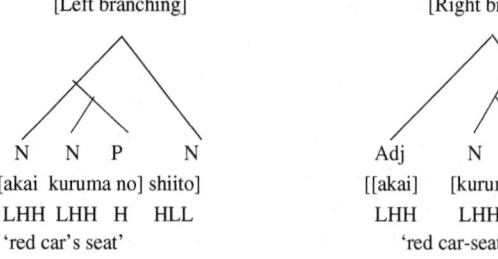

Figure 10.3 Branching structures

(a) Left-branching sentence

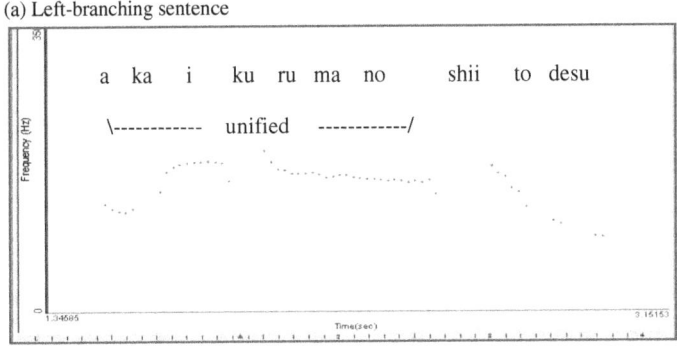

(b) Right-branching sentence

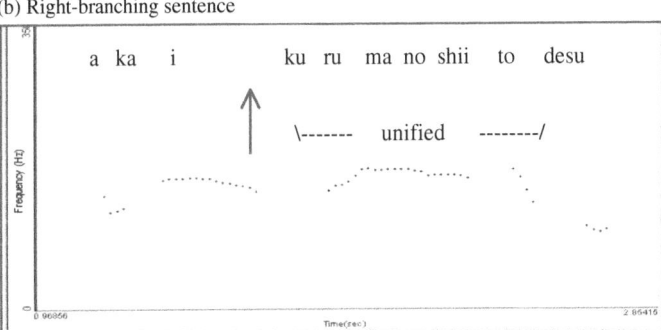

Figure 10.4 Sample intonation contours of *akai kuruma no shiito* by NS

a listener to understand the structure. As this sample shows, NSs tend to use a variety of more explicit prosodic markers for the right-branching sentences. This may be a consequence of the right-branching structure being the marked structure in Japanese (Kubozono, 1998).

For data collection, the JLs were told to say aloud the phrase in the frame of *Kore wa ___ desu.* ('This is ___.') once at normal speed. Four sets of syntactically ambiguous sentences were created for this task.[8] The target stimulus was presented with pictures of the target words on a computer screen as in Production Task 1; however, in order to clarify the meaning of the sentence, the English translation of the sentence was also provided on the screen. The subjects participated in a trial session prior to the data collection session. Because the sentences were very ambiguous, the participants were allowed to spend a few minutes to think about how to utter the sentence before the recording.

The oral productions were recorded using the same protocol used in Production Task 1.

For the analysis, only one set of sentences, *akai kuruma no shiito*, was chosen, and the rest of the sentences were treated as distracters. The data from Production Task 2 were rated by native judges for comprehensibility. The native judges who also participated in the native judgement task for the narratives listened to the branching sentences produced by the JLs. As a control, the samples taken from three NSs[9] were included in the tokens to be rated. The native judges were asked to determine whether a sentence token was left branching or right branching after listening to each sentence. In the stimulus presentation, the left- and right-branching sentences produced by one speaker were presented as a set. The order of structure types was randomised across the subjects. The F0s of words in the sentences produced by the JLs and the control NSs were analysed with Multi-Speech Signal Analysis (Kay Elemetrics Corp.) to identify the prosodic strategies that were used by the speaker.

Experimental data: Production Task 3

Production Task 3 was designed to examine the speaker's ability to produce interrogative sentential intonation in Japanese. Data were collected from both NSs and JLs. The participants were asked to produce the utterances associated with both roles of short conversations once at a normal speed as follows:

A: *Are wa hon desu.* ('That over there is a book.')
B: *Hon?* ('A book?')

In the sample conversation above, the target word is *hon* ('a book'), which carries an HL (high-low) accent pattern. The stimulus was presented with a picture and the target conversation written in English on a computer screen. The oral productions were recorded in the same manner as in Production Task 1. The intonation contours for the declarative and interrogative sentences were evaluated with Multi-Speech Signal Analysis (Kay Elemetrics Corp.), and the number of occasions that the speaker changed the intonation pattern from the declarative to the interrogative was tabulated.

Experimental data: Perception tasks

In previous studies, a variety of tasks were used to evaluate JLs' perceptual abilities. For perception of mora timing, researchers had participants detect segmental duration. For instance, Min (1993) administered a 2-Alternative-Forced-Choice-Identification task. He asked subjects to listen to items and to choose whether that stimulus was a geminate consonant or a singleton consonant (Min, 1993). With regard to the perception of word accent, listening tests have also been used. In these tests, subjects are instructed to designate the accent with a mark on a response sheet, while listening to the word (Ayusawa, 2003).

In this study, four perception tasks were developed, each of which tapped the subject's perceptual ability for a different prosodic feature. Both NSs and JLs participated in all of the four tasks. The task format was a 2-Alternative-Forced-Choice-Identification Task. Task 1 contained 70 words + *ga* produced with either correct or incorrect word accent. In Task 2, 22 words were presented in the *Kore wa ___ desu* ('This is ___'.) frame. Half of the words in Task 2 contained incorrect mora timing (e.g. 'gakko' ('school') was uttered as 'gako', and 'byooin' ('hospital') was uttered as 'byoin'). Task 3 contained 12 short conversations that consisted of declarative and interrogative sentences. In half of the conversations, the accent pattern differentiated between the declarative and interrogative utterances. The stimuli for Tasks 1, 2, and 3 were produced by one of the researchers. For Task 4, two NSs who participated in a pilot study produced four pairs of left- and right-branching sentences[10] that were syntactically and semantically ambiguous.

For Tasks 1, 2, and 3, there was approximately a one-second break between stimuli that were presented continuously with the computer's sound player. All participants were asked to judge whether the phrase/sentence was produced correctly or incorrectly. For Task 4, the subjects were allowed to listen to individual stimuli two to three times prior to deciding whether a sentence stimulus was a left-branching sentence or a right-branching sentence. The rationale for the different presentation protocol in Task 4 comes from the observation in a pilot study that even NSs found it difficult to figure out the meaning of the branching sentences with just a single exposure.

Results

Result of native judgements for narratives

The native judges clearly distinguished between the NSs' productions and the JLs' productions in terms of comprehensibility and accentedness. Table 10.2 shows the average ratings of comprehensibility for each group (the lower rating values indicate better comprehensibility). The NSs received a mean rating very close to '1' (1.04) and showed very little variation. For the JL groups, the judges rated them all as rather poor. Even the very advanced learners' narratives were given poor ratings (ADV: 4.10; INT: 4.44; NOV: 5.67).

Table 10.2 Average rating of comprehensibility in native judgement task

	NS	ADV	INT	NOV
Average	1.04	4.10	4.44	5.67
STD	0.07	0.93	0.87	0.82

NS, native speaker; ADV, advanced; INT, intermediate; NOV, novice.

For the evaluation of overall accentedness, the average of the five subcategory ratings was used (i.e. pronunciation of vowels/consonants, word accent, rhythm, segmentation, and intonation). The results of the overall accentedness, which are presented in Table 10.3, were very similar to those obtained for ratings of comprehensibility. As expected, the NSs' narratives were judged as being of native speaker quality (1.12). The judges' ratings consistently distinguished the NSs' narratives from those of the JLs' (ADV: 4.43; INT: 4.90; NOV: 5.73).

In order to examine the significance of the relationship between the proficiency test scores and the rating results, a Pearson's correlation was calculated. The results revealed that the learners' proficiency scores were positively correlated with their comprehensibility scores ($r = 0.69$, $p < 0.005$), as well as with their scores for overall accentedness ($r = 0.66$, $p < 0.0005$).

Results of production tasks

Results of mora timing

Tables 10.4 and 10.5 present data for two kinds of mora duration: moraic nasals[11] and long vowels. The values in the table are the mean proportion of the word duration by group. Because the nasal consonants and long vowels were produced in 4-mora words, the hypothetical isochronic duration (presented as proportion) for the moraic nasal [n] is 0.25, and for the long vowel 0.50, regardless of the speech rate. If the speaker produces isochronic mora timing (claimed by Abercrombie, 1967 and Pike, 1945, both cited in Beckman, 1992; Kitahara, 1999), we can expect to have a result that is close to this proportion. Note that the results for the NSs

Table 10.3 Average rating of overall accentedness in native judgement task

	NS	ADV	INT	NOV
Average	1.12	4.43	4.90	5.73
STD	0.10	0.95	0.78	0.48

NS, native speaker; ADV, advanced; INT, intermediate; NOV, novice.

Table 10.4 Averaged proportional duration of moraic nasals in 4-mora words

Moraic nasal (N)	Isochronic duration	NS	ADV	INT	NOV
Normal speed	0.25	0.23	0.21	0.19	0.18
Slow speed	0.25	0.26	0.24	0.19	0.18

NS, native speaker; ADV, advanced; INT, intermediate; NOV, novice.

Table 10.5 Averaged proportional duration of long vowels in 4-mora words

Long vowel (CVV)	Isochronic duration	NS	ADV	INT	NOV
Normal speed	0.50	0.54	0.52	0.49	0.47
Slow speed	0.50	0.51	0.51	0.47	0.44

NS, native speaker; ADV, advanced; INT, intermediate; NOV, novice.

in this study are not consistent with this claim. At normal speed, the NSs produced moraic nasals shorter (0.23, see Table 10.4), and long vowels longer (0.54, see Table 10.5) than the predicted isochronic duration. This finding was consistent with some previous acoustic studies of NS mora production that also found that the mora timing was not very isochronic (e.g. Toda, 2003; Warner & Arai, 2001).

On the other hand, the NSs in this study adjusted the duration of both types of morae at slow speaking rates. That is, they prolonged the duration of the moraic nasal (0.26) and shortened the duration of the long vowel (0.51). This appears to support the claim for an underlying isochronicity (Warner & Arai, 2001).

Previous studies of L2 mora timing found that JLs cannot produce native-like distinctions between a geminate and single consonant and between short and long vowels (Han, 1992; Toda, 1997, 2003). In this study, we observed that ADV subjects performed in a manner similar to NSs. They produced shorter moraic nasals (0.21) and longer long vowels (0.52) at normal speed, but they made the durations of these morae closer to the isochronic durations at the slow speaking rate (moraic nasal: 0.24; long vowel: 0.51). On the other hand, the INT and NOV subjects did not show such durational adjustments. Their moraic nasal durations were unchanged and shorter than isochronic duration at both speeds (0.19 by INT subjects and 0.18 by NOV subjects). For long vowels, the INTs and NOVs actually shortened the durations at slow speaking rates (INT: 0.49 at normal → 0.47 at slow, and NOV: 0.47 at normal → 0.44 at slow).

Results of word accent

Many studies that investigated word accent produced by JLs repeatedly reported that JLs could not produce accurate word accent patterns in Japanese (e.g. Ayusawa, 2003). The current study provides further evidence of JLs' difficulty with word accent production. As Table 10.6 shows, the ADV subjects could correctly produce correct word accent only 53% of the time, with the INT and NOV subjects producing the correct accent even less frequently.

Figure 10.5 presents the pitch contour of *'mizu ga'* ('water'). The accent pattern of this phrase is Low-High (High).[12] The upper contour was produced by one of the NSs, the middle contour was produced by one of the ADVs (four out of seven ADVs mis-produced this accent), and the lower panel shows an NOV production (six out of seven NOVs mis-produced this). Both the ADV and NOV subjects produced this word with the incorrect High-Low (Low) pattern.

Figure 10.6 shows the F0 difference between Mora 1 and Mora 2 and between Mora 2 and the particle for the 2-mora words. When the difference value is negative, the pitch goes up from the preceding mora to the following mora. When the difference value is positive, the pitch goes down. These figures display not only the remarkable differences between the NSs' word accent productions and those of the JLs, but they also indicate that the JLs' productions for all accent types were very similar. For LH(H) and LH(L) patterns (Figure 10.6(a) and (b)), the NSs produced a rising pitch from Mora 1 to Mora 2. From Mora 2 to the particle, they produced a gradual declining pitch for LH(H) and a steep falling pitch for LH(L), which represent the correct F0 patterns. For HL(L) words (Figure 10.6(c)), the NSs produced a sharp falling pitch from Mora 1 to the particle. On the other hand, all three JL groups produced a falling pitch, which was not very steep, regardless of the

Table 10.6 Mean of the correct word accent production in 2-mora words (%)

	NS	ADV	INT	NOV
Correct word accent	0.98	0.53	0.42	0.37

NS, native speaker; ADV, advanced; INT, intermediate; NOV, novice.

Prosody Acquisition by Japanese Learners 191

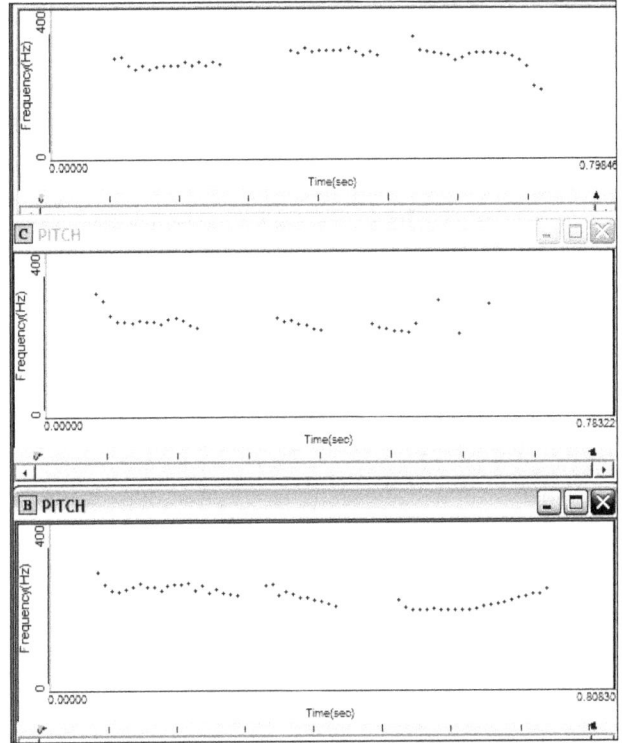

Figure 10.5 Sample intonation contours of *mizu ga*. Top panel, NS production; middle panel, ADV production; bottom panel, NOV production

accent patterns. This pattern of findings shows that the JLs lack the ability to produce word accent patterns accurately.

Results of branching sentences

Figure 10.7 shows the results of the native judgements for the productions of branching sentences. The left bar for each subject group represents the result for the left-branching structures, and the right bar the result for right-branching structures. Of the NSs' productions, 95% were understood correctly by the judges. The ADVs' productions of the left-branching sentences were correctly identified 88% of the time, but their productions of right-branching sentences were only correctly identified 74% of the time. The NOVs' productions were the least well identified

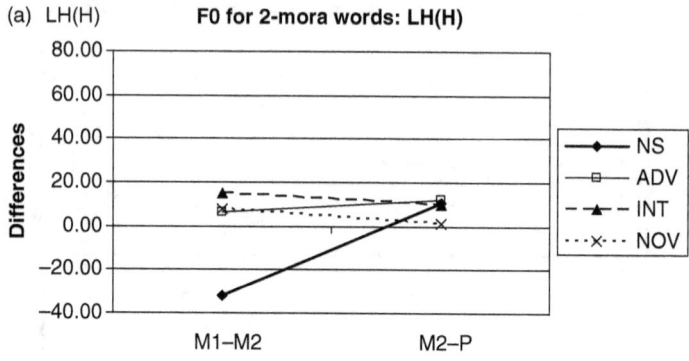
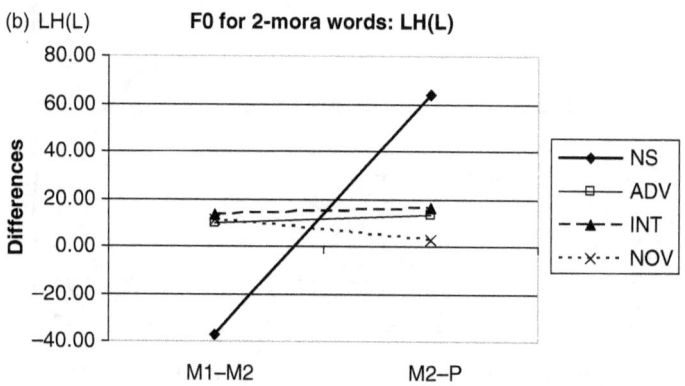
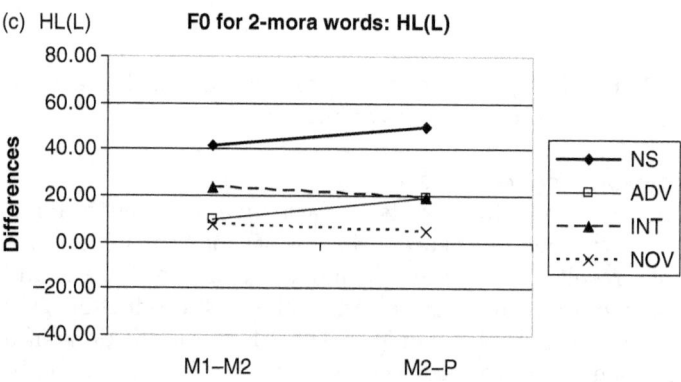

Figure 10.6 Differences of F0s between adjacent morae in 2-mora words

Comprehensibility of branching structures

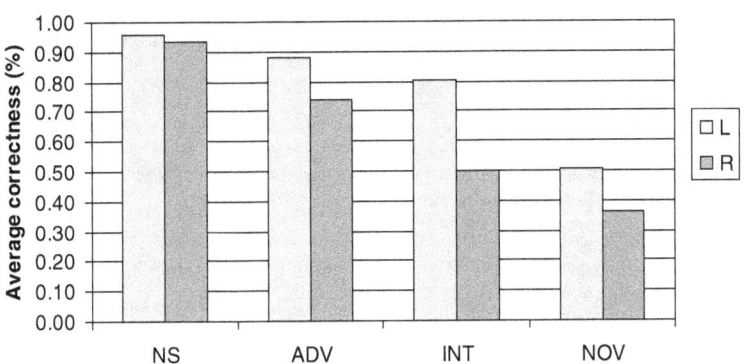

Figure 10.7 Comprehensibility of branching sentences in native judgement

(left branching sentences, 51%; right-branching sentences, 37%). The INTs' results fell between the NOV and ADV (left-branching sentences, 80%; right-branching sentences, 50%). These results also indicate that the native judges had more difficulty identifying JLs' right-branching sentences than their left-branching sentences.

The acoustic analysis revealed that the JLs used prosodic cues inappropriately. Table 10.7 presents a summary of the improper uses of prosodic cues by the JLs. For instance, for the left-branching sentences, the JLs placed a pause after *akai*, where there should be no phrasal boundary. For the right-branching sentences, they did not raise the pitch of *kuruma* and did not suppress the pitch of *shiito*. As seen, this improper use of

Table 10.7 Improper use of prosodic cues in the branching sentences by JLs (proportion)

	Left branching	*Right branching*	
	Pause after **akai**	Not raise the pitch for **kuruma**	Not suppress pitch for **shiito**
ADV	0.00	0.43	0.29
INT	0.11	0.33	0.67
NOV	0.43	0.43	0.71

ADV, advanced; INT, intermediate; NOV, novice.

prosodic signals occurred more often for the right-branching structures, which made it difficult for the judges to correctly identify those sentences. Note that the higher proficiency learners used less inappropriate cues than did the lower proficiency learners.

Results of interrogative sentences

Figure 10.8 presents sample pitch contours of *tabemono* (LHHL, 'food') in a declarative sentence (the left part of each panel: *Are wa tabemono desu.* 'That over there is food.') and an interrogative sentence (the right part of each panel: *Tabemono?* 'Food?'). The upper panel in the figure shows an example of a NS's production, which indicates that the word accent patterns of the two kinds of sentences are the same. On the other hand, the NOV's production (the lower panel) indicates that he produced the word with a slightly falling accent in the declarative sentence and changed it to the sharp rising pattern in the interrogative (four out of seven NOVs mis-produced this intonation pattern).

In Table 10.8, the number of occurrences of changing accent patterns and correct intonation patterns are displayed (presented as proportions). The NOVs most often changed the accent patterns (0.64), and the ADVs changed the patterns more often (0.38) than did the INTs (0.27). The

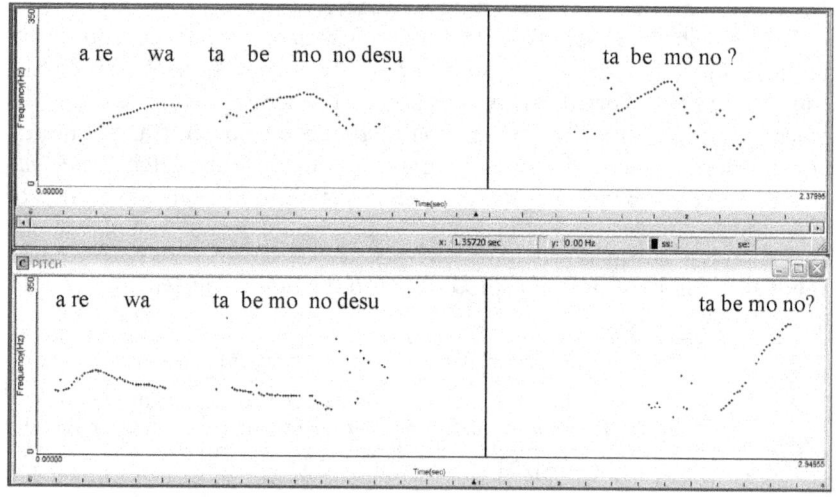

Figure 10.8 Intonation contours for declarative and interrogative sentences of *tabemono* (upper panel, NS's production; lower panel, NOV's production)

Table 10.8 Accent changes from declaratives to interrogatives and correct intonation (proportion)

	Accent change	Correct intonation	
		Declarative	Interrogative
ADV	0.38	0.50	0.55
INT	0.27	0.54	0.52
NOV	0.64	0.47	0.36

ADV, advanced; INT, intermediate; NOV, novice.
- For the accent change, the higher the number, the more often the speakers changed the accent.
- For the correct intonation, the higher the number, the more correctly the speakers produced the sentential intonation.

results for correct intonation productions were similar for the ADVs and INTs, and the lowest accuracy score was observed for the NOVs. This table presents the data collapsed over all accent types. Looking at individual accent patterns, we found that the ADVs could produce the flat accent pattern better than the other lower proficiency JLs (see Table 10.9). The JLs whose L1 is English tend to put a stress at the beginning of a Japanese word, which results in a falling intonation. Because of this tendency, the flat accent is very difficult for them to produce. The INTs did not change the accent pattern as often as the ADVs; however, the INTs did not produce an accurate flat accent as often as the ADVs. This result may suggest a complexity in the acquisition of word accent and sentential intonation.

Table 10.9 Correct intonation for flat accent and falling accent word (proportion)

		ADV	INT	NOV
Flat accent				
2-mora LH(H)	Declarative	0.43	0.06	0.00
	Interrogative	0.36	0.17	0.43
Falling accent				
2-mora HL(L)	Declarative	0.71	1.00	1.00
	Interrogative	0.86	0.93	0.43

ADV, advanced; INT, intermediate; NOV, novice.

Results of perception tasks

The results for the four perception tasks are presented with the scheme shown in Figure 10.9. In such a scheme, when a subject detects both the well-formed and ill-formed productions accurately, the square becomes larger, and when the subject cannot detect them, the square becomes smaller. The smaller square in the figure indicates that the subject's performance is a chance performance. For example, if this subject responded 'correct' for all items, he would receive a 50% correct judgement score.

Figure 10.10 presents the results for all subject groups. The NSs' performance is represented by the largest square, which shows their nearly perfect ability to detect the ill-formed productions of all kinds of prosodic cues. Over all, the JL groups' performances indicate that the higher their proficiency, the better their performance on the perceptual tasks. Nonetheless, the figure reveals that even ADVs could detect word accent no better than chance (ADV = 56%, INT = 49%, NOV = 47%). For mora timing, the ADVs did better than the INTs, and the NOVs did very poorly (ADV = 75%, INT = 62%, NOV = 45%). For interrogative

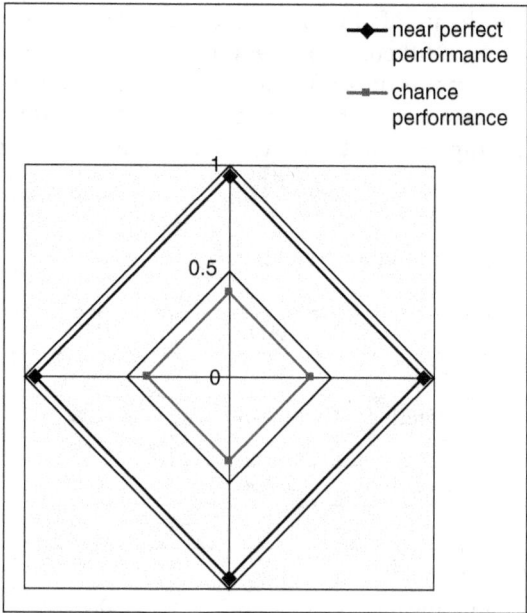

Figure 10.9 Scheme of perception test result

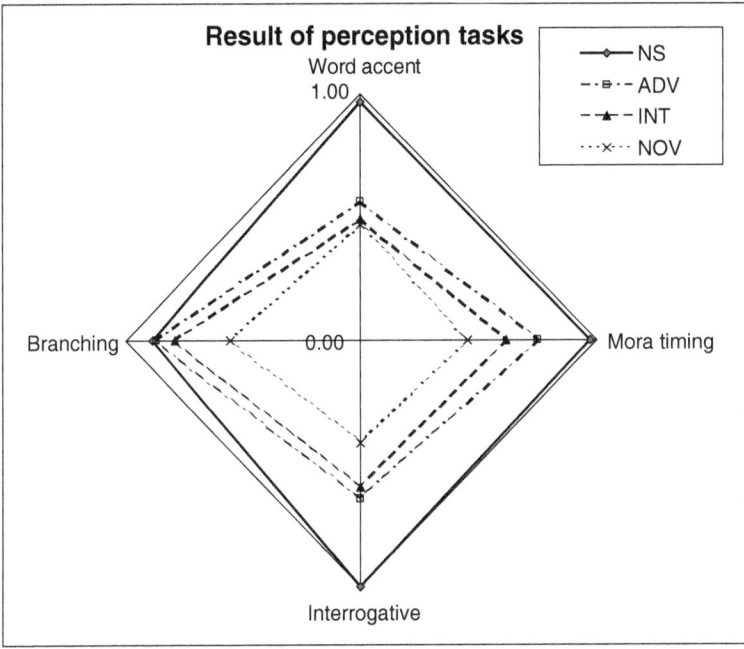

Figure 10.10 Result of perception task (proportion of items correctly identified)

intonation, the ADVs and INTs performed similarly (ADV = 64%, INT = 59%), but again the NOVs' result was much lower (NOV = 42%).

The score for perception of branching structures was much higher than that obtained for the other three tasks. It also differed from the rest of results in that the scores of NSs and ADVs were very similar. This indicates that even NSs had difficulty detecting the semantically and syntactically ambiguous sentences based only on the information in the acoustic signal. The result of NSs was 89%, and that of ADVs was 87%. INTs also performed fairly well, but the NOVs performed much more poorly (INT = 79%, NOV = 55%).

Discussion

Previous studies of L2 prosody acquisition have reported that even advanced learners have problems producing and perceiving various kinds of prosodic features, such as word accent and phrasal/sentential intonation. However, the majority of studies have focused on one or two prosodic features and have not viewed L2 prosody acquisition holistically. This study attempted to investigate the speaker's ability to produce and perceive Japanese prosody in terms of four kinds of information: segmental information, metrical information, syntactic information, and intentional meaning. These four kinds of information are considered to be fundamental to prosody generation in the L1 speech processing model (Levelt, 1989). The tasks in this study were designed to assess JLs' abilities to produce/perceive prosodic features. We also wanted to determine the comprehensibility and accentedness of spontaneous narratives collected from the same JLs, and relate them to the findings from the experimental production and perception tasks. An examination of how these findings are related can be used to develop a model of JLs' prosody acquisition.

Native judgement for narratives vs proficiency

Munro and Derwing (1995) reported that native judges detected heavy accents in the oral productions by non-native speakers of English, although the productions were not always incomprehensible. In this study, the native judgements of the narrative samples revealed that the scores of comprehensibility and accentedness were highly correlated ($r = 0.915$, $p < 0.0001$). This suggests that the more accented samples were also the least comprehensible. When looking at the relationship between the native judgement scores and the JLs' proficiency level, we see a moderate correlation for proficiency × comprehensibility ($r = -0.692$, $p < 0.001$) and for proficiency × accentedness ($r = -0.655$, $p < 0.001$). These r values are negative because the scale used for the native judgement assigned a '1' to the most native-like and a '9' to the most foreign. Thus as JLs' proficiency level improves, the comprehensibility and accentedness in their narrative productions also improves. Nevertheless, this study also revealed that even advanced learners' narrative production was perceived as having some degree of accentedness, which accounts for their lower comprehensibility when compared to NSs' productions. For example, one of the ADVs in this study scored 98% on the proficiency test; however, his narrative production was rated 2.94 on the comprehensibility scale and 3.04 on the accentedness scale.

Production tasks vs native judgement for narratives and proficiency

To understand why the narrative productions by JLs were perceived as foreign we need to look at the results of the production tasks and their interactions with the native judgement scores and the learner proficiency level scores. In this study we examined several different prosodic features in the production data. F0 was measured to assess word accent. The duration of segment was used to determine mora timing. The native judgement and F0 measurement were used in order to find how comprehensible the sentence was and what kind of prosodic cues the JLs used to distinguish syntactically ambiguous left- and right-branching sentences. Finally F0 contours used to distinguish declarative and interrogative were compared.

Table 10.10 presents the correlations (r) between the production data and the JLs' proficiency test results (%) and the accentedness of the native judgement for the narratives scores. The data show that the results for word accent and right-branching sentences do not have a strong correlation with the proficiency level; that is, even the highly proficient JLs could not produce those prosodic features. On the other hand, JLs can produce the native-like duration of long vowels and interrogative sentence intonation as they achieve greater L2 proficiency. The moderate correlation between left-branching sentence production and proficiency level indicates that some of JLs can produce appropriate prosodic cues for the left-branching sentence as their proficiency level goes higher.

The correlations between the results of production data and the accentedness ratings for the narratives (the lower row in Table 10.10) suggest that the appropriate production of word accent, mora timing, and interrogative intonation may be important to producing less accented narratives. We could not observe a significant correlation between the production of branching sentences and the accentedness ratings. This could in part be due to the fact that the JLs did not produce syntactically ambiguous branching structures in their narratives. In future studies, we will need to investigate narratives that contain syntactically more complex sentences such as noun modification structures.

Table 10.10 Correlations (r) between the results of production data and the proficiency test and the accentedness of native judgement (p-values are provided for significant correlations)

	Word accent	Long vowels (slow speed)	Left branching	Right branching	Interrogative sentences
Proficiency test	0.322	0.757 ($p < 0.0001$)	0.563 ($p < 0.006$)	0.344	0.696 ($p < 0.0003$)
Accentedness	−0.525 ($p < 0.002$)	−0.454 ($p < 0.003$)	−0.135	−0.040	−0.502 ($p < 0.002$)

Table 10.11 Correlations (*r*) among the four production results

	Word accent	Long vowels (slow speed)	Left branching	Right branching	Interrogative sentences
Word accent					
Long vowels (slow speed)	0.323				
Left branching	0.102	0.378			
Right branching	0.098	0.367	0.697 ($p < 0.0003$)		
Interrogative sentences	0.508 ($p < 0.02$)	0.586 ($p < 0.004$)	0.313	0.222	

When we examine the correlations between the different measures of production (Table 10.11) we see that JLs who could produce understandable left-branching sentences also could produce understandable right-branching sentences. Furthermore, those who could produce interrogative intonation properly could produce word accent and mora timing fairly well. Nonetheless, the results indicate that even though JLs could produce comprehensible branching sentences, not many of them could produce word accent correctly.

The comparison of the production data shows that the most difficult tasks for JLs in terms of producing Japanese prosody involve improving word accent and production of the proper prosodic cues for branching structures.

Perception tasks vs proficiency and accentedness

Besides improving their ability to produce prosodic features, JLs also need to improve the ability to perceive prosodic features. As Levelt's speech processing model assumes, the speaker needs to be able to comprehend whether the production is well- or ill-formed (Levelt, 1989). We looked at how the JLs' proficiency level relates to their perceptual ability and the native judgement of accentedness of their narratives. Table 10.12 presents the correlations between the proficiency test (%), the accentedness ratings and the correct detection of the prosodic features (%).

We see that the level of proficiency and the JLs' perception of prosodic features were moderately correlated, except the ability to detect correct word accent, which showed a lower though significant correlation. The

Table 10.12 Correlations (r) between the correct detection of prosodic features and proficiency test scores and the native judgement of accentedness for sample narratives

	Word accent	Mora timing	Interrogative intonation	Branching sentences
Proficiency test	0.493 ($p < 0.02$)	0.699 ($p < 0.0003$)	0.618 ($p < 0.002$)	0.618 ($p < 0.002$)
Accentedness	−0.555 ($p < 0.007$)	−0.719 ($p < 0.0002$)	−0.450 ($p < 0.04$)	−0.326

correlations with accentedness ratings reveal that when JLs are better at detecting word accent and mora timing, their narratives were perceived to be less accented. This result is similar to the one observed for the production data; that is, improving the perceptual ability for word accent is the hardest task for JLs. Table 10.13 illustrates the relationships among the different measures of the perceptual ability of prosodic features. The correlations among the perception results were stronger than those among the production results. This indicates that the ability to detect various prosodic features seems to be acquired in parallel.

Production vs perception

This study was not designed to determine whether or not perceptual abilities lead production abilities when it comes to mastery of prosody. However, the correlations of the production and perception scores show that the JLs in this study who could produce accurate prosodic features tended to also be able to perceive those features (Table 10.14).

Table 10.13 Correlations (r) among the four perception results

	Word accent	Mora timing	Interrogative intonation	Branching sentence
Word accent				
Mora timing	0.572 ($p < 0.005$)			
Interrogative intonation	0.625 ($p < 0.002$)	0.510 ($p < 0.02$)		
Branching sentence	0.483 ($p < 0.02$)	0.554 ($p < 0.007$)	0.403	

Table 10.14 Correlations (r) between the results of production and perception for the production of branching sentence

	Word accent	Mora timing	Interrogative intonation	Branching sentence
Correlation between production and perception	0.645 ($p < 0.0009$)	0.485 ($p < 0.02$)	0.675 ($p < 0.0005$)	0.588 ($p < 0.004$)

Note: The r values for the left- and right-branching sentence productions were averaged

Conclusions

The aim of this study was to depict L2 prosody acquisition from a holistic point of view for JLs whose L1 is English. We examined the JLs' productive and perceptual abilities for four prosodic features, word accent, mora timing, prosodic cues for syntactically and semantically ambiguous sentences (i.e. the sentences that contain left- and right-branching structures), and interrogative sentential intonation. These prosodic features carry essential information to generate a prosodic constituent (see the speech production processing model by Levelt, 1989). As a validation of the role of these features we also collected JLs' spontaneous narrative productions in order to see how these features are related to native judges' ratings of accentedness and how accentedness influences the comprehensibility of the narratives.

The native judgements of narrative productions revealed that native judges perceived some degree of foreign accent in even very advanced JLs' narratives, and the ratings of accentedness and comprehensibility were strongly related.

The production tasks showed that the JLs had difficulty producing the word accent of 2-mora and 4-mora words. They could not differentiate the word accent properly, and they tended to produce a slightly falling accent regardless of the original word accent. As for mora timing, the lower the proficiency score of the JLs, the less native-like were their productions of mora timing for long vowels and nasal consonants at slow speech rates.

The productions of branching sentences by JLs were evaluated by the native judges in terms of the comprehensibility. We found that the JLs' branching sentences, especially right-branching sentences, were hard to comprehend for the judges. The JLs' right-branching sentences contained improper prosodic signals, which would lead to difficulty of comprehension.

The analyses of interrogative sentential intonation revealed a complex relationship between word accent and sentential intonation. The ADVs could produce a flat word accent (the most difficult Japanese word accent pattern for English speakers) in interrogative sentences better than INTs. In Japanese, the word accent stays the same regardless of the type of sentence. It was expected that more proficient learners could produce the same accent pattern in declarative and interrogative sentences. Nonetheless, the ADVs changed the word accent pattern when producing declarative and interrogative sentences more often than the INTs. Because we did not investigate the JLs' knowledge of interrogative intonation, we cannot conclusively account for this finding.

The results of the perception tasks indicated that JLs could not detect ill-formed word accent regardless of their proficiency level. The highly proficient JLs could detect the ill-formed mora timing and interrogative intonation better than the JLs with lower proficiency, even though the results were much lower than for the NSs.

The correlations between proficiency level and the results of production tasks indicated that, for the JLs in this study, to produce word accent and prosodic cues for right-branching sentences was the hardest skill to achieve. This can be taken as evidence that the ability to produce various prosodic features does not emerge all at once. Some prosodic features (in this study, word accent and right-branching sentences) seem to be mastered later than the other prosodic features (i.e. mora timing, interrogative intonation, and left-branching sentences in this study). This is also supported by the finding that the ability to produce word accent and interrogative intonation is related to the perceived accentedness of the spontaneous narrative productions. The development of perceptual ability follows a similar trajectory. The ability to perceive some prosodic features (i.e. word accent in this study) takes longer to develop than other prosodic features (i.e. mora timing, interrogative intonation, and branching sentences in this study). Interestingly, we observed that better perception of word accent and mora timing was associated with lower accentedness ratings of the spontaneous narratives.

L2 prosody acquisition is not a simple process. In order to improve the accentedness and comprehensibility of JLs' productions, it will be necessary to develop pedagogical materials that will allow JLs to improve their productive and perceptual abilities of word accent. The production and perception of word accent and branching sentences appear to need intensive instruction. At this point it is difficult to determine whether the JLs' performance was due to lack of knowledge, lack of exercise, or a combination of the two. In future studies, we need to investigate how

JLs' knowledge of Japanese prosody influences their production/perception of prosodic cues.

Notes

1. Mora is the unit of phonetic and phonological duration (Kubozono & Ohta, 1998). For instance, native speakers of Japanese perceive that *ii* (a 2-mora word, 'good') is twice longer than *i* (a 1-mora word, 'stomach').
2. Although the JLs were categorised into groups by their proficiency scores, their backgrounds with respect to their Japanese learning experience varied in terms of gender, Japanese class level, length of study in high school and/or college in the United States, experience with Japanese study abroad, and length of stay in Japan. However, in this study, we could not consider those differences in their performance. It will be done in the future study.
3. Pictures drawn by Norman Rockwell (1894–1978) were used.
4. Two of the NSs were teaching assistants of Japanese, and one was an undergraduate student, all attending a midwestern university.
5. Because of time restriction, some of the NSs who participated in the production and perception tasks could not participate in this native judgement task. The additional native judges speak a variety of dialects of Japanese.
6. The sample excerpts were taken from two JLs in the pilot study, which was executed prior to the main data collection.
7. The stimuli for the word accent/mora timing data collection were selected from *Nakama* 1 (Makino *et al.*, 1998).
8. The stimuli for Production Task 2 were taken from the textbook *Nakama* 1, except the woman's name 'Naomi' and a noun 'shiito' ('seat'). The nouns and adjectives in the target phrases contain two to four morae. The target phrases were as follows:

    Target 1: *Akai kuruma no shiito* (it means 'a red-car's seat' in the left and 'a red car-seat' in the right)

    Target 2: *Kiree na Naomi no tokee* (it means 'beautiful Naomi's watch' in the left and 'Naomi's beautiful watch' in the right)

    Target 3: *Suteki na tomodachi no kaban* (it means 'nice friend's bag' in the left and '(my) friend's nice bag' in the right)

    Target 4: *Yuumee na Naomi no inu* (it means 'famous Naomi's dog' in the left and 'Naomi's famous dog' in the right)

9. These NSs' data were collected in the pilot study by one of the researchers. All of three NSs were speakers of Tokyo dialect.
10. The target sentences were the same as the ones for Production Task 2 (see Note 8 above).
11. A mora-counting language like Japanese considers a coda nasal as an independent unit. For instance, *ten* ('point') is considered a 2-mora word in Japanese. On the other hand, a syllable-counting language like English does not consider a coda nasal as an independent unit. Therefore, *ten* in English is considered a one-syllable word.
12. The pitch height in parentheses indicates that of the particle (*ga*).

Chapter 11
Recognition and Production of Formulas in L2 Pragmatics

KATHLEEN BARDOVI-HARLIG

This chapter addresses the question of how recognition relates to production in the acquisition of second language pragmatics. It adopts a rather narrow focus to investigate how learners' recognition of formulas relates to their use of the same formulas in written production tasks.

Literature on interlanguage pragmatics often appeals to formulas. The term *formula* has at least three uses in interlanguage pragmatics: one which describes a stage of the acquisition process, one which describes the end point, or target, and one which describes components of a speech act, or *semantic formulas* (Bardovi-Harlig, 2006b). In this chapter I investigate the second type, target (or social) formulas. Most definitions of formulas describe them as multimorphemic expressions that are stored and retrieved as a single lexical unit. Definitions of social formulas predictably also include conditions of use. Coulmas (1981: 1–17) offers a classic definition of formulas as 'highly conventionalized prepatterned expressions whose occurrence is tied to more or less standardized communication situations'. Myles *et al.* (1998) describe formulas as being situationally dependent and community-wide in use.

House (1996: 227–228) describes the importance of formulas in second language learning: 'From a sociolinguistic point of view, it is important to learn routines at any learning stage because they embody the societal knowledge that members of a given community share ...routine formulas are thus essential in the verbal handling of everyday life'. Roever (2005) identifies the knowledge of formulas as part of pragmalinguistic knowledge, the linguistic resources to express pragmatic functions. (See also Nattinger & DeCarrico, 1992; for overviews of the role of formulas in acquisition more broadly, see Weinert, 1995; Wray & Perkins, 2000.)

Although some researchers of pragmatic development have reported that some learners use L2 formulas (Achiba, 2003; R. Ellis, 1992; Kasper & Rose, 2002; Scarcella, 1979; Schmidt, 1983), other researchers have identified patterns that suggest that learners do not use formulas where native speakers (NSs) often do (Blum-Kulka & Olshtain, 1986; Edmondson & House, 1991; Kecskes, 2000, 2003). Blum-Kulka and Olshtain (1986) report that intermediate and advanced learners produced longer responses than native speakers on written production questionnaires, known as discourse completion tasks (DCTs). Edmondson and House (1991) acknowledge that, on the one hand, learner response length may be an effect of the DCT, but they also report that learners and NSs responded to the task differently, suggesting that task effect is not completely responsible. Edmondson and House interpret the longer responses of the learners to be an indication that learners do not use formulas. Like Edmondson and House, Kecskes (2003) found that some learners used too much talk and too few formulas. Edmondson and House suggest that learners are wordy because they are not confident that they are getting their illocutionary point across: 'We suggest that learners are, at least in part, "insecure" because they do not have ready access to, and therefore do not make use of, standardized routines for meeting the social imposition...as native speakers do' (Edmondson & House 1991: 284). Thus, length (or the *waffle* as they call it) is a compensatory strategy, used to make up for what the learner perceives to be a deficiency in pragmatic competence.

Although many tasks have been developed to elicit production in L2 pragmatics, many fewer tasks have been developed to test interpretation (what learners think expressions mean), and still fewer to test recognition (whether learners are familiar with an expression and their degree of familiarity). Production studies often report that learners do not use formulas where native speakers may do so, but they are not designed to determine why learners do not use target formulas. One possible explanation for this lack of use is that learners do not know the formulas. The present study explores the question of whether learners recognise target formulas.

Two recent studies in interlanguage pragmatics have tested learners' recognition and interpretation of target formulas (Kecskes, 2000; Roever, 2005). A native-like interpretation of a formula suggests that a learner is familiar with the formula, without requiring the learner to produce it. Roever's web-based study included learners at a range of proficiency levels in English as a second language (ESL) (host) and English as a foreign language (EFL) (foreign) settings, and Kecskes's study included advanced learners in the ESL setting.

Of particular relevance to this investigation are the designs used by these studies. In order to test learners' recognition of target formulas as appropriate in particular contexts, Roever (2005) employed a multiple-choice identification test consisting of a scenario, a prompt, and four choices, as in (1). The learners chose among the three distracters and one right answer.

(1) Claudia calls her friend Dennis. Dennis is not home but Claudia would like the person who answered the phone to tell Dennis something.
What would Claudia probably say?
(a) 'Can you write something?'
(b) 'Can I give you information?'
(c) 'Can you take a note?'
(d) 'Can I leave a message?' (Roever, 2005, item 309)

The test included 12 items, with a range of responses from 'hello' to increasingly less common formulas. (Even single, monomorphemic words are sometimes described as formulas in the literature on social formulas.) It seems that some of the items are more difficult than others, not necessarily because of the targeted formulas, but because of the relation of the targeted formula to the distracters. For example, in some items both the target formula and the distracters are likely formulas as well, although the distracters are not appropriate in the specific context; in others, the target formulas contrast with distracters in which none of the choices seems especially formulaic (or even conventional). In fact, the most critical comments about the task from native speakers during the retrospective interviews centred on alternatives when they preferred an answer other than the ones listed (Roever, 2005: 75). Constructing the distracters seems to be one of the challenges in creating the multiple-choice items.

In contrast to Roever's task, which asked whether learners recognise pragmatic formulas in given settings, Kecskes (2000) asked whether learners know what formulas mean. Kecskes used three tasks: a dialogue interpretation task, a dialogue completion task in which learners supplied missing turns in short dialogues, and a discourse completion task in which learners supplied a response to a scenario. The dialogue interpretation task included idioms that had both a possible literal and idiomatic reading (e.g. *OK, shoot* 'go ahead', *Get out of here* 'don't fool me', and *Piece of cake* 'easy'). Kecskes (2000, 2003) reported that the advanced nonnative speakers he tested did not recognise the metaphorical use of formulas. Of greater relevance to the current study, Kecskes also reported that the same non-native speakers did not use target expressions in the production tasks, whereas native speakers did. For example, when given a scenario describing a TV anchor breaking for a commercial, native speakers supplied responses such as *Stay tuned, We'll be right back, We'll have to take a break, Don't go away,* and *Stick around,* whereas learners whose length of residence was a year or less supplied non-formulaic responses such as *Keep your channel* and *When we come back we will an action* (Kecskes 2003: 185).

In addition to under-using formulas, learners may over-use formulas. Kecskes's report of overgeneralisation of formulas also emphasises the need to test production along with recognition. One learner used the same formula, *Sure, no problem,* in response to both requests and offers. This resulted in felicitous replies to the requests, *Can I borrow your pen?* and *Can I talk to you after class?*, but not to the offer, *Would you like some candy?* (Kecskes, 2000: 155).

The studies by Roever and Kecskes suggest possible designs for the investigation of learners' recognition and interpretation of formulas and expressions. As Roever shows through retrospective interviews, one of the challenges in item construction is the distracters. Moreover, the multiple-choice format allows learners to arrive at a response by various routes. A learner may recognise only one formula and select it, a learner may reject formulas and select the remaining formula(s), or a learner may recognise all of the formulas, in which case the task may require learners to reject the distracters as well as to recognise the correct formula, thus, testing preference in addition to recognition. In this way, a multiple-choice task may be more complex than necessary in order to determine a learner's familiarity with an expression, which is the goal of the present study.

To begin the exploration of recognition and production of formulas in second language pragmatics, the present study addresses two research questions: Do learners report recognising expressions in recognition tasks? Do learners use those same expressions in production tasks?

The Study

Participants

In total, 61 intermediate to advanced ESL learners in an intensive English programme completed the tasks. They were enrolled in levels 4–7 of instruction in a seven-level programme. Fourteen languages were represented, distributed across levels (Korean, 18; Chinese, 8; Spanish, 7; Thai, 7; Japanese, 6; Portuguese, 3; Turkish, 2; Mongolian,

Pashto, Russian, Slovak, Tajik, Urdu, Vietnamese, 1 each; 3 undisclosed). Because the learners' recognition is being compared to their own production, no control group was tested in this phase of the study (although NS responses are available for the scenarios from Roever, 2005).

Tasks

To test the recognition of formulas, this study adapts two measures used by vocabulary researchers, substituting formulaic sequences for individual words. The two measures are self-report of recognition (Meara & Buxton, 1987) and the multilevel Vocabulary Knowledge Scale (VKS; Wesche & Paribakht, 1996), an instrument that combines self-report and performance items to elicit both self-perceived and demonstrated knowledge of specific words (in this task, *formulas*). The recognition tasks are supplemented by production tasks.

Learners completed four timed tasks, each of which was collected upon completion, prior to beginning the next portion. These included a self-report of recognition (Task 1), identification of likely contexts for expressions (Task 2), a written discourse completion task (DCT; Task 3), and a modified VKS (Task 4). The total time allotted for data collection was just over half an hour (33 minutes). The amount of time allowed for each section was determined in discussion with the programme ESL teachers. The idea was to encourage learners to respond quickly, as automaticity is thought to be a characteristic of formula retrieval (Weinert, 1995; Wray & Perkins, 2000). Approximately 15 seconds were allotted for each item on the recognition task, 30 seconds for each item on the context identification task, and 1.5 minutes for each item on the production tasks (the DCT and the VKS). Observers reported that learners finished the recognition and context identification tasks more quickly than anticipated and that lower-level learners could have used more time on the production tasks.

Recognition task

The self-report recognition task instructed learners to circle all the expressions that they knew or recognised. There were 63 items, 59 of which were expressions in American English, and 4 of which were not. It was anticipated that unfamiliar expressions would serve as controls for familiar ones. The list was constructed from expressions in a variety of published sources including pragmatics studies such as Kecskes (2000) and Roever (2005), formula lists such as Nattinger and DeCarrico (1992), and current usage (such as *my bad*) suggested by ESL teachers.

Learners were given 8 minutes to complete this section. The task had the format in Example (2).

(2) Self-report recognition task
Instructions: Circle all the expressions that you know or recognise
Beg your pardon?
Can I ask you a favor?
Can I leave a message?
My bad
Can I get a ride?
Could you do me a favor?
Do you have a piece of paper I can borrow?
Do you have the time?

Context identification

The next part of the task asked learners to identify the general situations in which they usually hear expressions. This task was an attempt to discover if learners associated expressions with broad contexts such as stores, phone calls, or television. The list of contexts, which was chosen to reflect the usage of the expressions, was the same for each item. Sixteen expressions were presented and learners were given 7 minutes for the task. A test item appears in Example (3).

(3) Context identification item
Instructions: Where are you likely to hear the following expressions? Circle ALL that apply (more than one answer is OKAY)
Stay tuned
   With friends
   In a store
   On the phone
   On TV
   At a fast-food restaurant
   On campus
   Don't know where
   Haven't heard it

Written DCT

Six scenarios were presented to the learners who were given 8 minutes to complete them. Three of the scenarios were used by Roever (2005), and three were written for this study. All the scenarios provided a possible context for the use of one or more expressions in the recognition task. An example is provided in (4); the full task is provided in the Appendix.

(4) Written DCT
Instructions: Please fill in the blank with your part of the conversation.
You are in class, but have forgotten your notebook. You ask your friend for some paper.
You say: _____

Modified VKS
The final task was a modification of the multilevel Vocabulary Knowledge Scale (Wesche & Paribakht, 1996), an instrument that combines self-report and performance items to elicit both self-perceived and demonstrated knowledge of specific words. The task was modified to include expressions rather than individual words. The scale ratings range from complete unfamiliarity, through recognition of the formula and some idea of its meaning, to the ability to use the formula with grammatical and semantic accuracy in a sentence, and in this modification, pragmatic appropriateness.

The task asked learners to rate six expressions and an example was provided. Four of the six expressions were used by Roever (2005), and two came from common usage (e.g. *help yourself*). Two of the six expressions were also appropriate responses to contexts presented on the DCT (Task 3). All of the expressions also appeared in Task 1. Learners had 10 minutes for this task. The example that was presented to the learners appears in (5).

(5) Modified VKS
Instructions: Choose the ONE answer that best describes your knowledge. Circle the letter.
Example: *A piece of cake*
(a) I don't remember having heard this expression before.
(b) I have heard this expression before, but I don't know what it means.
(c) I have heard this expression before, and I think it means _____
(d) I know this expression. It means   *Something is easy*
(e) I can use this expression in a conversation. Give an example: *I can do that. It's a piece of cake.*
If you do this section, please also do (d) above.

Given the order of presentation, the recognition task served as a priming task to the DCT and the modified VKS. Thus, when completing the third task, the learners had already seen items appropriate for use on the DCT; however, given that each task was collected immediately after completion, learners did not have access to the full list of expressions from the recognition task during the subsequent activities.

Analysis

The responses to all the tasks were recorded and analysed by instructional level. Responses to the self-report recognition task were coded for each expression individually as 'known' (indicated by circling) or 'unknown'. The total number of 'known' items for each level was calculated by dividing the number of known expressions by the number of respondents, yielding the percentage of respondents that reported recognizing the expression. Responses to the context identification tasks were tallied for each expression. Responses to the DCT were coded according to expressions and key parts of expressions. Responses to the VKS were first tallied for level of familiarity and then by expression supplied as for the DCT. The total number of occurrences of an expression was divided by the total number of responses yielding the percentage of use of an individual expression.

For purposes of comparison, only items that appeared on both the recognition task (Task 1) and were potential responses to the DCT (Task 3) were included in the analysis for this report. Expressions that were included on both the recognition and production tasks are found in (6).

(6)
    (a) Do you have a piece of paper I can borrow?
    (b) Can I leave a message?
    (c) No thanks, I'm full
    (d) Excuse me
    (e) No problem / It's OK / That's OK
    (f) You're welcome

The VKS (Task 4) also included the expressions in (6c) *No thanks, I'm full* and (6d) *Excuse me* and these are also discussed in the results. The context identification task (Task 2) did not discriminate among items, and thus is not discussed in the results section.

Results

The results show that learners reported high rates of recognition, but even with priming of the recognition task (Task 1) to the DCT (Task 3), they show much lower rates of production.

Recognition

Of the eight formulas discussed in this chapter, seven were reported as recognised by 100% of the learners in Levels 5 and 7. Level 6 reported recognising six at 100%, with one each at 90% and 95%. All of the Level 4 learners (100%) also reported that they recognised two formulas, 93% reported recognising three others, and between 79% and 86% of the Level 4 learners reported recognising the remaining three (Table 11.1).

Table 11.1 Recognition of formulas by percent of respondents

	Level			
Expression	4	5	6	7
Do you have a piece of paper I can borrow?	79%	100%	90%	100%
Can I leave a message?	86%	100%	100%	100%
No thanks, I'm full	93%	100%	100%	100%
Excuse me	100%	100%	100%	100%
You're welcome	86%	100%	100%	100%
No problem	100%	92%	95%	100%
It's okay	93%	100%	100%	100%
That's okay	93%	100%	100%	92%

DCT responses

In contrast to the consistently high levels of self-reported recognition at each level, fewer learners actually produced the targeted formulas. Although 79% of the learners in Level 4, 90% of the learners in Level 6, and 100% of the learners in Levels 5 and 7 reported recognizing 'Do you have a piece of paper I can borrow?' in response to the paper borrowing scenario, only two learners attempted to use that expression. One learner (in Level 5) used it correctly, and the other learner (in Level 6) broke it into two sentences (*Do you have a piece of paper? Can I borrow?*). As Table 11.2 shows, learners favoured verbs other than *borrow*, a result also reported by Blum-Kulka and Levenston (1987) for learners of L2 Hebrew. No single expression or verb emerged as a clear favourite of the learners.

Reported rates of recognition for *Can I leave a message?* in the telephone scenario were even higher than the reported rates of recognition for *Do you have a piece of paper I could borrow?* 86% of the learners in Level 4 and all of the learners in Levels 5–7 reported recognising this expression

Table 11.2 Production responses to scenarios 1–3 by percent use

Expression or key words	Level			
	4	5	6	7
Do you have a piece of paper I can borrow?				
Borrow	50%	23%	38%	35%
Give	36%	62%	43%	27%
Lend	0%	15%	10%	8%
Other	14%	0%	10%	31%
Can I leave a message?				
Modal+I leave a message	43%	46%	71%	46%
Modal you	43%	31%	9%	46%
Imperative	7%	8%	14%	8%
No thanks, I'm full				
No thanks, I'm full	0%	8%	29%	15%
No thanks	33%	38%	57%	30%
Thank you but	14%	15%	24%	23%
Thank you	35%	8%	5%	39%
Sorry	0%	15%	0%	8%
I'm full	62%	46%	52%	54%
I'm (intensifier) full	0%	15%	14%	8%
I am full	15%	15%	14%	23%

Note. Italics indicate the expression used in the recognition task (Task 1).

(Table 11.2). Nevertheless, exact usage of *Can I leave a message?* was low, at 13% overall. However, if the formula is understood, following Nattinger and DeCarrico (1992), as combining a modal expression (*can/could/may*) with speaker orientation (*I leave a message*), we see that modal + speaker orientation is used approximately 43–46% of the time by Levels 4, 5, and 7, and 71% by Level 6 (Table 11.2). Hearer-oriented expressions (*could you, will you*) strongly compete in all levels except 6, with the imperative a weak third.

Responses to the scenario in which a host offers a guest more food suggest that learners may construct responses in parts. A high of 93% of the Level 4 learners and 100% of Levels 5–7 report recognition of

Recognition and Production of Formulas in L2 Pragmatics 215

Table 11.3 Production responses to scenarios 4–6 by percent use

Expression or key words	Level			
	4	5	6	7
Use of alerters				
Excuse me	43%	54%	43%	46%
Excuse me + sorry	43%	8%	14%	15%
Sorry	7%	0%	9%	8%
I'm sorry to interrupt you	0%	0%	19%	0%
Responses to a minor infraction				
No problem	21%	39%	24%	8%
That's OK	14%	0%	14%	15%
It's OK	23%	29%	23%	0%
Never mind	0%	23%	5%	0%
Don't worry	7%	8%	10%	0%
Minimisers				
You (x) welcome	42%	85%	71%	61%
No problem	14%	8%	5%	15%
My pleasure	7%	0%	5%	8%
Not at all	0%	0%	10%	0%

this expression. Whereas very few learners responded with the targeted *No thanks, I'm full*, with Level 6 again showing the highest score at 29% of the responses, many more learners used either *no thanks* (highest score of 57% in Level 6) or a variant of *I am full* (a high of 85% in Level 7), but not both (Table 11.2). Learners seem to treat *I (x) full* as the key component of the response in this scenario.

The next three scenarios were intended to elicit very brief formulas. Of the learners, 100% report recognising *excuse me*, whereas only 43–54% use it to attract the clerk's attention in Scenario 4 (Table 11.3). Responses to an apology for a minor infraction (Scenario 5) may involve expressions such as *it's okay, that's okay*, and *no problem* which learners report recognising at very high levels. In Scenario 6, in which the speaker has given a ride to someone who lives next door, a minimiser such as *no problem* might be an appropriate response to an expression of gratitude. Whereas both *you're welcome* and *no problem* show high rates

Table 11.4 Production of *you* (*x*) *welcome* on DCT (item 4) by percent use

Expression or key words	Level			
	4	5	6	7
You're welcome	21%	54%	52%	46%
You are welcome	14%	31%	19%	15%
You welcome	1%	0%	0%	0%

of recognition (86–100% and 92–100%, respectively), only *you (x) welcome* is used with frequency (42–85%), and *no problem* shows very little use (5–15%). Even in the case of the relatively simple *you're welcome*, as Table 11.4 shows, only 21–54% of the learners produce the contracted form of the recognition task, while 19–31% use the full form *you are welcome*.

Modified VKS

The modified VKS offered an opportunity to investigate self-reported recognition and production in the same task. The modified VKS shared two items with the recognition task and the DCT, *no thanks I'm full* and *excuse me*.

The responses to the VKS suggest learners know what *no thanks, I'm full* means. However, 10% of all learners, or 17% (6/35) of those learners who supplied examples in part (e), 'I can use this expression in a conversation', used *I'm full* without the thanking component, even though the complete expression appeared on the task. This corroborates the findings on the DCT which suggest the learners take the concept 'full' to be the core of the expression and build around that.

(7) Production responses using *full* on the modified VKS
   (a) Level 4
       The foods are very good, but I'm full
       I can't eat too much, I'm full
   (b) Level 6
       It's very delicious, but I'm full
       I'm sorry, but I'm full now
   (c) Level 7
       I am very thankful to you but sully, I am full.
       I am full, I am not going to eat more

In contrast, *excuse me* is used more idiomatically in the DCT and in the examples on the modified VKS, but there is less agreement by the learners on what *excuse me* means. A number of learners identified *excuse me* as an alerter explaining 'if somebody is interrupted and you want to be polite' (Learner 6.02) or 'an expression before you are going to do something unexpecting and botherable' (Learner 6.21).

The most common alternative interpretation is 'sorry', with 26% of all learners offering that interpretation in part (d), 'I know this expression. It means___.' The close relation of *excuse me* and *sorry* has been known for some time, first identified by Borkin and Reinhart (1978) in a paper entitled 'Excuse me and I'm sorry'. The interpretation and example provided by a single learner can provide different pictures of the learner's understanding of a formula: For example, target-like interpretations of *excuse me* are sometimes accompanied by examples in which the formula is employed in a manner that does not entirely match the tone of the interpretation, as shown in (8) and (9).

(8) Explanation: 'Some kind of information that please accept my interruption on conversation or walking'
Example: Excuse me. You are in my way now. (Learner 6.08)
(9) Explanation: 'Please allow me to bother you.'
Example: Excuse me, but would you please shut up here? (Learner 6.13)

The importance of using various methods to elicit knowledge of expressions is that it reveals that the targeted knowledge is multi-layered. Recognition, articulation of meaning, production of form, and use all seem to develop at different rates even for individual learners (cf. Shibata & Hurtig, this volume).

Discussion

This study set out to investigate the reason that learners do not seem to use formulas in pragmatic production tasks, focusing specifically on recognition of expressions. It addressed two questions: Do learners report recognising expressions in recognition tasks? and Do learners use those same expressions in production tasks? Learners reported very high rates of recognition, but they produced the same expressions at much lower rates. The instructional level of the learners seemed to influence the self-reported recognition with Level 4 learners reporting lower rates than Levels 5–7. There was not a clear increase in the use of expressions by level, but the groups are relatively small, and no statistical tests were conducted. Although these findings should be considered preliminary and open to further investigation through more rigorous tasks, they bear discussion to that end.

There are two possible interpretations of the first result – that learners recognise the formulas tested – and both lead to refining the tasks: either the self-report of recognition was too generous as a task of recognition, and it overestimates the learners' recognition of the expressions or the task was appropriate, and the self-report accurately represents the learners' recognition.

If we assume the former interpretation – that self-report of recognition seems to yield a very generous assessment of what learners recognise – then the recognition task needs to be revised. Although it has the advantage of allowing learners to respond to a large number of items in a short time, more rigorous tasks like the modified VKS may need to be used in lieu of self-report alone. Recognition tasks could be also be paired with multiple-choice questionnaires like those used by Roever (2005), Rose (1994), and Rose and Ono (1995) in L2 pragmatics, and Schmitt et al. (2004) in general formula research. Responses on multiple-choice questionnaires could then be compared to production. A final adjustment could be made to the mode of delivery. All studies so far have asked learners to identify written expressions. Because the study of L2 pragmatics is essentially concerned with conversational formulas, and conversation is spoken, the recognition (and production) tasks should be listening (and speaking) tasks (Bardovi-Harlig, 2006b). A listening-based recognition task could yield more modest self-reports.

The second task, context identification, did not discriminate among items, and therefore was not informative. The contexts turned out to be too open, and respondents saw the 'on campus' setting as a place where they might hear all of the expressions; 'television' was also frequently cited. Context identification might be useful if further refined. Learners could be asked to evaluate an expression or a range of expressions for their appropriateness or felicity in a single explicit (linguistic) environment (Dekydtspotter & Edmonds, personal communication, October 2005), thus both constraining the context task and avoiding the problem of having to reject alternatives, as is the case with the multiple-choice task.

In comparing the results from multiple-choice questionnaires (Roever, 2005), we see that the selection rates are lower than those for the recognition task, but higher than those for the production tasks. Comparing the recognition task and the DCT to the multiple-choice questionnaire for the three DCT scenarios that are directly comparable shows that learners report recognising formulas without context to a greater extent than they can select them given a context in a multiple-choice questionnaire. The targeted formulas are selected on the multiple-choice questionnaire fully constructed, with no formally close distracters, at higher rates than they are produced by learners. *Can I leave a message* was selected by learners in 74% of the responses to the multiple-choice questionnaire (compared to 13% exact production on the DCT). *No thanks, I'm full* was selected in 67% of the responses (compared to 29% production) and *that's ok* was selected 57% (compared to 15% production).

If we assume the latter interpretation, that learner self-report yields an adequate picture of familiarity, then we must still explain why learners do not use the expressions in production tasks. (Learners did report that some formulas on the task such as *my bad* and *think nothing of it* were unfamiliar.) Again, there are at least two possible answers: The first lies in the format of the production task and the second calls on the learners' difficulty in accessing even familiar formulas to explain the recognition–production disparity.

The format of the production task allows learners to use alternatives to the primed and targeted expressions. Even when learners are primed for formulas use through other tasks, we still have to deal with the fact that on a task like a DCT, learners have many options for how to respond. This is always the case with pragmatic production tasks (whether DCTs, role plays, or spontaneous conversation), but it is even more obvious in this study, where I have attempted to compare recognition and production. On the one hand, this could (and possibly should) lead to the development of another production task in which a learner would be more constrained to produce a formula if they knew one. In a study of the knowledge of formulas in second language acquisition more generally, Schmitt et al. (2004) used a contextualised c-test in which the first letter(s) of the content words in a formula were given (e.g. fi__ of a__ is given for the target formula *first of all*). Such a task could be adapted for use with the type of DCT scenarios currently used in interlanguage pragmatics research. For example, in the telephone scenario (DCT item 2), the targeted response, *Can I leave a message?* might be cued as C__ I le__ a m_____? This type of production is highly controlled, but especially in comparison with the work of Schmitt and colleagues, may yield an informative picture of control of pragmatic formulas. A less controlled, but promising format, would be to present a frame. Continuing with the same example, a response may be cued with speaker-orientation *Can I____?* (e.g. *Can I leave a message?*), hearer orientation *Could you____?* (e.g. *Could you take a message?*), or neutral orientation *Would it____?* (e.g. *Would it be possible to leave a message?*).

Pursuing the second explanation, recognition and production seem to be linked by an intermediate step of retrieval. Cohen's (1996) term *sociolinguistic ability* – defined as a speaker's control over his or her selection of language forms used to realise a speech act – reminds us that access is part of pragmatic competence. Established psycholinguistic measurements, such as response time to retrieval, may help distinguish levels of familiarity in a recognition task or ease or difficulty of accessing a formula in a production task.

Regardless of the interpretation of the task that we adopt, the selection of the expressions needs to be carefully considered. In addition to selecting expressions that are attested in the responses of native speakers (as was done here), the type of expression must also be taken into account. Formulaic expressions run the gamut from unanalysable idioms to rather loose collocations (Nattinger & DeCarrico, 1992). Pragmatic formulas fall somewhere in between. The target expressions should either be equally conventional or vary by degree of conventionality, which is controlled. In their study of L2 formula knowledge, Schmitt *et al.* (2004) consulted word frequency lists, and although an equivalent resource does not exist for pragmatics, a similar attempt should be made to ascertain the frequency of target pragmatic expressions. This procedure would likely eliminate the target expression *Do you have a piece of paper I could borrow* does not seem to be highly conventional. (There do seem to be at least two collocations in the expression – *piece of paper* and *(that) I could borrow* – and at least the latter should be relevant for making requests for loans of certain types.) Han (personal communication, April 2006) also suggested checking ESL/EFL textbooks as sources of both target-like and non-target-like sources of formula use.

The learners' responses to the production tasks also lead to the observation that expressions may be built up by learners around key lexical items, in a process similar to what Peters (1983) called *fusion*. This observation – that learners build up formulas – suggests an additional avenue of investigation. The responses to the DCT suggest that learners build up the formulas *no thanks, I'm full* around the semantic centre, *I'm full*. Similarly, as noted by Blum-Kulka and Levenston (1987), learners in this task did not use *borrow* in the request scenario (e.g. *can I borrow x?, do you have an x I can borrow?*); in addition, learners who do use *borrow* show some difficulties in sorting out agent and recipient roles. These data suggest that, at least in some cases, learners build expressions rather than use formulas as unanalysed wholes. New research designs (including longitudinal observation) would have to be implemented to investigate whether expressions are built up or learned whole. A well-known alternative interpretation to the building of formulas through fusion is the breaking down of formulas through analysis (N. Ellis, 2002). Although it is possible that learners also move from formulas to rule-governed production, this process is less consistent with these data because the analysis of formulas would not lead to the pattern observed of recognition without corresponding production.

Conclusion

As the reader is by now aware, the research question posed at the outset of the study, whether learners recognise target formulas, and how this influences production, cannot be answered satisfactorily with the present data. Both the recognition and the production tasks need to be further modified. The VKS is a promising instrument for one task in a set of tasks, but is not likely to be sufficient alone for the study of formula use in pragmatics because the production portion is intentionally open-ended. The results also suggest that the recognition – production relation that this study set out to investigate is too simplistic and it must admit an intervening step of recognition – access – production. Refinement of existing tasks, incorporation of standard psycholinguistic measurements, and development of new tasks is a crucial step in the investigation of the relation of recognition, access, and production in the development of L2 pragmatic competence.

Acknowledgements

Thanks go to the Second Language Studies research group at Indiana University for helpful comments on this study. I am indebted to Amanda Edmonds for extensive and insightful discussion of this project.

Appendix

Part I: DCT

Please fill in the blank with what you would say in the situation.

(1) You are in class, but have forgotten your notebook. You ask your friend for some paper.
(2) You call your friend, John, but his roommate answers the phone and tells you that your friend is not home. You would like the roommate to tell John something. (Roever, 2005, item 309)

(3) You are having dinner at a friend's house. Your friend offers you more food, but you couldn't possibly eat another bite. (Roever, 2005, item 305)
(4) You go to the bookstore between classes for some pens and paper, but you can't find what you want. You need help, but the student-employees are having a friendly conversation with each other. You have a test in your next class, so you can't wait until they finish.
(5) A woman on a crowded bus steps on your foot, but it didn't hurt you. She says, 'I'm sorry'. (Roever, 2005, item 312).
(6) You drive a friend home in your car. She lives in the same dorm as you. She says 'Thank you'.

Part II: Modified VKS (Vocabulary Knowledge Scale) for expressions (items used for comparison)

(2) *No thanks, I'm full*
  (a) I don't remember having heard this expression before.
  (b) I have heard this expression before, but I don't know what it means.
  (c) I have heard this expression before, and I think it means _____
  (d) I know this expression. It means _____
  (e) I can use this expression in a conversation: _____

  (If you do this section, please also do (d).)   →
  go to next page

(6) *Excuse me*
  (a) I don't remember having heard this expression before.
  (b) I have heard this expression before, but I don't know what it means.
  (c) I have heard this expression before, and I think it means _____
  (d) I know this expression. It means _____
  (e) I can use this expression in a conversation:_____

  (If you do this section, please also do (d).)

References

Abercrombie, D. (1967) *The Elements of General Phonetics*. Chicago: Aldine Publishing Company.
Achiba, M. (2003) *Learning to Request in a Second Language: A Study of Child Interlanguage Pragmatics*. Clevedon, England: Multilingual Matters.
Allport, A. (1988) What concept of consciousness? In A.J. Marcel and E. Bisiach (eds) *Consciousness in Contemporary Science* (pp. 159–182). London: Clarendon Press.
Anderson-Hsieh, J., Johnson, R. and Koehler, K. (1992) The relationship between native speaker judgments of nonnative pronunciation and deviance in segmentals, prosody, and syllable structure. *Language Learning* 42, 529–555.
Armand, F. (2000) Le rôle des capacités métalinguistiques et de la compétence langagière orale dans l'apprentissage de la lecture en français langue première et seconde. *The Canadian Modern Language Review/La Revue Canadienne des Langues Vivantes* 56, 469–495.
Armand, F. (2005) Capacités métalinguistiques d'élèves immigrants nouvellement arrivés situation de grand retard scolaire. *Revue des Sciences de l'éducation* 31, 441–469.
Armand, F., Lefrançois, P., Baron, A., Gomez, M.-C. and Nuckle, S. (2004) Improving reading and writing learning in underprivileged pluriethnic settings. *British Journal of Educational Psychology* 74, 437–459.
Athanasopoulos, P. (2001) L2 acquisition and bilingual conceptual structure. Unpublished master's thesis, University of Essex, United Kingdom.
Athanasopoulos, P. (2006) Effects of the grammatical representation of number on cognition in bilinguals. *Bilingualism: Language and Cognition* 9 (1), 89–96.
Athanasopoulos, P., Sasaki, M. and Cook, V.J. (2004) *Do bilinguals think differently from monolinguals?* Paper presented at EUROSLA, San Sebastian, September 2004.
Ayusawa, T. (2003) Acquisition of Japanese accent and intonation by foreign learners. *Journal of Phonetic Society of Japan* 7 (2), 47–58.
Ayusawa, T. and Taniguchi, S. (1991) Nihongo onsee no inritsuteki tokuchoo [Prosodic properties in Japanese]. In O. Mizutani *et al.* (eds) *Nihongo no inritsu ni mirareru bogo no kanshoo – Onkyoo onseegakuteki taishoo kenkyuu – <D1-han> Nihongo onsee ni okeru inritsuteki tokuchoo no jittai to sono kyooiku ni kansuru soogooteki kenkyuu – Gaikokujin o taishoo to suru nihongo kyooiku ni okeru onsee kyooiku no hoosaku ni kansuru kenkyuu – Heesee 2 nendo Kenkyuu seika hookokusho [L1 transfer in Japanese prosody – Comparative studies of acoustic analysis – <Group D1> Studies of characteristics of Japanese prosody and teaching the prosody – Studies of strategies of teaching Japanese prosody for foreign learners – Reports of the studies in Heesee 2]* (pp. 1–24).
Baddeley, A. (2003) Working memory and language: An overview. *Journal of Communication Disorders* 36 (3), 189–208.

Bailey, N., Madden, C. and Krashen, S. (1974) Is there a 'natural sequence' in adult second language learning? *Language Learning* 24 (2), 235–243.
Balcom, P. (2003) Crosslinguistic influence of L2 English on middle constructions in L1 French. In V.J. Cook (ed.) *Effects of the L2 on the L1*. Clevedon: Multilingual Matters.
Barcroft, J. (2002) Semantic and structural elaboration in L2 lexical acquisition. *Language Learning* 52, 323–363.
Barcroft, J. (2004) Theoretical and methodological issues in research on semantic and structural elaboration in lexical acquisition. In B. VanPatten, J. Williams, S. Rott and M. Overstreet (eds) *Form–Meaning Connections in Second Language Acquisition* (pp. 219–234). Mahwah, NJ: Lawrence Erlbaum.
Barcroft, J. (2006) Can writing a new word detract from learning it? More negative effects of forced output during vocabulary learning. *Second Language Research* 24, 487–497.
Bardovi-Harlig, K. (1992a) The relationship of form and meaning: A cross-sectional study of tense and aspect in the interlanguage of learners of English as a second language. *Applied Psycholinguistics* 13, 253–278.
Bardovi-Harlig, K. (1992b) The use of adverbials and natural order in the development of temporal expression. *International Review of Applied Linguistics* 30, 299–320.
Bardovi-Harlig, K. (2006a) Interlanguage development: Main routes and individual paths. *AILA Review* 19, 69–82.
Bardovi-Harlig, K. (2006b) On the role of formulas in the acquisition of L2 pragmatics. In K. Bardovi-Harlig, C. Félix-Brasdefer and A.S. Omar (eds) *Pragmatics and Language Learning* (Vol. 11, pp. 1–28). Honolulu, HI: Second Language Teaching and Curriculum Center, University of Hawaii, Manoa.
Bardovi-Harlig, K. and Dörnyei, Z. (1998) Do language learners recognize pragmatic violations? Pragmatic vs. grammatical awareness in instructed L2 learning. *TESOL Quarterly* 32, 233–259.
Barss, A. (1986) Chains and anaphoric dependence. PhD thesis, MIT.
Barss, A. (1988) Paths, connectivity, and featureless empty categories. In A. Sardinaletti, G. Cinque and G. Giusti (eds) *Constituent Structure* (pp. 9–34). Dordrecht: Foris.
Barss, A. (1993) Sentence processing and the grammar of anaphora. In G. Altmann and R. Shillcock (eds) *Cognitive Models of Speech Processing* (pp. 401–451). Hilldale, NJ: Lawrence Erlbaum.
Barss, A. (1994) Derivations and reconstruction. *Studies in the Linguistic Sciences* 24 (1), 19–38.
Barss, A. (2001) Syntactic reconstruction effects. In M. Baltin and C. Collins (eds) *The Handbook of Contemporary Syntactic Theory* (pp. 670–696). Oxford: Blackwell.
Bassetti, B. (2004) Second language reading and second language awareness in English-speaking learners of Chinese as a foreign language. Unpublished doctoral dissertation, University of Essex, United Kingdom.
Bautier-Castaing, E. (1977) Comparative acquisition of French syntax by francophone and non-francophone children. *Etudes de Linguistique Appliquée* 27, 19–41.
Beckman, M.E. (1992) Evidence for speech rhythm across languages. In Y. Tohkura, E. Vatikiotis-Bateson and Y. Sagisaka (eds) *Speech Perception, Production and Linguistic Structure* (pp. 457–463). Tokyo: Ohmsha.

Beckman, M.E. (1996) The parsing of prosody. *Language and Cognitive Process* 11, 17–67.
Belletti, A., Bennati, E. and Sorace, A. (2005) Revising the null parameter from an L2 developmental perspective: Pronominal subjects and postverbal subjects in L2 near native Italian. Paper presented at the XXXI Generative Grammar Meeting. Rome, February 2005.
Bennett, S. (1994) Interpretation of English reflexives by adolescent speakers of Serbo-Croatian. *Second Language Research* 10 (2), 125–156.
Bennett, S. and Progovac, L. (1998) Morphological status of reflexives in second language acquisition. In S. Flynn, G. Martohardjono and W. O'Neil (eds) *The Generative Study of Second Language Acquisition* (pp. 187–214). Mahwah, NJ: Lawrence Erlbaum.
Berent, G.P. (1996) The acquisition of English syntax by deaf learners. In W. Ritchie and T. Bhatia (eds) *Handbook of Second Language Acquisition* (pp. 469–506). San Diego: Academic Press.
Berent, G.P. (2004) Sign language-spoken language bilingualism: Code-mixing and mode-mixing by ASL-English bilinguals. In T.K. Bhatia and W.C. Ritchie (eds) *The Handbook of Bilingualism* (pp. 312–335). Malden, MA: Blackwell Publishing.
Berent, G.P. (2005a) Coding deaf and hard-of-hearing students' successful and unsuccessful English productions. In D. Janáková (ed.) *Proceedings 2004: Teaching English to Deaf and Hard-of-Hearing Students at Secondary and Tertiary Levels of Education in the Czech Republic* (pp. 109–115). Prague, Czech Republic: Eurolex Bohemia.
Berent, G.P. (2005b) Input-enhancement in teaching English to deaf and hard-of-hearing students. In D. Janáková (ed.) *Proceedings 2004: Teaching English to Deaf and Hard-of-Hearing Students at Secondary and Tertiary Levels of Education in the Czech Republic* (pp. 75–87). Prague, Czech Republic: Eurolex Bohemia.
Berent, G.P., Kelly, R.R., Aldersley, S., Schmitz, K.L., Khalsa, B.K., Panara, J. and Keenan, S. (2007) Focus-on-form instructional methods promote deaf college students' improvement of English grammar. *Journal of Deaf Studies and Deaf Education* 12, 8–24.
Berent, G.P., Samar, V.J., Kelly, R., Berent, R., Bochner, J., Albertini, J. and Sacken, J. (1996). Validity of indirect assessment of writing competency for deaf and hard-of-hearing college students. *Journal of Deaf Studies and Deaf Education* 1, 167–178.
Bialystok, E. (1988) Levels of bilingualism and levels of linguistic awareness. *Developmental Psychology* 24, 560–567.
Bialystok, E. (1990) Connaissances linguistiques et contrôle des activités de langage. In D. Gaonac'h (ed.) *Acquisition et Utilisation d'une Langue Étrangère: l'Approche Cognitive* (pp. 50–58). Paris: Hachette.
Bialystok, E. (1993) Metalinguistic awareness: The development of children's representations of language. In C. Pratt and A.F. Garton (eds) *Systems of Representation in Children. Development and Use* (pp. 211–233). New York: John Wiley and Sons.
Bialystok, E. (1994) Analysis and control in the development of second language proficiency. *Studies in Second Language Acquisition* 17, 157–168.
Bialystok, E. (2001a) Metalinguistic aspects of bilingual processing. *Annual Review of Applied Linguistics* 21, 169–181.

Bialystok, E. (2001b) *Bilingualism in Development: Language, Literacy, & Cognition.* New York: Cambridge University Press.
Bialystok, E. and Ryan, E.B. (1985a) Toward a definition of metalinguistic. *Merrill-Palmer Quarterly* 31, 229–251.
Bialystok, E. and Ryan, E.B. (1985b) A metacognitive framework for the development of first and second language skills. In D.L. Forrest-Pressley, G.E. Mackinon and T.G. Waller (eds) *Meta-cognition, Cognition, and Human Performance* (pp. 207–252). New York: Academic Press.
Bialystok, E. and Ryan, E.B. (1985c) On precision and the virtue of simplicity in metalinguistics: A reply to Menyuk. *Merrill-Palmer Quarterly* 31, 261–264.
Bilmes, J. (1986) *Discourse and Behavior.* New York: Plenum.
Birdsong, D. (1989) *Metalinguistic Performance and Interlinguistic Competence.* Berlin: Springer-Verlag.
Bjork, R.A. (1994) Memory and metamemory considerations in the training of human beings. In J. Metcalfe and A. Shimamura (eds) *Metacognition: Knowing about Knowing* (pp. 185–205). Cambridge, MA: MIT Press.
Bjork, R.A. and Linn, M.C. (2006) The science of learning and the learning of science: Introducing desirable difficulties. *APS Observer* 19. On WWW at http://www.psychologicalscience.org/observer/getArticle.cfm?id = 1952. Accessed 04.10.06.
Blackmore, A.M. and Pratt, C. (1997) Grammatical awareness and reading in Grade 1 children. *Merrill-Palmer Quarterly* 43, 567–590.
Blamey, P.J. (2003) Development of spoken language by deaf children. In M. Marschark and P.E. Spencer (eds) *Oxford Handbook of Deaf Studies, Language, and Education* (pp. 232–246). New York: Oxford University Press.
Blaxton, T.A. (1989) Investigating dissociations among memory measures: Support for a transfer-appropriate processing framework. *Journal of Experimental Psychology: Learning, Memory, Cognition* 15, 657–668.
Bley-Vroman, R. (1983) The comparative fallacy in interlanguage studies: The case of systematicity. *Language Learning* 33 (1), 1–17.
Blum-Kulka, S. and Levenston, W.A. (1987) Lexico-grammatical pragmatic indicators. *Studies in Second Language Acquisition* 9, 155–170.
Blum-Kulka, S. and Olshtain, E. (1986) Too many words: Length of utterance and pragmatic failure. *Studies in Second Language Acquisition* 8, 165–180.
Bongaerts, T., van Summeren, C., Planken, B. and Schils, E. (1997) Age and ultimate attainment in the pronunciation of a foreign language. *Studies in Second Language Acquisition* 19 (4), 447–465.
Borkin, A. and Reinhart, S.M. (1978) Excuse me and I'm sorry. *TESOL Quarterly* 12, 57–70.
Bowey, J.A. (1986) Syntactic awareness and verbal performance from preschool to fifth grade. *Journal of Psycholinguistic Research* 13, 285–308.
Bowles, M. (2003) The effects of textual input enhancement on language learning: An online/offline study of fourth-semester Spanish students. In P. Kempchinski and P. Pineros (eds) *Theory, Practice, and Acquisition: Papers from the 6th Hispanic Linguistic Symposium and the 5th Conference on the Acquisition of Spanish & Portuguese* (pp. 359–411). Somerville, MA: Cascadilla Press.
Braidi, S.M. (2002) Reexamining the role of recasts in native-speaker/nonnative-speaker interactions. *Language Learning* 52 (1), 1–42.

Brock, C., Crookes, G., Day, R. and Long, M. (1986) The differential effects of corrective feedback in native speaker/non-native speaker conversation. In R. Day (ed.) *Talking to Learn: Conversation in Second Language Acquisition* (pp. 327–351). Rowley, MA: Newbury House.
Brown, R. (1973) *A First Language*. Cambridge, MA: Harvard University Press.
Brown, T.S. and Perry, F.L. (1991) A comparison of three learning strategies for ESL vocabulary acquisition. *TESOL Quarterly* 25, 655–670.
Bryant, P., Devine, M., Ledward, A. and Nunes, T. (1997) Spelling with apostrophes and understanding possession. *British Journal of Educational Psychology* 67, 91–110.
Cadierno, T. and Lund, K. (2004) Cognitive linguistics and second language acquisition: Motion events in a typological framework. In B. VanPatten, J. Williams and S. Rott (eds) *Form–Meaning Connections in Second Language Acquisitions* (pp. 139–154). Lawrence Erlbaum Associates, Inc.
Campbell, D.T. and Stanley, J.C. (1963) *Experimental and Quasi-Experimental Designs for Research*. Chicago, IL: Rand McNally College Publishing Co.
Caramazza, A. and Brones, I. (1979) Lexical access in bilinguals. *Bulletin of the Psychonomic Society* 13, 212–214.
Carlisle, J.F., Beeman, M., Davis, L. and Spharim, G. (1999) Relationship of metalinguistic capabilities and reading achievement for children who are becoming bilingual. *Applied Psycholinguistics* 20, 459–478.
Carpenter, H., Jeon, S., MacGregor, D. and Mackey, A. (2006) Learners' interpretations of recasts. *Studies in Second Language Acquisition* 28 (2), 209–236.
Carroll, S. (1999) Adults' sensitivity to different sorts of input. *Language Learning* 49, 37–92.
Carroll, S. (2001) *Input and Evidence*. Amsterdam: John Benjamins.
Carroll, S. (2005) Input and SLA: Adults' sensitivity to different sorts of cues to French gender. In R. DeKeyser (ed.) *Grammatical Development in Language Learning* (pp. 79–138). Best of Language Learning Series, Malden, MA: Blackwell.
Chiappe, P. and Siegel, L.S. (1999) Phonological awareness and reading acquisition in English and Punjabi-speaking Canadian children. *Journal of Educational Psychology* 20, 275–303.
Cho, Y.-M., Lee, H.S., Schulz, C., Sohn, H.-M., and Sohn, S.-O. (2001) *Integrated Korean: Beginning 1*. KLEAR Textbooks in Korean Language. Honolulu: University of Hawaii Press.
Chomsky, N. (1981) *Lectures on Government and Binding*. Dordrecht: Foris.
Chomsky, N. (1986) *Knowledge of Language: Its Nature, Origin and Use*. NY: Praeger.
Chomsky, N. (1993) A minimalist program for linguistic theory. In K. Hale and J. Kester (eds) *The View from Building 20: Essays in Honor of Sylvain Bromberger* (pp. 1–50). Cambridge, MA: MIT Press.
Chomsky, N. (1995) *The Minimalist Program*. Cambridge, MA: MIT Press.
Chun, D.M. (2002) *Discourse Intonation in L2: From Theory and Research to Practice*. Philadelphia: John Benjamins Publishing Company.
Cinque, G. (1982) *Constructions with Left-Peripheral Phrases, 'Connectedness,' Move A and ECP*. Ms., University of Venice.
Clahsen, H. (1984) The acquisition of German word order: A test case for cognitive approaches to L2 development. In R. Anderson (ed.) *Second Languages* (pp. 219–242). Rowley, MA: Newbury House.

Clahsen, H. and Felser, C. (2006) Grammatical processing in language learners. *Applied Psycholinguistics* 27 (1), 3–42.
Cleeremans, A. (2001) Conscious and unconscious processes in cognition. In N.J. Smelser and P.B. Baltes (eds) *International Encyclopedia of Social and Behavioral Sciences* (Vol. 4, pp. 2584–2589). London: Elsevier.
Cleeremans, A. (2005) Computational correlates of consciousness. *Progress in Brain Research* 150, 81–98.
Clements, G.N. and Keyser, S.J. (1983) From CV phonology: A generative theory of the syllable. In J.A. Goldsmith (ed.) (1999) *Phonological Theory: The Essential Readings* (pp. 185–200). Malden, MA: Blackwell Publishers.
Cohen, A.D. (1996) Developing the ability to perform speech acts. *Studies in Second Language Acquisition* 18, 253–267.
Cole, P. and Sung, L. (1994) Head movement and long-distance reflexives. *Linguistic Inquiry* 25 (3), 355–406.
Commission Scolaire de Montréal (2005) *Profil sociolinguistique des élèves du secteur des jeunes de la Commission scolaire de Montréal – Année scolaire 2004–2005*. On WWW at http://www.csdm.qc.ca/CSDM/pdf/sociolinguistique.pdf.
Cook, V.J. (1990) The I-language approach and classroom observation. *English Language Teaching Documents* 133 (1), 71–80.
Cook, V.J. (1991) The poverty-of-the-stimulus argument and multi-competence. *Second Language Research* 7 (2), 103–117.
Cook, V.J. (1997) Monolingual bias in second language acquisition research. *Revista Canaria de Estudios Ingleses* 34, 35–50.
Cook, V.J. (1999) Going beyond the native speaker in language teaching. *TESOL Quarterly* 33 (2), 185–209.
Cook, V.J. (2001) Using the first language in the classroom. *Canadian Modern Language Review* 57 (3), 402–423.
Cook, V.J. (ed.) (2002) *Portraits of the L2 User*. Clevedon: Multilingual Matters.
Cook, V.J. (ed.) (2003) *Effects of the Second Language on the First*. Clevedon: Multilingual Matters.
Cook, V.J. (2004) *The English Writing System*, London: Edward Arnold.
Cook, V.J. (2006a) The nature of the L2 user: Language and community in second language acquisition. Plenary talk at EUROSLA, Antalya.
Cook, V.J. (2006b) Interlanguage, multi-competence and the problem of the 'second language.' *Rivista di Psicolinguistica Applicata* VI, 3.
Cook, V.J. (2007) The goals of ELT: Reproducing native-speakers or promoting multi-competence among second language users? In J. Cummins and C. Davison (eds) *Handbook on English Language Teaching* (pp. 237–248). Amsterdam: Kluwer.
Cook, V.J. (in press) Developing links between second language acquisition research and language teaching. In K. Knapp and B. Seidlhofer (eds) *Handbooks of Applied Linguistics Vol. 6: Foreign Language Communication and Learning*. Berlin: Mouton.
Cook, V.J. and Bassetti, B. (eds) (2005) *Second Language Writing Systems*, Clevedon: Multilingual Matters.
Cook, V.J., Bassetti, B., Kasai, C., Sasaki, M. and Takahashi, J.A. (2006) Do bilinguals have different concepts? The case of shape and material in Japanese L2 users of English. *International Journal of Bilingualism* 10 (2), 137–152.

Cook, V.J., Iarossi, E., Stellakis, N. and Tokumaru, Y. (2003) Effects of the second language on the syntactic processing of the first language. In V.J. Cook (ed.) *Effects of the Second Language on the First* (pp. 214–233). Clevedon: Multilingual Matters.
Cook, V.J., Kasai, C. and Sasaki, M. (2005) 'Syntactic differences of bilingual speakers: The case study of Japanese' poster presentation at EUROSLA, Dubrovnik.
Cook, V.J. and Newson, M. (2007) *Chomsky's Universal Grammar* (3rd edn). Oxford: Blackwell Publishing.
Coppieters, R. (1987) Competence differences between native and near-native speakers. *Language* 63 (3), 544–573.
Corder, S. (1967) The significance of learners' errors. *International Review of Applied Linguistics* 5, 161–170.
Corder, S. (1981) *Error Analysis and Interlanguage*. Oxford: Oxford University Press.
Correa, J. (2004) A avaliação da consciência sintática na criança: Uma análise metodológica. *Psicologia: Teoria e Pesquisa* 20, 69–75.
Coulmas, F. (1981) Introduction: Conversational routine. In F. Coulmas (ed.) *Conversational Routine: Explorations in Standardized Communication Situations and Prepatterned Speech* (pp. 1–17). The Hague: Mouton.
Cowan, R. and Hatasa, Y.A. (1994) Investigating the validity and reliability of native speaker and second-language learner judgments about sentences. In E.E. Tarone, S.M. Gass and A.D. Cohen (eds) *Research Methodology in Second-Language Acquisition* (pp. 287–302). Hillsdale, NJ: Lawrence Erlbaum Associates.
Craik, F.I.M. (2002) Levels of processing: Past, present ... and future? *Memory* 10, 305–318.
Craik, F.I.M. and Lockhart, R.S. (1972) Levels of processing: A framework for memory research. *Journal of Verbal Learning and Verbal Behavior* 11, 671–684.
Craik, F.I.M. and Tulving, E. (1975) Depth of processing and the retention of words in episodic memory. *Journal of Experimental Psychology: General* 104, 268–294.
Cuculick, J.A. and Kelly, R.R. (2003) Relating deaf students' reading and language scores at college entry to their degree completion rates. *American Annals of the Deaf* 148 (4), 279–286.
Culicover, P. (1997) *Principles and Parameters: An Introduction to Syntactic Theory*. Oxford: Oxford University Press.
Cummins, J. (1986) Empowering minority students: A framework for intervention. *Harvard Education Review* 56, 18–36.
Cummins, J. (1991) Interdependence of first- and second-language proficiency in bilingual children. In E. Bialystok (ed.) *Language Processing in Bilingual Children* (pp. 70–89). Cambridge: Cambridge University Press.
Cutler, A. (2001) Listening to a second language through the ears of a first. *Interpreting* 5, 1–18.
Dalrymple, M., Shieber, S. and Pereira, F. (1991) Ellipsis and higher-order unification. *Linguistics and Philosophy* 14 (4), 399–452.
Day, R., Chenoweth, N., Chun, A. and Luppescu, S. (1983) Foreign language learning and the treatment of spoken errors. *Language Learning and Communication* 2, 215–224.
de Bot, K. (1992) A bilingual production model: Levelt's 'speaking' model adapted. *Applied Linguistics* 13, 1–24.
De Groot, A.M.B. (2002) 'Lexical representation and lexical processing in the L2 user.' In V.J. Cook (ed.) *Portraits of the L2 User* (pp. 29–64). Clevedon: Multilingual Matters.

DeKeyser, R. (1995) Learning second language grammar rules: An experiment with a miniature linguistics system. *Studies in Second Language Acquisition* 17, 379–410.
DeKeyser, R. (1998) Beyond focus on form: Cognitive perspectives on learning and practicing second language grammar. In C. Doughty and J. Williams (eds) *Focus on Form in Classroom Second Language Acquisition* (pp. 42–63). Cambridge: Cambridge University Press.
DeKeyser, R. (2003) Implicit and explicit learning. In C. Doughty and M.H. Long (eds) *The Handbook of Second Language Acquisition* (pp. 313–348). Oxford: Blackwell Publishing.
DeKeyser, R. (2005) What makes learning second language grammar difficult? A review of issues. *Language Learning* 55, 1–25.
DeKeyser, R.M. (2007) Introduction: Situating the concept of practice. In R.M. DeKeyser (ed.) *Practice in a Second Language: Perspectives from Applied Linguistics and Cognitive Psychology*. Cambridge: Cambridge University Press.
Demont, E. (1994) Développement métalinguistique et apprentissage de la lecture. Unpublished doctoral thesis, Université de Bourgogne, Dijon.
Demont, E. and Gombert, J.E. (1996) Phonological awareness as a predictor of recoding skills and syntactic awareness as a predictor of comprehension skills. *British Journal of Educational Psychology* 66, 315–323.
Dempster, F.N. (1996) Distributing and managing the conditions of encoding and practice. In E.L. Bjork and R.A. Bjork (eds) *Memory* (pp. 317–344). San Diego: Academic Press.
de Saussure, F. (1976) *Cours de linguistique générale*. Edited by C. Bally and A. Sechehaye (1915) Critical edition by T. de Maurio Payothèque. Payot: Paris.
de Villiers, J.G. and de Villiers, P.A. (1972) Early judgments of semantic and syntactic acceptability by children. *Journal of Psycholinguistic Research* 1, 299–310.
de Villiers, J. and de Villiers, P. (1973) A cross-sectional study of the acquisition of grammatical morphemes in child speech. *Journal of Psycholinguistic Research* 2 (3), 267–278.
de Villiers, J.G. and de Villiers, P.A. (1974) Competence and performance in child language: Are children really competent to judge? *Journal of Child Language* 1, 11–22.
Doughty, C. (2001) Cognitive underpinnings of focus on form. In P. Robinson (ed.) *Cognition and Second Language Instruction* (pp. 206–238). Cambridge: Cambridge University Press.
Doughty, C. (2003) Instructed SLA: Constraints, compensation, and enhancement. In C. Doughty and M. Long (eds) *Handbook of Second Language Acquisition* (p. 298). Oxford: Blackwell.
Doughty, C. and Long, M. (2003) *Handbook of Second Language Acquisition*. Oxford: Blackwell.
Doughty, C. and Varela, E. (1998) Communicative focus on form. In C. Doughty and J. Williams (eds) *Focus on Form in Classroom Second Language Acquisition* (pp. 114–138). Cambridge: Cambridge University Press.
Doughty, C. and Williams, J. (eds) (1998a) *Focus on Form in Classroom Second Language Acquisition*. New York: Cambridge University Press.

Doughty, C. and Williams, J. (1998b) Pedagogical choices in focus on form. In C. Doughty and J. Williams (eds) *Focus on Form in Classroom Second Language Acquisition* (pp. 197–262). Cambridge: Cambridge University Press.

Doughty, C. and Williams, J. (1998c) Issues and terminology. In C. Doughty and J. Williams (eds) *Focus on Form in Classroom Second Language Acquisition* (pp. 1–11). New York: Cambridge University Press.

Doughty, C., Izumi, S., Maciukaite, S. and Zapata, G. (1999) *Recasts, Focused Recasts, and Models: Effects on L2 Spanish Word Order*. Paper presented at the Second Language Research Forum, University of Minnesota.

Dulay, H. and Burt, M. (1973) Should we teach children syntax? *Language Learning* 23 (2), 245–258.

Dulay, H.C., Burt, M. and Krashen, S. (1982) *Language Two*. Rowley, MA: Newbury House.

Edmondson, W. and House, J. (1991) Do learners talk too much? The waffle phenomenon in interlanguage pragmatics. In R. Phillipson, E. Kellerman, L. Selinker, M. Sharwood Smith and M. Swain (eds) *Foreign/Second Language Pedagogy Research: A Commemorative Volume for Claus Faerch* (pp. 273–287). Clevedon: Multilingual Matters.

Ellis, N.C. (2001) Memory for language. In P. Robinson (ed.) *Cognition and Second Language Instruction* (pp. 33–68). Cambridge: Cambridge University Press.

Ellis, N.C. (2002) Frequency effects in language acquisition: A review with implications for theories of implicit and explicit language acquisition. *Studies in Second Language Acquisition* 24 (2), 143–188.

Ellis, N.C. (2003) Constructions, chunking and connectionism: The emergence of second language structure. In C. Doughty and M.H. Long (eds) *The Handbook of Second Language Acquisition* (pp. 63–103). Oxford: Blackwell Publishing.

Ellis, N.C. (2005) At the interface: Dynamic interactions of explicit and implicit language knowledge. *Studies in Second Language Acquisition* 27 (2), 305–352.

Ellis, N.C. (2006a) Selective attention and transfer phenomena in L2 acquisition: Contingency, cue competition, salience, interference, overshadowing, blocking, and perceptual learning. *Applied Linguistics* 27 (2), 164–194.

Ellis, N.C. (2006b) Language acquisition as rational contingency learning. *Applied Linguistics* 27 (1), 1–24.

Ellis, N.C. and Larsen-Freeman, D. (2006) Language emergence: Implications for applied linguistics. *Applied Linguistics* 27 (4), 558–589.

Ellis, R. (1992) Learning to communicate in the classroom: A study of two language learners' requests. *Studies in Second Language Acquisition* 14, 1–23.

Ellis, R. (1994) A theory of instructed second language acquisition. In N. Ellis (ed.) *Implicit and Explicit Learning of Languages* (pp. 79–114). NY: Academic Press.

Ellis, R. (2001a) Preemptive focus on form in the ESL classroom. *TESOL Quarterly* 35 (4), 407–432.

Ellis, R. (2001b) Investigating form-focused instruction. *Language Learning* 51 (Suppl. 1), 1–46.

Ellis, R. (2002) The place of grammar instruction in the second/foreign language curriculum. In E. Hinkel and S. Fotos (eds) *New Perspectives on Grammar Teaching in Second Language Classrooms* (pp. 17–34). Mahwah, NJ: Lawrence Erlbaum.

Ellis, R. (2003) *Task-Based Language Learning and Teaching*. Oxford: Oxford University Press.

Ellis, R. (2005) Measuring implicit and explicit knowledge of a second language: A psychometric study. *Studies in Second Language Acquisition* 27 (2), 141–172.
Ellis, R. (2007) The effect of corrective feedback on the L2 acquisition of different grammatical structures. In A. Mackey (ed.) *Conversational Interaction in Second Language Acquisition: A Series of Empirical Studies* (chapter 14). Oxford: Oxford University Press.
Eskey, D.E. (2005) Reading in a second language. In E. Hinkel (ed.) *Handbook of Research in Second Language Teaching and Learning* (pp. 563–579). Mahwah, NJ: Lawrence Erlbaum.
ETS (1986) *The Test of Written English*. Princeton, NY: Educational Testing Service.
Everett, D. (2005) Cultural constraints on grammar and cognition in Pirahã. *Current Anthropology* 46 (4), 621–646.
Fanselow, J. (1987) *Breaking Rules: Generating and Exploring Alternatives in Language Teaching*. White Plains: Longman.
Fanselow, J. (1992) *Try the Opposite*. Tokyo: SIMUL.
Fiengo, R. and May, R. (1994) *Indices and Identity*. Cambridge, MA: MIT Press.
Fischer, S.D. and van der Hulst, H. (2003) Sign language structures. In M. Marschark and P.E. Spencer (eds) *The Handbook of Deaf Studies, Language, and Education* (pp. 319–331). New York: Oxford University Press.
Foley, C., Nuñez del Prado, Z., Barbier, I. and Lust, B. (1997) Operator variable binding in the initial state: An argument from VP Ellipsis. In S. Somashekar et al. (eds) *Papers on Language Acquisition: Cornell Working Papers in Linguistics* (Vol. 15, pp. 1–19). Ithaca, NY: Cornell University, Department of Linguistics.
Foster, P. and Ohta, A. (2005) Negotiation for meaning and peer assistance in second language classrooms. *Applied Linguistics* 26, 402–430.
Franceschina, F. (2005) *Fossilized Second Language Grammars: The Acquisition of Grammatical Gender*. Amsterdam: John Benjamins.
Franks, J.J., Bilbrey, C.W., Lien, K.G. and McNamara, T.P. (2000) Transfer-appropriate processing (TAP) and repetition priming. *Memory and Cognition* 28, 1140–1151.
Gagné, J. (2003) Développement des habiletés langagières orales de décontextualisation chez des élèves allophones sous-scolarisés. Unpublished doctoral thesis, Université Laval, Québec.
Galambos, S.J. and Goldin-Meadow, S. (1990) The effects of learning two languages on levels of metalinguistic awareness. *Cognition* 34, 1–56.
Gass, S. (1997) *Input, Interaction and the Second Language Learner*. Mahwah, NJ: Lawrence Erlbaum.
Gass, S. (2003) Input and interaction. In C. Doughty and M. Long (eds) *The Handbook of Second Language Acquisition* (pp. 224–255). Malden, MA: Blackwell Publishing.
Gass, S. and Selinker, L. (2001) *Second Language Acquisition: An Introductory Course*. NJ: Erlbaum Associates.
Gass, S., Svetics, I. and Lemelin, S. (2003) Differential effects of attention. *Language Learning* 53, 497–545.
Gatbonton, E. and Segalowitz, N. (1988) Creative automatization: Principles for promoting fluency within a communicative framework. *TESOL Quarterly* 22, 473–492.
Gatbonton, E. and Segalowitz, N. (2005) Rethinking communicative language teaching: A focus on ACCESS to fluency. *Canadian Modern Language Review* 61, 325–353.

Gaux, C. and Gombert, J-E. (1997) Conscience phonologique, syntaxique et lecture. Étude chez les jeunes enfants et les pré-adolescents. In C. Barré-de Miniac and B. Lété (eds) *L'illétrisme, de la prévention chez l'enfant aux stratégies de fonction chez l'adulte* (pp. 203–223). Paris: DeBoeck & Larcier.
Gaux, C. and Gombert, J-E. (1999a) Implicit and explicit syntactic knowledge and reading in pre-adolescents. *British Journal of Developmental Psychology* 17, 169–188.
Gaux, C. and Gombert, J-E. (1999b) La conscience syntaxique chez les préadolescents: Question de méthodes. *L'année psychologique* 99, 45–74.
Geeslin, K. and Guijarro-Fuentes, P. (2006) Second language acquisition of variable structures in Spanish by Portuguese speakers. *Language Learning* 56 (1), 53–107.
Geva, E. and Ryan, E.B. (1993) Linguistic and cognitive correlates of academic skills in first and second language. *Language Learning* 43 (1), 5–42.
Goldschneider, J. and DeKeyser, R. (2001) Explaining the 'natural order of L2 morpheme acquisition' in English: A meta-analysis of multiple determinants. *Language Learning* 51, 27–77.
Gombert, J.E. (1990) *Le Développement Métalinguistique.* Paris: Presses Universitaires de France.
Gombert, J.E. (1992) *Metalinguistic Development.* Chicago: Chicago University Press.
Gombert, J.E., Gaux, C. and Demont, E. (1994) Capacité métalinguistique et lecture. Quels liens? *Repères* 9, 61–73.
González-Nueno, M. (1997) VOT in the perception of foreign accent. *International Review of Applied Linguistics* XXXV (4), xxx–261.
Gotteri, N. and Michalak-Gray, J. (1997) *Polish.* London: Teach Yourself Books.
Graddol, D. (2006) *English Next.* On WWW at http://www.britishcouncil.org/files/documents/learning-research-english-next.pdf. Accessed 09.12.06.
Haegeman, L. (1994) *Introduction to Government & Binding Theory* (2nd edn). Oxford: Blackwell.
Hakes, D.T. (1980) *The Development of Metalinguistic Abilities in Children.* Berlin u.a.: Springer.
Hakuta, K. (1976) A case study of a Japanese child learning ESL. *Language Learning* 26, 321–352.
Hakuta, K. and Cancino, H. (1977) Trends in second language acquisition research. *Harvard Educational Review* 47 (3), 294–316.
Han, M.S. (1992) The timing control of geminate and single stop consonants in Japanese: a challenge for nonnative speakers. *Phonetica* 49, 102–127.
Han, Z-H. (1998) Fossilization: An investigation into advanced L2 learning of a typologically distant language. Unpublished PhD dissertation, University of London, London.
Han, Z-H. (2000) Persistence of the implicit influence of NL: The case of the pseudo-passive. *Applied Linguistics* 21 (1), 78–105.
Han, Z-H. (2001) Fine-tuning corrective feedback. *Foreign Language Annals* 34, 582–594.
Han, Z-H. (2002) A study of the impact of recasts on tense consistency in L2 output. *TESOL Quarterly* 36 (4), 543–572.
Han, Z-H. (2004a) To be a native speaker means not to be a nonnative speaker. *Second Language Research* 20 (2), 166–167.
Han, Z-H. (2004b) Review of Cook (ed.) 2003, *Studies in Second Language Acquisition* 26 (3), 488–489.

Han, Z-H. (2004c) *Fossilization in Adult Second Language Acquisition*. Clevedon: Multilingual Matters.
Han, Z-H. (2005) Input Enhancement: Untangling the Tangles. Plenary speech given at the 27th NYS TESOL Winter Applied Linguistics Conference. New York, NY.
Han, Z-H. (2006) Can grammaticality judgment be a reliable source of evidence on fossilization? In Z-H. Han and T. Odlin (eds) *Studies of Fossilization in Second Language Acquisition* (pp. 56–58). Clevedon: Multilingual Matters.
Han, Z-H. and Kim, J.H. (in press) Recasts: What teachers might want to know? *Journal of Language Learning*.
Han, Z-H. and Larsen-Freeman, D. (2005) On the Role of 'Meaning' in Focus on Form. Paper presented at the 28th SLRF conference. Teachers College, Columbia University, NY.
Han, Z-H. and Odlin, T. (eds) (2006) *Studies of Fossilization in Second Language Acquisition*. Clevedon: Multilingual Matters.
Han, Z-H., Park, E.S. and Combs, C. (2005) Input Enhancement: A Critical Meta-synthesis of the Research. Manuscript, Teachers College, Columbia University.
Han, Z-H. and Peverly, S. (2007) Input processing: A study of ab initio learners with multilingual backgrounds. *The International Journal of Multilingualism* 4 (1), 17–37.
Han, Z-H. and Selinker, L. (1999) Error resistance: Towards an empirical pedagogy. *Language Teaching Research* 3 (3), 248–275.
Harley, B. (1993) Instructional strategies and SLA in early French immersion. *Studies in Second Language Acquisition* 15, 245–259.
Harley, B. (1994) Appealing to consciousness in the L2 classroom. In J. Hulstijn and R. Schmidt (eds) *Consciousness in Second Language Learning. AILA Review* 11 (pp. 57–68).
Harrington, M. and Sawyer, M. (1992) L2 working memory capacity and L2 reading skill. *Studies in Second Language Acquisition* 14, 25–38.
Hasegawa, M., Carpenter, P.A. and Just, M.A. (2002) An fMRI study of bilingual sentence comprehension and workload. *Neuroimage* 15, 647–660.
Hatch, E. and Lazaraton, A. (1991) *The Research Manual. Design and Statistics for Applied Linguistics*. Boston, MA: Heinle & Heinle Publishers.
Hauser, E. (2005) Coding 'corrective recasts': The maintenance of meaning and more fundamental problems. *Applied Linguistics* 26 (3), 293–316.
Hayes, B. (1989) Compensatory lengthening in moraic phonology. In J.A. Goldsmith (ed.) (1999) *Phonological Theory: The Essential Readings* (pp. 351–369). Malden, MA: Blackwell Publishers.
Hestvik, A. (1995) Reflexives and ellipsis. *Natural Language Semantics* 3 (2), 211–237.
Heycock, C. (1995) Asymmetries in reconstruction. *Linguistic Inquiry* 26 (5), 547–570.
Hilles, S. (1986) Interlanguage and the PRO-drop parameter. *Second Language Research* 2 (1), 33–52.
Hoffman, E. (1989) *Lost in Translation: A Life in a New Language*. New York: Penguin Books.
Hopp, H. (2003) Syntax and its interfaces in L2 grammars-situating L1 effects. In J. van Kampen and S. Baauw (eds) *Proceedings of GALA 2003*. LOT, The Netherlands.

Hopp, H. (2005) Constraining second language word order optionality: Scrambling in advanced English-German and Japanese-German interlanguage. *Second Language Research* 21 (1), 34–71.
Hollywood and Broadway. (n.d.). On WWW at http://www.geocities.com/yamataro670/hollywood-broadway.htm/. Accessed 01.09.04.
House, J. (1996) Developing pragmatic fluency in English as a foreign language: Routines and metapragmatic awareness. *Studies in Second Language Acquisition* 17, 225–252.
Howatt, A.P.R. (1984) *A History of English Language Teaching.* Oxford: Oxford University Press.
Huang, C-T.J. (1987) Comments on Hasegawa's paper. In Y. Hirakawa (ed.) *Proceedings of the Japanese Syntax Workshop: Issues on Empty Categories* (pp. 56–78). New London: Connecticut College.
Huang, C-T.J. (1993) Reconstruction and the structure of VP: Some theoretical consequences. *Linguistic Inquiry* 24 (2), 103–138.
Huang, C-T.J. (1994) More on Chinese word order and parametric theory. In B. Lust, G. Hermon and J. Kornfilt (eds) *Syntactic Theory and First Language Acquisition: Cross Linguistic Perspectives* (Vol. 1, pp. 15–35). Mahwah, NJ: Lawrence Erlbaum Associates.
Hulstijn, J. (2001) Intentional and incidental second language vocabulary learning: A reappraisal of elaboration, rehearsal and automaticity. In P. Robinson (ed.) *Cognition and Second Language Instruction* (pp. 258–286). Cambridge: Cambridge University Press.
Hulstijn, J. (2002) Towards a unified account of the representation, processing and acquisition of second language knowledge. *Second Language Research* 18, 193–223.
Hulstijn, J. (2003) Incidental and intentional learning. In C.J. Doughty and M.H. Long (eds) *The Handbook of Second Language Acquisition* (pp. 349–381). Oxford: Blackwell.
Institut de la statistique du Québec (2005) *La situation démographique au Québec. Bilan 2005.* On WWW at http://www.stat.gouv.qc.ca/publications/demograp/pdf2005/Bilan2005c8.pdf.
Ioup, G., Boustagui, E., El Tigi, M. and Moselle, M. (1994) Reexamining the critical period hypothesis: A case study of successful adult SLA in a naturalistic environment. *Studies in Second Language Acquisition* 16 (1), 73–98.
Iwasaki, N. (2000) Speaking Japanese: L1 and L2 grammatical encoding of case particles and adjectives/adjectival nouns. Unpublished doctoral dissertation, University of Arizona.
Iwashita, N. (1999) The role of task-based conversation in the acquisition of Japanese grammar and vocabulary. Unpublished PhD dissertation, University of Melbourne.
Izumi, S. (2002) Output, input enhancement, and the noticing hypothesis: An experimental study on ESL relativization. *Studies in Second Language Acquisition* 24, 541–577.
Izumi, S. (2003) Comprehension and production processes in second language learning: In speech of psycholinguistic rationale of the output hypothesis. *Applied Linguistics* 24, 168–196.
Izumi, S. and Bigelow, M. (2000) Does output promote noticing and second language acquisition? *TESOL Quarterly* 34, 239–278.

Izumi, S., Bigelow, M., Fujiwara, M. and Fearnow, S. (1999) Testing the output hypothesis: Effects of output on noticing and second language acquisition. *Studies in Second Language Acquisition* 21, 421–452.

Jacoby, L.L. (1978) On interpreting the effects of repetition: Solving a problem versus remembering a solution. *Journal of Verbal Learning and Verbal Behavior* 22, 485–508.

Jackendoff, R. (1987) *Consciousness and the Computational Mind*. Cambridge, MA: MIT Press.

Jiang, N. (2004) Morphological insensitivity in second language processing. *Applied Psycholinguistics* 25, 603–634.

Jourdenais, R., Ota, M., Stauffer, S., Boyson, B. and Doughty, C. (1995) Does textual enhancement promote noticing? A think-aloud protocol analysis. In R. Schmidt (ed.) *Attention and Awareness in Foreign Language Learning* (pp. 183–216). Honolulu: University of Hawaii Press.

Juffs, A. (2005) The influence of first language on the processing of *wh*-movement in English as a second language. *Second Language Research* 21 (2), 121–151.

Juffs, A. (2006) Processing reduced relative versus main verb ambiguity in English as a second language: A replication study with working memory. In R. Slabakova, S. Montrul and P. Prévost (eds) *Inquiries in Linguistic Development in Honor of Lydia White* (pp. 213–232). Amsterdam: John Benjamins.

Just, M.A. and Carpenter, P.A. (1992) A capacity theory of comprehension: Individual differences in working memory. *Psychological Review* 99, 122–149.

Just, M.A., Carpenter, P.A. and Woolley, J.D. (1982) Paradigms and processes in reading comprehension. *Journal of Experimental Psychology: General* 111, 228–238.

Kaiser, G.A. (1994) More about INFL-ection and agreement: The acquisition of clitic pronouns in French. In J.M. Meisel (ed.) *Bilingual First Language Acquisition: French and German Grammatical Development* (pp. 131–159). Amsterdam: John Benjamins.

Kasper, G. and Kellerman, E. (eds) (1997) *Communication Strategies: Psycholinguistic and Sociolinguistic Perspectives*. London: Longman.

Kasper, G. and Rose, K.R. (2002) *Pragmatic Development in a Second Language*. Mahwah, NJ: Blackwell.

Kato, K. (2004) Second Language (L2) Segmental speech learning: Perception and production of L2 English by Japanese native speakers. Unpublished doctoral dissertation, University of Essex, UK.

Kehoe, M., Lleo, C. and Rakow, M. (2004) Voice onset time in German/Spanish bilinguals. *Bilingualism: Language and Cognition* 7 (1), 71–88.

Kecskes, I. (2000) Conceptual fluency and the use of situation-bound utterances. *Links & Letter* 7, 145–161.

Kecskes, I. (2003) *Situation-Bound Utterances in L1 and L2*. Berlin: Mouton.

Kecskes, I. and Papp, T. (2000) *Foreign Language and Mother Tongue*. Hillsdale, NJ: Lawrence Erlbaum.

Kellerman, E. (1983) Now you see it, now you don't. In S. Gass and L. Selinker (eds) *Language Transfer in Language Learning* (pp. 112–134). Rowley, MA: Newbury House.

Kellerman, E. (1995) Crosslinguistic influence: Transfer to nowhere. *Annual Review of Applied Linguistics* 15, 125–150.

Kim, J.H. and Han, Z-H. (2007) Recasts in communicative EFL classes: Do teacher intent and learner interpretation overlap? In A. Mackey (ed.) *Conversational Interaction in Second Language Acquisition: A Series of Empirical Studies*. Oxford: Oxford University Press.
Kitagawa, Y. (1991) Copying identity. *Natural Language and Linguistic Theory* 9 (4), 497–536.
Kitahara, M. (1999) Studies on rhythm in speech production and perception as an interface between Phonetics and Cognitive Science. *Journal of the Phonetic Society of Japan* 3 (1), 41–47.
Klein, W. (1986) *Second Language Acquisition*. Cambridge: Cambridge University Press.
Klein, W. and Perdue, C. (1997) The basic variety (or: couldn't natural languages be much simpler?). *Second Language Research* 13 (4), 301–347.
Koopman, H. and Sportiche, D. (1991) The position of subjects. *Lingua* 85 (2), 211–258.
Krashen, S. (1976) Formal and informal linguistic environments in language acquisition and language learning. *TESOL Quarterly* 10, 157–68.
Krashen, S. (1978) The monitor model for second language acquisition. In R. Gingras (ed.) *Second Language Acquisition and Foreign Language Teaching*. Arlington, VA: Center for Applied Linguistics.
Krashen, S. (1982) *Principles and Practice in Second Language Acquisition*. Oxford: Pergamon.
Krashen, S. (1985) *The Input Hypothesis: Issues and Implications*. New York: Longman.
Kroll, J. and Sunderman, G. (2003) Cognitive processes in second language learners and bilinguals: The development of lexical and conceptual representations. In C. Doughty and M. Long (eds) *The Handbook of Second Language Acquisition* (pp. 104–129). Oxford: Blackwell.
Kroll, J. and Dussias, P. (2004) The comprehension of words and sentences in two languages. In T. Bhatia and W. Ritchie (eds) *Handbook of Bilingualism* (pp. 169–200). Cambridge, MA: Blackwell Publishers.
Kroll, J.F., Michael, E., Tokowicz, N. and Dufour, R. (2002) The development of lexical fluency in a second language. *Second Language Research* 18, 137–171.
Kubozono, H. (1998) *Eigogaku enshuu shiriizu: Onseegaku/On'inron [Seminar Series in English Linguistics: Phonetics/Phonology]*. Tokyo: Kurosio Shuppan.
Kubozono, H. and Ohta, S. (1998) *Onin koozoo to akusent [Phonological Structure and Accent]*. Tokyo: Kenkyuusha.
Labov, W. (1969) The logic of non-standard English. *Georgetown Monographs on Language and Linguistics* 22, 1–31.
Ladefoged, P. (2001) *Vowels and Consonants: An Introduction to the Sounds of Languages*. Malden, MA: Blackwell Publishing.
Lakshmanan, U. and Teranishi, K. (1994) Preferences versus grammaticality judgements: Some methodological issues concerning the governing category parameter in second-language acquisition. In E. Tarone, S. Gass and A. Cohen (eds) *Research Methodology in Second Language Acquisition* (pp. 185–206). Hillsdale, NJ: Lawrence Erlbaum.
Lambert, W.E., Tucker, G.R. and d'Anglejan, A. (1973) Cognitive and attitudinal consequences of bilingual schooling. *Journal of Educational Psychology* 85 (2), 141–159.

Lapkin, S., Swain, M. and Smith, M. (2002) Reformulating and the learning of French pronominal verbs in a Canadian French immersion context. *The Modern Language Journal* 86, 485–507.

Lardiere, D. (2007) *Ultimate Attainment in Second Language Acquisition: A Case Study*. Mahwah, NJ: Lawrence Erlbaum.

Larsen-Freeman, D. (1975) The acquisition of grammatical morphemes by adult ESL students. *TESOL Quarterly* 9 (4), 409–420.

Larsen-Freeman, D. (2001) Teaching grammar. In M. Celce-Murcia (ed.) *Teaching English as a Second or Foreign Language* (3rd edn, pp. 251–266). Boston: Heinle & Heinle.

Larsen-Freeman, D. (2003) *Teaching Language: From Grammar to Grammaring*. Boston: Thomson/Heinle.

Larsen-Freeman, D. (2006a) The emergence of complexity, fluency, and accuracy in the oral and written production of five Chinese learners of English. *Applied Linguistics* 27 (4), 590–619.

Larsen-Freeman, D. (2006b) Second language acquisition and the issue of fossilization: There is no end, and there is no state. In Z-H. Han and T. Odlin (eds) *Studies of Fossilization in Second Language Acquisition* (pp. 189–200). Clevedon: Multilingual Matters.

Lasnik, H. (1999) *Minimalist Analysis*. Oxford: Blackwell.

Lasnik, H. (2001) Derivation and representation in modern transformational syntax. In M. Baltin and C. Collins (eds) *The Handbook of Contemporary Syntactic Theory* (pp. 62–88). Oxford: Blackwell.

Laufer, B. (2003) The influence of L2 on L1 collocational knowledge and on L1 lexical diversity in free written expression. In V.J. Cook (ed.) *L2 Effects on the L1* (pp. 19–31). Clevedon: Multilingual Matters.

Laufer, B. and Hulstijn, J. (2001) Incidental vocabulary acquisition in a second language: The construct of task-induced involvement. *Applied Linguistics* 22, 1–26.

Lee, J.F. (1999) On levels of processing and levels of comprehension. In J. Gutiérrez-Rexach and F. Martínez-Gil (eds) *Advances in Hispanic Linguistics* (pp. 42–59). Somerville, MA: Cascadilla Press.

Lee, J.F. (2002) The incidental acquisition of Spanish future morphology through reading in a second language. *Studies in Second Language Acquisition* 24, 55–80.

Lee, J.F., Cadierno, T., Glass, W.R. and VanPatten, B. (1997) The effects of lexical and grammatical cues on processing past temporal reference in second language input. *Applied Language Learning* 8, 1–23.

Leeman, J. (2003) Recasts and second language development: Beyond negative evidence. *Studies in Second Language Acquisition* 25 (1), 37–64.

Leeser, M. (2004) The effects of topic familiarity, mode, and pausing on second language learners' comprehension and focus on form. *Studies in Second Language Acquisition* 26, 587–615.

Lefrançois, P. and Armand, F. (2003) The role of phonological and syntactic awareness in second language reading. The case of Spanish-speaking learners of French. *Reading and Writing: An Interdisciplinary Journal* 16, 219–246.

Lenneberg, E. (1967) *Biological Foundations of Language*. New York: Wiley.

Leow, R. (1993) To simplify or not to simplify: A look at intake. *Studies in Second Language Acquisition* 15, 333–355.

Leow, R. (1995) Modality and intake in second language acquisition. *Studies in Second Language Acquisition* 17, 79–89.
Leow, R. (1997a) Attention, awareness and foreign language behavior. *Language Learning* 47, 467–505.
Leow, R. (1997b) The effects of input enhancement and text length on adult L2 learners' comprehension and intake in second language acquisition. *Applied Language Learning* 8, 151–182.
Leow, R. (1998) Toward operationalizing the process of attention in SLA: Evidence for Tomlin and Villa's (1994) fine-grained analysis. *Applied Psycholinguistics* 19, 133–159.
Leow, R. (2000) A study of the role of awareness in foreign language behavior: Aware versus unaware learners. *Studies in Second Language Acquisition* 22, 557–584.
Leow, R. (2001) Attention, awareness and foreign language behavior. *Language Learning* 51 (Suppl. 1), 113–155.
Leow, R. (2002) Models, attention, and awareness in SLA: A response to Simard and Wong's 'Alertness, orientation, and detection: The conceptualization of attentional functions in SLA.' *Studies in Second Language Acquisition* 24, 113–119.
Leow, R. and Morgan-Short, K. (2004) To think aloud or not to think aloud. *Studies in Second Language Acquisition* 26 (1), 35–57.
Levelt, W.J.M. (1989) *Speaking: From Intention to Articulation*. Cambridge, MA: MIT Press.
Levelt, W.J.M. (1999) Models of word production. *Trends in Cognitive Sciences* 3 (6), 223–232.
Levelt, W.J.M., Roelofs, A. and Meyer, A.S. (1999) A theory of lexical access in speech production. *Behavioral and Brain Science* 22, 1–75.
Levelt, W.J. and Wheeldon, L. (1994) Do speakers have access to a mental syllabary? *Cognition* 50, 239–269.
Levinson, S.C. (1996) Relativity in spatial conception and description. In J.J. Gumperz and S.C. Levinson (eds) *Rethinking Linguistic Relativity* (pp. 177–202). Cambridge: Cambridge University Press.
Levinson, S. (1997) From outer to inner space: Linguistic categories and non-linguistic thinking. In J. Nuyts and E. Pederson (eds) *Language and Linguistic Categorization* (pp. 13–45). Cambridge: Cambridge University Press.
Levitt, H. (1989) Speech and hearing in communication. In M.C. Wang, M.C. Reynolds and H.J. Walberg (eds) *Handbook of Special Education: Research and Practice* (Vol. 3, pp. 23–46). New York: Pergamon Press.
Lightbown, P.M. (1983) Exploring relationships between developmental and instructional sequences in L2 acquisition. In H. Seliger and M.H. Long (eds) *Classroom Oriented Research in Second Language Acquisition* (pp. 217–243). Rowley, MA: Newbury House.
Lightbown, P.M. (1985) Input and acquisition for second language learners in and out of classrooms. *Applied Linguistics* 6, 263–273.
Lightbown, P.M. (1991) What have we here? Some observations on the role of instruction in second language acquisition. In R. Phillipson, E. Kellerman, L. Selinker, M. Sharwood Smith and M. Swain (eds) *Foreign/Second Language Pedagogy Research: A Commemorative Volume for Claus Faerch* (pp. 197–212). Clevedon: Multilingual Matters.

Lightbown, P.M. (1998) The importance of timing in focus on form. In C. Doughty and J. Williams (eds) *Focus on Form in Classroom Second Language Acquisition* (pp. 177–196). Cambridge: Cambridge University Press.
Lightbown, P.M. (2000) Anniversary article: Classroom SLA research and second language teaching. *Applied Linguistics* 21 (4), 431–462.
Lightbown, P.M. and Spada, N. (2006) *How Languages are Learned* (3rd edn). Oxford: Oxford University Press.
Lin, T. (1998) Investigating the perceived relationship between Chinese adult students' early school language learning experiences and current American ESL teaching methods. Unpublished doctoral dissertation, The Florida State University, FL.
Lipka, O., Siegel, L.S. and Vukivic, R. (2005) The literacy skills of English language learners in Canada. *Learning Disabilities Research & Practice* 20, 39–49.
Livingston, S. (1997) *Rethinking the Education of Deaf Students: Theory and Practice from a Teacher's Perspective*. Portsmouth, NH: Heinemann.
Llurda, E. (ed.) (2005) *Non-Native Teachers*. New York: Springer.
Locastro, V. (1987) Aizuchi: A Japanese conversational routine. In L.E. Smith (ed.) *Discourse Across Cultures* (pp. 101–113). New York: Prentice Hall.
Lockhart, R.S. (2002) Levels of processing, transfer-appropriate processing, and the concept of robust encoding. *Memory* 10, 397–403.
Long, M. (1991) Focus on form: A design feature in language teaching methodology. In K. de Bot, D. Coste, C. Kramsch and R. Ginsberg (eds) *Foreign Language Research in a Cross-Cultural Perspective* (pp. 39–52). Amsterdam: John Benjamins.
Long, M.H. (1996) The role of the linguistic environment in second language acquisition. In W.C. Ritchie and T.K. Bhatia (eds) *Handbook of Second Language Acquisition* (pp. 413–468). New York: Academic Press.
Long, M. (2000) Focus on form in task-based language teaching. In R. Lambert and E. Shohamy (eds) *Language Policy and Pedagogy: Essays in Honor of A. Ronald Walton* (pp. 179–192). Philadelphia: John Benjamins.
Long, M. (2003) Stabilization and fossilization in interlanguage development. In C. Doughty and M. Long (eds) *The Handbook of Second Language Acquisition* (pp. 487–536). Oxford: Blackwell.
Long, M. (2007) Recasts: The story so far. In *Problems in SLA* (pp. 75–118). Mahwah, NJ: Lawrence Erlbaum.
Long, M., Inagaki, S. and Ortega, L. (1998) The role of implicit negative feedback in SLA: Models and recasts in Japanese and Spanish. *Modern Language Journal* 82 (3), 357–371.
Long, M. and Robinson, P. (1998) Focus on form: Theory, research, and practice. In C. Doughty and J. Williams (eds) *Focus on Form in Classroom Second Language Acquisition* (pp. 15–41). Cambridge: Cambridge University Press.
Lyster, R. (1994) The effect of functional-analytic teaching on aspects of French immersion students' sociolinguistic competence. *Applied Linguistics* 15, 263–287.
Lyster, R. (1998) Recasts, repetition, and ambiguity in L2 classroom discourse. *Studies in Second Language Acquisition* 20 (1), 51–81.
Lyster, R. (2001) Negotiation of form, recasts, and explicit correction in relation to error types and learner repair in immersion classrooms. *Language Learning* 51 (Suppl. 1), 265–301.

Lyster, R. (2004) Differential effects of prompts and recasts in form-focused instruction. *Studies in Second Language Acquisition* 26 (3), 399–432.
Lyster, R. and Ranta, L. (1997) Corrective feedback and learner uptakes: Negotiation of form in communicative classrooms. *Studies in Second Language Acquisition* 19 (1), 37–66.
Lyster, R. and Mori, H. (2006) Interactional feedback and instructional counterbalance. *Studies in Second Language Acquisition* 28, 321–341.
Macaro, E. (1997) *Target Language, Collaborative Learning and Autonomy*. Clevedon: Multilingual Matters.
Mackey, A. (ed.) (2006) *Studies in Second Language Acquisition*. Special Issue 28 (2).
Mackey, A. (ed.) (2007) *Conversational Interaction in Second Language Acquisition: A Series of Empirical Studies*. Oxford: Oxford University Press.
Mackey, A. and Philp, J. (1998) Conversational interaction and second language development: Recasts, responses, and red herrings. *Modern Language Journal* 82, 338–356.
Mackey, A., Gass, S. and McDonough, K. (2000) How do learners perceive interactional feedback? *Studies in Second Language Acquisition* 22 (4), 471–497.
Mackey, A. and Goo, J. (2007) Interaction research in SLA: A meta-analysis and research synthesis. In A. Mackey (ed.) *Conversational Interaction in Second Language Acquisition: A Series of Empirical Studies*. Oxford: Oxford University Press.
MacLaughlin, D. (1998) The acquisition of morphosyntax of English reflexives. In M. Beck (ed.) *Morphology and its Interfaces in Second Language Knowledge* (pp. 195–226). Amsterdam: John Benjamins.
MacWhinney, B. (2001) The competition model: The input, the context, and the brain. In P. Robinson (ed.) *Cognition and Second Language Instruction* (pp. 69–70). Cambridge: Cambridge University Press.
MacWhinney, B. (2005) A unified model of language acquisition. In J. Kroll and A.M.B. de Groot (eds) *Handbook of Bilingualism* (pp. 49–67). Oxford: Oxford University Press.
MacWhinney, B. (2006) Emergent fossilization. In Z-H. Han and T. Odlin (eds) *Studies of Fossilization in Second Language Acquisition* (pp. 134–156). Clevedon: Multilingual Matters.
Major, R.C. (2001) *Foreign Accent: The Ontogeny and Phylogeny of Second Language Prosody*. London: Lawrence Erlbaum Associates.
Makino, S., Hatasa, Y.A. and Hatasa, K. (1998) *Nakama I: Japanese Communication, Culture, Context*. Boston: Houghton Mifflin Co.
Mangubhai, F. (1991) The processing behaviors of adult second language learners and their relationship to second language proficiency. *Applied Linguistics* 12, 268–297.
Marinis, T., Roberts, L., Felser, C. and Clahsen, H. (2005) Gaps in second language processing. *Studies in Second Language Acquisition* 27 (1), 53–78.
Mayer, C. and Akamatsu, C.T. (2003) Bilingualism and literacy. In M. Marschark and P.E. Spencer (eds) *Oxford Handbook of Deaf Studies, Language, and Education* (pp. 136–147). Oxford: Oxford University Press.
Mayer, C. and Wells, G. (1996) Can the linguistic interdependence theory support a bilingual – bicultural model of literacy education for deaf students? *Journal of Deaf Studies and Deaf Education* 1, 93–107.

McDonough, K. (2004) Learner–learner interaction during pair and small group activities in a Thai EFL context. *System* 32, 207–224.
McDonough, K. and Mackey, A. (2006) Responses to recasts: Repetitions, primed production and linguistic development. *Language Learning* 56 (4), 693–720.
McLaughlin, B. (1990) Restructuring. *Applied Linguistics* 11, 113–128.
McNeill, D. (1966) Developmental psycholinguistics. In F. Smith and G.A. Miller (eds) *The Genesis of Language: a Psycholinguistic Approach*. Cambridge MA: MIT Press.
Meara, P. and Buxton, B. (1987) An alternative to multiple choice vocabulary tests. *Language Testing* 4, 142–154.
Meisel, J., Clahsen, H. and Pienemann, M. (1981) On determining developmental stages in natural second language acquisition. *Studies in Second Language Acquisition* 3 (2), 109–135.
Mennen, I. (2004) Bi-directional interference in the intonation of Dutch speakers of Greek. *Journal of Phonetics* 32, 543–563.
Michigan Test of English Language Proficiency (1977) Ann Arbor, MI: University of Michigan, English Language Institute.
Min, K.J. (1993) Nihongo sokuon no chooshu handan ni kansuru kenkyuu [The study of perceptual judgment of Japanese geminate consonants]. *Sekai no Nihongo Kyooiku* 3, 237–249.
Ministère de l'Éducation du Québec (1996) Le point sur les services d'accueil et de francisation de l'école publique québécoise. Pratiques actuelles et résultats des élèves. Québec: Direction des services aux communautés culturelles du gouvernement du Québec.
Miyake, A. and Friedman, N.P. (1998) Individual differences in second language proficiency: Working memory as language aptitude. In F. Healy and L.E. Bourne (eds) *Foreign Language Learning: Psychometric Studies on Training and Retention* (pp. 339–364). Mahwah, NJ: Lawrence Erlbaum.
Mondria, J-A. and Wit-de-Boer, M. (1991) The effects of contextual richness on the guessability and the retention of words in a foreign language. *Applied Linguistics* 12, 249–267.
Morris, D.D., Bransford, J.D. and Franks, J.J. (1977) Levels of processing versus transfer appropriate processing. *Journal of Verbal Learning and Verbal Behavior* 16, 519–533.
Müller, N. and Hulk, A. (2001) Cross-linguistic influence in bilingual first language acquisition: Italian and French as recipient languages. *Bilingualism: Language and Cognition* 4, 1–21.
Munro, M.J. (1995) Nonsegmental factors in foreign accent: Ratings of filtered speech. *Studies in Second Language Acquisition* 17, 17–34.
Munro, M.J. (1998) The effects of noise on the intelligibility of foreign-accented speech. *Studies in Second Language Acquisition* 20, 139–154.
Munro, M.J. and Derwing, T.M. (1995) Foreign accent, comprehensibility, and intelligibility in the speech of second language learners. *Language Learning* 45, 73–97.
Munro, M.J. and Derwing, T.M. (1998) The effect of speaking rate on listener evaluation of native and foreign-accented speech. *Language Learning* 48, 159–182.
Munro, M.J. and Derwing, T.M. (2001) Modeling perceptions of the accentedness and comprehensibility of L2 speech: The role of speaking rate. *Studies in Second Language Acquisition* 23, 451–468.

Murphy, V.A. (1997) The effect of modality on grammaticality judgement task. *Second Language Research* 13, 34–65.
Musumeci, D. (1989) The ability of second language learners to assign tense at the sentence level: A cross-linguistic study. Unpublished PhD thesis, University of Illinois at Urbana-Champaign, IL.
Myles, F. (2004) From data to theory: The over-representation of linguistic knowledge in SLA. *Transactions of the Philological Society* 102, 139–168.
Myles, F., Hooper, J. and Mitchell, R. (1998) Rote or rule? Exploring the role of formulaic language in classroom foreign language learning. *Language Learning* 48 (3), 323–363.
Nabei, T. and Swain, M. (2002) Learner awareness of recasts in classroom interaction: A case study of an adult EFL student's second language learning. *Language Awareness* 11 (1), 43–63.
Nairne, J.S. (2002) The myth of the encoding – retrieval match. *Memory* 10, 389–395.
Nation, K. and Snowling, M.J. (2000) Factors influencing syntactic awareness skills in normal readers and poor comprehenders. *Applied Psycholinguistics* 21, 229–241.
Nattinger, J.R. and DeCarrico, J.S. (1992) *Lexical Phrases and Language Teaching*. Oxford: Oxford University Press.
Nelson, K.E. (1987) Some observations from the perspective of the rare event cognitive comparison theory of language acquisition. In K.E. Nelson and A. van Kleeck (eds) *Children's Language* (pp. 289–331). Hillsdale, NJ: Lawrence Erlbaum.
Newmeyer, F. (1998) *Language Form and Language Function*. Cambridge, MA: MIT Press.
Nicholas, H., Lightbown, P. and Spada, N. (2001) Recasts as feedback to language learners. *Language Learning* 51 (4), 719–758.
Norenzayan, A., Smith, E.E., Kim, B.J. and Nisbett, R.E. (2002) Cultural preferences for formal versus intuitive reasoning. *Cognitive Science* 26, 653–684.
Norris, J.M. and Ortega, L. (2000) Effectiveness of L2 instruction: A research synthesis and quantitative meta-analysis. *Language Learning* 50 (3), 417–528.
Nunnally, J.C. (1967) *Psychometric Theory*. New York, NY: McGraw-Hill.
Obler, L. (1982) The parsimonious bilingual. In L. Obler and L. Menn (eds) *Exceptional Language and Linguistics* (pp. 339–346). New York: Academic Press.
Odlin, T. (2003) Cross-linguistic influence. In C. Doughty and M. Long (eds) *Handbook of Second Language Acquisition* (pp. 436–486). Oxford: Blackwell.
Odlin, T. (2005) Crosslinguistic influence and conceptual transfer: What are the concepts? *Annual Review of Applied Linguistics* 25, 3–25.
Oliver, R. (1995) Negative feedback in child NS–NNS conversation. *Studies in Second Language Acquisition* 17 (4), 459–481.
Ortega, L. and Long, M. (1997) The effects of models and recasts on the acquisition of object topicalization and adverb placement in L2 Spanish. *Spanish Applied Linguistics* 1, 65–86.
Osaka, M. and Osaka, N. (1992) Language-independent working memory as measured by Japanese and English reading span tests. *Bulletin of the Psychonomic Society* 30, 287–289.

Osaka, M., Osaka, N. and Groner, R. (1993) Language-independent working memory: Evidence from German and French reading span tests. *Bulletin of the Psychonomic Society* 31, 117–118.

Overstreet, M. (1998) Text enhancement and content familiarity: The focus of learner attention. *Spanish Applied Linguistics* 2, 229–258.

Panova, I. (2005) *Focus on L2 Nominal Morphology Patterns of Corrective Feedback in the Adult ESL.* Paper presented at the 28th SLRF Conference, New York, NY.

Park, D.C., Welsh, R.C., Marschuetz, C., Gutchess, A.H., Mikels, J., Polk, T.A., Noll, D.C. and Taylor, S.F. (2003) Working memory for complex scenes: Age differences in frontal and hippocampal activations. *Journal of Cognitive Neuroscience* 15 (8), 1122–1134.

Park, E.S. (2004) Constraints of implicit focus on form: Insights from a study of input enhancement. *Teachers College, Columbia University Working papers in TESOL & Applied Linguistic* 4 (2). On WWW at http://www.tc.edu/tesolalwebjournal/Park.pdf. Accessed 07.09.05.

Park, E.S. (2007) Learner-generated noticing of L2 input: An exploratory study. Unpublished doctoral dissertation, Teachers College, Columbia University, NY.

Pavlenko, A. (2003) 'I feel clumsy speaking Russian': L2 influence on L1 in narratives of Russian L2 users of English. In V.J. Cook (ed.) *Effects of the Second Language on the First* (pp. 32–61). Clevedon: Multilingual Matters.

Peters, A.M. (1983) *The Units of Language Acquisition.* Cambridge: Cambridge University Press.

Pica, T. (2002) Subject-matter content: How does it assist the interactional and linguistic needs of classroom language learners? *The Modern Language Journal* 86 (1), 1–19.

Pickering, L. (2001) The role of tone choice in improving ITA communication in the classroom. *TESOL Quarterly* 35 (2), 233–255.

Philp, J. (2003) Constraints on 'noticing the gap'. Nonnative speakers' noticing of recasts in NS–NNS interaction. *Studies in Second Language Learning* 25, 99–126.

Pienemann, M. (1984) Psychological constraints on the teachability of languages. *Studies in Second Language Acquisition* 6 (2), 18–214.

Pienemann, M. (1985) Learnability and syllabus construction. In K. Hyltenstam and M. Pienemann (eds) *Modeling and Assessing Second Language Acquisition* (pp. 23–112). Clevedon: Multilingual Matters.

Pienemann, M. and Johnston, M. (1987) Factors influencing the development of language proficiency. In D. Nunan (ed.) *Applying Second Language Acquisition Research* (pp. 45–141). Adelaide, Australia: National Curriculum Resource Centre, AMEP.

Pierrehumbert, J. and Beckman, M. (1988) *Japanese Tone Structure.* Cambridge, MA: MIT Press.

Pike, K.L. (1945) *The Intonation and American English.* Ann Arbor: The University of Michigan Press.

Pinker, S. (1997) *How the Mind Works.* New York: Norton.

Plunkett, B. (1999) Targeting complex structure in French questions. *Proceedings of the Annual Boston University Conference on Language Development* 23, 764–775.

Posner, M. and Petersen, E. (1990) The attention system of the human brain. *Annual Review of Neuroscience* 13, 25–42.

Power, D. and Leigh, G.R. (2000) Principles and practices of literacy development for deaf learners: A historical perspective. *Journal of Deaf Studies and Deaf Education* 5, 3–8.
Progovac, L. (1992) Relativized SUBJECT: Long-distance reflexives without movement. *Linguistic Inquiry* 23 (5), 671–680.
Progovac, L. (1993) Long-distance reflexives: Movement-to-Infl versus relativized SUBJECT. *Linguistic Inquiry* 24 (6), 755–772.
Queen, R.M. (2001) Bilingual intonation patterns: evidence of language change from Turkish–German bilingual children. *Language in Society* 30, 55–80.
Quigley, S.P. and King, C.M. (1980) Syntactic performance of hearing impaired and normal hearing individuals. *Applied Psycholinguistics* 1, 329–356.
Raimes, A. (2002) Errors: Windows into the mind. In G. DeLuca, L. Fox, M. Johnson and M. Kogen (eds) *Dialogue on Writing: Rethinking ESL, Basic Writing, and First-Year Composition* (pp. 279–287). Mahwah, NJ: Lawrence Erlbaum.
Rast, R. (2003) Le tout début de l'acquisition: Le traitement initial d'une langue non maternelle par l'apprenant adulte [Acquisition begins: The initial analysis of an additional language by adult learners]. Unpublished doctoral dissertation, Université de Paris VIII.
Rast, R. and Dommergues, J.-Y. (2003) Towards a characterization of saliency on first exposure to a second language. In S. Foster-Cohen and S. Pekarek-Doehler (eds) *EUROSLA Yearbook: Papers from the Annual Conference of the European Second Language Association* (Vol. 3, pp. 131–156). Amsterdam: Benjamins.
Rayner, K. (1998) Eye movements in reading and information processing: Twenty years of research. *Psychological Bulletin* 3, 372–422.
Rayner, K. and Pollatsek, A. (1989) *The Psychology of Reading*. Hillsdale, NJ: Lawrence Erlbaum Associates.
Reinhart, T. (1986) Center and periphery in the grammar of anaphora. In B. Lust (ed.) *Studies in the Acquisition of Anaphora* (Vol. 1, pp. 123–150). Dordrecht: Reidel.
Reuland, E. and Everaert, M. (2001) Deconstructing binding. In M. Baltin and C. Collins M. (eds) *The Handbook of Contemporary Syntactic Theory* (pp. 670–696). Oxford: Blackwell.
Ricciardelli, L.A. (1993) Two components of metalinguistic awareness: Control of linguistic processing and analysis of linguistic knowledge. *Applied Psycholinguistics* 14, 349–367.
Riegel, M., Pellat, J.-M. and Rioul, R. (2004) *Grammaire méthodique du français*. Paris: Presses universitaires de France.
Rizzi, L. (1982) *Issues in Italian Syntax*. Dordrecht: Foris.
Roberson, D., Davies, I. and Davidoff, J. (2000) Colour categories are not universal: Replications and new evidence from a stone-age culture. *Journal of Experimental Psychology: General* 129, 369–398.
Roberts, I. (1997) *Comparative Syntax*. London: Arnold.
Robinson, P. (1995) Review article: Attention, memory and the noticing hypothesis. *Language Learning* 45, 283–331.
Robinson, P. (2001) Task complexity, second language development and syllabus design: A triadic framework for examining task influences in SLA. In P. Robinson (ed.) *Cognition and Second Language Instruction* (pp. 287–318). Cambridge: Cambridge University Press.

Robinson, P. (2003) Attention and memory in SLA. In C. Doughty and M. Long (eds) *Handbook of Second Language Acquisition* (pp. 631–678). Oxford: Blackwell.
Roediger, H.L. and Karpicke, J.D. (2005) Learning and memory. *Encyclopedia of Social Measurement* 2, 479–486.
Roediger, H.L., Gallo, D.A. and Geraci, L. (2002) Processing approaches to cognition: The impetus from the levels-of-processing framework. *Memory* 10, 319–332.
Roever, C. (2005) *Testing ESL Pragmatics: Development and Validation of a Web-Based Assessment Battery*. Berlin: Peter Lang.
Rosa, E. and O'Neill, M. (1999) Explicitness, intake, and the issue of awareness: Another piece to the puzzle. *Studies in Second Language Acquisition* 21, 511–533.
Rose, K. (1994) On the validity of discourse completion tests in non-Western contexts. *Applied Linguistics* 15, 1–14.
Rose, K. and Ono, R. (1995) Eliciting speech act data in Japanese: The effect of questionnaire type. *Language Learning* 45, 191–223.
Rossomondo, A.E. (2003) The role of lexical temporal indicators in the incidental acquisition of the Spanish future tense. PhD Thesis: Indiana University.
Rutherford, W. and Sharwood Smith, M. (1989) Consciousness raising and Universal Grammar. In W. Rutherford and M. Sharwood Smith (eds) *Grammar and Second Language Teaching: A Book of Readings* (pp. 107–116). NY: Newbury House.
Safir, K. (2004) *The Syntax of Anaphora*. NY: Oxford University Press.
Sag, I. (1976) Deletion and logical form. PhD dissertation, MIT.
Sagarra, N. (2002) The role of syntactic modifications on L2 oral comprehension. In C. Wiltshire and J. Camps (eds) *Romance Phonology and Variation* (pp. 197–210). Amsterdam: John Benjamins.
Sagarra, N. (2001). What remains after comprehension: Meaning, form, or both? Paper presented at the conference *Form-Meaning Connections in Second Language Acquisition*. The University of Illinois at Chicago, IL, February 2001.
Sagarra, N. (2007) From CALL to face-to-face interaction: The effect of computer-delivered recasts and working memory on L2 development. In A. Mackey (ed.) *Conversational Interaction in Second Language Acquisition: A Series of Empirical Studies* (chapter 9). Oxford: Oxford University Press.
Sagarra, N. and Dussias, P.E. (2001). Attention allocation to morphological cues during L2 sentence processing: Evidence from eye-movement. Paper presented at the *V Hispanic Linguistics Symposium*. University of Illinois at Urbana-Champaign, IL, October 2001.
Sagarra, N., Bozhak, M. and Pfursich, J. (2005) Working memory and processing of redundant L2 morphosyntactic cues. Paper presented at the *Second Language Research Forum*. New York, NY.
Sasaki, M. (2005) The effect of L1 reading processes on L2: A crosslinguistic comparison of Italian and Japanese users of English. In V.J. Cook and B. Bassetti (eds) *Second Language Writing Systems* (pp. 289–308). Clevedon: Multilingual Matters.
Sato, C. (1986) Conversation and interlanguage development: Rethinking the connection. In R. Day (ed.) *Talking to Learn: Conversation in Second Language Acquisition* (pp. 23–48). Rowley, MA: Newbury House.
Sato, C. (1991) Sociolinguistic variation and language attitudes in Hawaii. In J. Cheshire (ed.) *English Around the World: Sociolinguistic Perspectives* (pp. 647–663). Cambridge: Cambridge University Press.

Sato, T. (1995) Tan-on to inritsu ga nihongo onsee no hyooka ni ataeru eikyooryoku no hikaku [Comparison of influences between single sounds and prosody in judgment of naturalness of Japanese]. *Sekai no Nihongo Kyoiku* 5, 139–154.
Saxton, M. (1997) The contrast theory of negative input. *Journal of Child Language* 24, 139–161.
Scarcella, R. (1979) Watch up! *Working Papers in Bilingualism* 19, 79–88.
Schachter, J. (1974) An error in error analysis. *Language Learning* 2, 205–214.
Schachter, J. (1996) Maturation and the issue of Universal Grammar in second language acquisition. In W. Ritchie and T. Bhatia (eds) *Handbook of Second Language Acquisition* (pp. 159–194). San Diego: Academic Press.
Schirmer, B.R. and Williams, C. (2003) Approaches to teaching reading. In M. Marschark and P.E. Spencer (eds) *Oxford Handbook of Deaf Studies, Language, and Education* (pp. 110–122). Oxford: Oxford University Press.
Schmidt, R. (1983) Interaction, acculturation, and the acquisition of communicative competence: A case study of an adult. In E. Judd and N. Wolfson (eds) *Sociolinguistics and Language Acquisition* (pp. 137–174). Rowley, MA: Newbury House.
Schmidt, R. (1990) The role of consciousness in second language learning. *Applied Linguistics* 11 (2), 129–158.
Schmidt, R. (1993) Awareness and second language acquisition. *Annual Review of Applied Linguistics* 13, 206–226.
Schmidt, R. (1994a) Deconstructing consciousness in search of useful definitions for applied linguistics. *AILA Review* 11, 11–26.
Schmidt, R. (1994b) Implicit learning and the cognitive unconscious: Of artificial grammars and SLA. In N. Ellis (ed.) *Implicit and Explicit Learning of Languages* (pp. 165–209). San Diego: Academic Press.
Schmidt, R. (1995) Consciousness and foreign language learning: A tutorial on the role of attention and awareness in learning. In R. Schmidt (ed.) *Attention and Awareness in Foreign Language Learning* (pp. 217–258). Honolulu: University of Hawaii Press.
Schmidt, R. (2001) Attention. In P. Robinson (ed.) *Cognition and Second Language Instruction* (pp. 3–32). Cambridge: Cambridge University Press.
Schmidt, R.A., Young, D.E., Swinnen, S. and Shapiro, D.C. (1989) Summary knowledge of results for skill acquisition: Support for the guidance hypothesis. *Journal of Experimental Psychology: Learning, Memory, & Cognition* 15, 352–359.
Schmitt, N., Dörnyei, Z., Adolphs, S. and Durow, V. (2004) Knowledge and acquisition of formulaic sequences. In N. Schmitt (ed.) *Formulaic Sequences: Acquisition, Processing and Use* (pp. 55–86). Amsterdam: Benjamins.
Schwartz, B.D. (1999) Let's make up your mind: 'Special nativist' perspectives on language, modularity of mind, and nonnative language acquisition. *Studies in Second Language Acquisition* 21, 635–655.
Seabrook, R., Brown, G.D.A. and Solity, J.E. (2005) Distributed and massed practice: From laboratory to classroom. *Applied Cognitive Psychology* 19, 107–122.
Sebastián-Gallés, N. and Bosch, L. (2005) Phonology and bilingualism. In J.F. Kroll and A.M.B. de Groot (eds) *Handbook of Bilingualism: Psycholinguistic Approaches* (pp. 68–87). Oxford: Oxford University Press.
Segalowitz, N. and Lightbown, P.M. (1999) Psycholinguistic approaches to SLA. *Annual Review of Applied Linguistics* 19, 23–43.
Seliger, H. (1996) Primary language attrition in the context of bilingualism. In W. Ritchie and T. Bhatia (eds) *The Handbook of Second Language Acquisition* (pp. 605–625). New York: Academic Press.

Selinker, L. (1972) Interlanguage. *International Review of Applied Linguistics* 10 (3), 209–231.
Selinker, L. (2006) Afterword: Fossilization 'or' does your mind? In Z-H. Han and T. Odlin (eds) *Studies of Fossilization in Second Language Acquisition* (pp. 201–210). Clevedon: Multilingual Matters.
Selinker, L. and Lakshmanan, U. (1992) Language transfer and fossilization: The multiple effects principle. In S.M. Gass and L. Selinker (eds) *Language Transfer in Language Learning* (pp. 190–216). Philadelphia: John Benjamins.
Selkirk, E.O. (1982) The syllable. In J.A. Goldsmith (ed.) (1999) *Phonological Theory: The Essential Readings* (pp. 328–350). Malden, MA: Blackwell Publishers.
Selkirk, E.O. (1984) *Phonology and Syntax: The Relation Between Sound and Structure.* Cambridge, MA: MIT Press.
Shah, A. and Baum, S. (2006) Perception of lexical stress by brain-damaged individuals: Effects on lexical-semantic activation. *Applied Psycholinguistics* 27 (2), 143–156.
Sharwood Smith, M.A. (1981) Consciousness-raising and the second language learner. *Applied Linguistics* 2 (2), 159–168.
Sharwood Smith, M. (1986) Comprehension vs. acquisition: Two ways of processing input. *Applied Linguistics* 7 (3), 239–256.
Sharwood Smith, M. (1991) Speaking to many minds: On the relevance of different types of language information for the L2 learner. *Second Language Research* 7 (2), 118–132.
Sharwood Smith, M. (1993) Input enhancement in instructed SLA. *Studies in Second Language Acquisition* 15, 165–179.
Sharwood Smith, M.A. (1994) *Second Language Acquisition: Theoretical Foundations.* London: Longman.
Sharwood Smith, M. (1996) Metalinguistic ability and primary linguistic data: Response to Samuel Epstein, Suzanne Flynn & Gita Martohardjono. *Behavioural and Brain Science* 19, 740–741.
Sharwood Smith, M. (2002) *Losing LAD and getting MAD: On acquiring parallel language systems.* Paper presented at Department of Linguistics and English Language Colloqium series. Durham University, England, UK.
Sharwood Smith, M. (2004) In two minds about grammar: On the interaction of linguistic and metalinguistic knowledge in performance. *Transactions of the Philological Society* 102, 255–280.
Sheen, Y. (2004) Corrective feedback and learner uptake in communicative classrooms across instructional settings. *Language Teaching Research* 8 (3), 263–300.
Shibata, T. (2005) Prosody acquisition of Japanese as a second language: View from an integrative perspective. Unpublished doctoral dissertation, University of Iowa.
Shieber, S., Pereira, F. and Dalrymple, M. (1996) Interaction of scope and ellipsis. *Linguistics and Philosophy* 19 (4), 527–552.
Shin, S. and Milroy, L. (1999) Bilingual language acquisition by Korean school children in New York City. *Bilingualism: Language and Cognition* 2 (2), 147–167.
Simard, D. and Wong, W. (2001) Alertness, orientation and detection: the conceptualization of attentional functions in SLA. *Studies in Second Language Acquisition* 23, 103–124.

Skehan, P. (1998) *A Cognitive Approach to Language Learning.* Oxford: Oxford University Press.
Skehan, P. and Foster, P. (2001) Cognition and tasks. In P. Robinson (ed.) *Cognition and Second Language Instruction* (pp. 183–205). Cambridge: Cambridge University Press.
Slamecka, N.J. and Graf, P. (1978) The generation effect: Delineation of a phenomenon. *Journal of Experimental Psychology: Human Learning and Memory* 4, 592–604.
Slobin, D.I. (1973) Cognitive prerequisites for the development of grammar. In C. Ferguson and D.I. Slobin (eds) *Studies of Child Language Development* (pp. 175–208). New York: Rinehart and Winston.
Slobin, D. (1993) Adult language acquisition: A view from child language study. In C. Perdue (ed.) *Adult Second Language Acquisition: Cross-Linguistic Perspectives* (pp. 239–252). Cambridge: Cambridge University Press.
Slobin, D. (1996) From 'thought and language' to 'thinking for speaking.' In J.J. Gumperz and S.C. Levinson (eds) *Rethinking Linguistic Relativity* (pp. 70–96). Cambridge: Cambridge University Press.
Snow, M.A., Met, M. and Genesee, F. (1992) A conceptual framework for the integration of language and content instruction. In P.A. Richard-Amato and M.A. Snow (eds) *The Multicultural Classroom: Readings for Content-Area Teachers.* Reading, MA: Addison-Wesley.
Smith-Lock, K.M. (1995) Morphological usage and awareness in children with and without specific language impairment. *Annals of Dyslexia* 45, 163–185.
Smith-Lock, K.M. and Rubin, H. (1993) Phonological and morphological analysis skills in young children. *Journal of Child Language* 20, 437–454.
Sorace, A. (1985) Metalinguistic knowledge and language use in acquisition-poor environments. *Applied Linguistics* 6, 239–254.
Sorace, A. (1993) Incomplete vs. divergent representations of unaccusativity in near-native grammars of Italian. *Second Language Research* 9, 22–47.
Sorace, A. (2000) Syntactic optionality in non-native grammars. *Second Language Research* 16 (2), 93–102.
Sorace, A. (2003) Near-nativeness. In C. Doughty and M. Long (eds) *The Handbook of Second Language Acquisition* (pp. 130–152). Oxford: Blackwell.
Sorace, A. (2005) Selective optionality in language development. In L. Cornips and K. Corrigan (eds) *Biolinguistic and Sociolinguistic Accounts of Syntactic Variation.* (pp. 111–160). Amsterdam: Benjamins.
Spada, N. and Lightbown, P. (1993) Instruction and the development of questions in the L2 classroom. *Studies in Second Language Acquisition* 15, 205–221.
Spada, N. and Lightbown, P. (1999) Instruction, first language influence and developmental readiness in SLA. *Modern Language Journal* 83, 1–21.
Spada, N., Lightbown, P.M. and White, J.L. (2005) The importance of form/meaning mappings in explicit form-focussed instruction. In A. Housen and M. Pierrard (eds) *Current Issues in Instructed Second Language Learning* (pp. 199–234). Berlin: Mouton de Gruyter.
Spivey, M.J. and Marian, V. (1999) Cross talk between native and second languages: Partial activation of an irrelevant lexicon. *Psychological Science* 10, 181–184.
Stanislas, D. and Changeux, J.P. (2004) Neural mechanisms for access to consciousness. In M. Gazzaniga (ed.) *The Cognitive Neurosciences* (3rd edn) (pp. 1145–1157). New York: Norton.

Strauss, S., Lee, J. and Ahn, K. (2006) Applying conceptual grammar to advanced-level language teaching: The case of two completive constructions in Korean. *Modern Language Journal* 90 (2), 185-209.
Strong, M. (1995) A review of bilingual/bicultural programs for deaf children in North America. *American Annals of the Deaf* 140, 84-94.
Supalla, S.J. (1991) Manually coded English: The modality question in signed language development. In P. Siple and S.D. Fischer (eds) *Theoretical Issues in Sign Language Research* (Vol. 2): *Psychology* (pp. 85-109). Chicago: University of Chicago Press.
Swain, M. (1988) Manipulating and complementing content teaching to maximize second language learning. *TESL Canada Journal* 6, 68-83.
Swain, M. (1993) The output hypothesis: Just speaking and writing aren't enough. *The Canadian Modern Language Review* 50, 158-164.
Swain, M. (1995) Three functions of output in second language learning. In G. Cook and B. Seidlhofer (eds) *Principle and Practice in Applied Linguistics* (pp. 125-144). Oxford: Oxford University Press.
Swain, M. (1998) Focus on form through conscious reflection. In C. Doughty and J. Williams (eds) *Focus on Form in Classroom Second Language Acquisition* (pp. 64-82). New York: Cambridge University Press.
Takano, Y. (1995) Predicate fronting and internal subjects. *Linguistic Inquiry* 26 (3), 327-340.
Terrell, T. (1991) The role of grammar instruction in the communicative approach. *Modern Language Journal* 75, 52-63.
Thomas, M. (1995) Acquisition of the Japanese reflexive *zibun* and movement of anaphors in Logical Form. *Second Language Research* 11 (2), 206-234.
Tiegs, E.W. and Clark, W.W. (1957) *California Achievement Tests—Junior High Level*. Monterey, CA: California Test Bureau.
Tocalli-Beller, A. and Swain, M. (2005) Reformulation: The cognitive conflict and L2 learning it generates. *International Journal of Applied Linguistics* 15, 5-28.
Toda, T. (1997) Strategies for producing mora timing by non-native speakers of Japanese. *Acquisition of Japanese as a Second Language* 1, 157-197.
Toda, T. (2003) Acquisition of special morae in Japanese as a second language. *Journal of Phonetic Society of Japan* 7 (2), 70-83.
Tomlin, R. and Villa, H. (1994) Attention in cognitive science and second language acquisition. *Studies in Second Language Acquisition* 16 (2), 183-203.
Toothtaker, L. (1991) *Multiple Comparisons for Researchers*. London: Sage Publications.
Toscano, R.M., McKee, B. and Lepoutre, D. (2002) Success with academic English: Reflections of deaf college students. *American Annals of the Deaf* 147, 5-23.
Traxler, C.B. (2000) The Stanford Achievement Test, 9th edn: National norming and performance standards for deaf and hard-of-hearing students. *Journal of Deaf Studies and Deaf Education* 5, 337-348.
Trenkic, D. and Sharwood Smith, M. (2002) *Reevaluating Theoretical and Methodological Aspects of Focus on Form Research*. Presentations at EUROSLA 11, University of Paderborn, Germany.
Trenkic, D. and Sharwood Smith, M. (2003) *Reevaluating Theoretical and Methodological Aspects of Focus on Form Research*. On WWW at http://www.hw.ac.uk/langWWW/icsla/ICSLABIB.htm.

Trofimovich, P. (2005) Spoken-word processing in a native and a second language: An investigation of auditory word priming. *Applied Psycholinguistics* 26, 479–504.
Trofimovich, P. and Gatbonton, E. (2006) Repetition and focus on form in L2 Spanish word processing: Implications for pronunciation instruction. *Modern Language Journal* 90, 519–535.
Truscott, J. (1996) The case against grammar correction in L2 writing classes. *Language Learning* 46, 327–369.
Truscott, J. (1998) Noticing in second language acquisition: A critical review. *Second Language Research* 14 (2), 103–135.
Truscott, J. and Sharwood Smith, M. (2004a) Acquisition by processing: a modular perspective on language development. *Bilingualism: Language and Cognition* 7 (1), 1–2.
Truscott, J. and Sharwood Smith, M. (2004b) How APT is your theory: present status and future prospects. *Bilingualism: Language and Cognition* 7 (1), 43–47.
Tsimpli, T., Sorace, A., Heycock, C. and Filiaci, F. (2004) First language attrition and syntactic subjects: A study of Greek and Italian near native speakers of English. *International Journal of Bilingualism* 3, 257–278.
Tunmer, W.E. (1990) The role of language prediction skills in beginning reading. *New Zealand Journal of Educational Studies* 25, 95–114.
Tunmer, W.E., Nesdale, A.R. and Wright, A.D. (1987) Syntactic awareness and reading acquisition. *British Journal of Developmental Psychology* 5, 25–34.
Tunmer, W.E., Herriman, M.L. and Nesdale, A.R. (1988) Metalinguistic abilities and reading acquisition. *British Journal of Developmental Psychology* 5, 25–34.
Ueyama, M. (2003) Awareness of L2 syllable structures: The case of L2 Japanese and L2 English. *Journal of the Phonetic Society of Japan* 7 (2), 84–100.
van Heuven, W. (2005) Bilingual interactive activation models of word recognition in a second language. In V.J. Cook and B. Bassetti (eds) *Second Language Writing Systems* (pp. 260–288). Clevedon: Multilingual Matters.
VanPatten, B. (1990) Attending to form and content in the input. *Studies in Second Language Acquisition* 12, 287–301.
VanPatten, B. (1991) *Grammar Instruction and Input Processing*. Paper presented at the special colloquium on the role of grammar instruction in communicative language teaching, Concordia University and McGill University, Montreal.
VanPatten, B. (1996) *Input Processing and Grammar Instruction: Theory and Research*. Norwood, NH: Ablex.
VanPatten, B. (2004a) *Processing Instruction*. Mahwah, NJ: Lawrence Erlbaum.
VanPatten, B. (2004b) Input processing in SLA. In B. VanPatten (ed.) *Processing Instruction: Theory, Research, and Commentary* (pp. 5–32). Mahwah, NJ: Lawrence Erlbaum Associates.
VanPatten, B. and Cadierno, T. (1993) Explicit instruction and input processing. *Studies in Second Language Acquisition* 15, 225–243.
VanPatten, B., Williams, J. and Rott, S. (2004) Form–meaning connections in second language acquisition. In B. VanPatten, J. Williams, S. Rott and M. Overstreet (eds) *Form–Meaning Connections in Second Language Acquisition* (pp. 1–28). Mahwah, NJ: Lawrence Erlbaum.
Varela, E., Thompson, E. and Rosch, E. (1991) *The Embodied Mind*. Cambridge, MA: MIT Press.

Venditti, J.J. (1994) The influence of syntax on prosodic structure in Japanese. *Ohio State University Working Papers in Linguistics* 44, 191–223.
von Humboldt, W. (1836) *Über die Verschiedenheit des menschlichen sprachbaues und ihren Einfluss auf die geistige Entwickelung des Menschengeschlechts. [On the Diversity of Human Language Construction and Its Influence on Human Development].* Bonn: Dümmler.
von Stutterheim, C. and Klein, W. (1987) A concept-oriented approach to second language studies. In C. Pfaff (ed.) *First and Second Language Acquisition Process* (pp. 191–205). Cambridge, MA: Newbury House.
Vos, S.H., Gunter, T.C., Schriefers, H. and Friederici, A.D. (2001) Syntactic parsing and working memory: The effects of syntactic complexity, reading span and concurrent load. *Language and Cognitive Processes* 16, 65–103.
Walter, G.G. (1988) *Characteristics and Success of Deaf College Students in Three Types of Educational Environments.* Technical report, National Technical Institute for the Deaf, Rochester Institute of Technology.
Warner, N. and Arai, T. (2001) Japanese mora-timing: A review. *Phonetica* 58, 1–25.
Warren-Leuckerber, A. and Warren Cater, B. (1988) Reading and growth in metalinguistic awareness: Relations to socioeconomic status and reading readiness skills. *Child Development* 59, 728–742.
Waters, G.S. and Caplan, D. (1996) The measurement of verbal working memory capacity and its relation to reading comprehension. *Quarterly Journal of Experimental Psychology* 49 (A), 51–79.
Waters, G.S., Caplan, D. and Hildebrand, N. (1987) Working memory and written sentence comprehension. In M. Coltheart (ed.) *Attention and Performance XII: The Psychology of Reading* (pp. 531–555). Hillsdale, NJ: Lawrence Erlbaum.
Weinert, R. (1995) The role of formulaic language in second language acquisition: A review. *Applied Linguistics* 16, 180–205.
Weinreich, U. (1953) *Languages in Contact.* The Hague: Mouton.
Wesche, M. and Paribakht, T.S. (1996) Assessing second language vocabulary knowledge: Depth vs. Breadth. *Canadian Modern Language Review* 53, 13–40.
Wheeldon, L.R. (2000) Generating prosodic structure. In L.R. Wheeldon (ed.) *Aspects of Language Production* (pp. 249–274). Philadelphia, PA: Taylor & Francis.
White, L. (1987) Against comprehensible input: The Input Hypothesis and the development of L2 competence. *Applied Linguistics* 8, 95–110.
White, L. (1991) Adverb placement in second language acquisition: some effects of positive and negative evidence in the classroom. *Second Language Research* 7 (2), 133–161.
White, L. (1995) Chasing after linguistic theory. In L. Eubank, L. Selinker and M. Sharwood-Smith (eds) *The Current State of Interlanguage* (pp. 63–71). Amsterdam: John Benjamins.
White, L. (2001) Crosslinguistic influence revisited: An L2 perspective. *Bilingualism: Language and Cognition* 4, 46–48.
White, L., Hirakawa, M. and Kawasaki, T. (1996) Second language acquisition of long distance reflexives: Effects and non-effects of input manipulation. *McGill Working Papers in Linguistics* (pp. 1–22). McGill University, Canada.
Whorf, B.L. (1940) Science and linguistics. *Technology Review* 42 (6), 229–231.
Williams, E. (1977) Discourse and logical form. *Linguistic Inquiry* 8 (1), 101–139.

Williams, J. (2001) Learner-generated attention to form. *Language Learning* 51 (Suppl. 1), 303–346.
Williams, J. and Evans, J. (1998) What kind of focus on form and on which forms? In C. Doughty and J. Williams (eds) *Focus on Form in Classroom Second Language Acquisition* (pp. 139–155). Cambridge: Cambridge University Press.
Williams, J., Mobius, P. and Kim, C. (2001) Native and non-native processing of English *wh*-questions: Parsing strategies and plausibility constraints. *Applied Psycholinguistics* 22 (4), 509–540.
Willows, D. and Bouchard Ryan, E. (1986) The development of grammatical sensitivity and its relationship to early reading achievement. *Reading Research Quarterly* 21, 253–266.
Wode, H. (1981) Language-acquisitional universals: A unified view of language acquisition. In H. Winitz (ed.) *Native Language and Foreign Language Acquisition* (Vol. 379). New York: Annals of the New York Academy of Sciences.
Wong, W. (2001) Modality and attention to meaning and form in the input. *Studies in Second Language Acquisition* 23, 345–368.
Wong, W. (2004a) *Input Enhancement: From Theory and Research to the Classroom.* San Francisco, CA: McGraw-Hill.
Wong, W. (2004b) The nature of processing instruction. In B. VanPatten (ed.) *Processing Instruction: Theory, Research, and Commentary* (pp. 33–63). Mahwah, NJ: Lawrence Erlbaum.
Wong, W. and VanPatten, B. (2003) The evidence is IN: Drills are OUT. *Foreign Language Annals* 36, 403–423.
Wray, A. and Perkins, M.R. (2000) The functions of formulaic language: An integrated model. *Language and Communication* 20, 1–28.
Yelland, G.W., Pollard, J. and Mercuri, A. (1993), The metalinguistic benefits of limited contact with a second language. *Applied Psycholinguistics* 14, 423–444.
Ying, H. (1999) Access to UG and language transfer: A study of L2 learners' interpretation of reconstruction in Chinese. *Second Language Research* 15 (1), 41–72.
Ying, H. (2000) *Interpretation of Reflexive Binding and the Internal Subject Hypothesis by Chinese-Speaking Learners of English: A Timed Sentence Judgment Task.* Paper presented at the Bi-Annual Meeting of Generative Approaches to Second Language Acquisition (GASLA). MA: MIT.
Ying, H. (2003) *Investigating Reconstruction in a Second Language.* Muenchen: Lincom Europa Academic Publishers.
Yip, V. and Tang, G. (1998) Acquisition of English reflexive binding by Cantonese learners: testing the positive transfer hypothesis. In M-L. Beck (ed.) *Morphology and Its Interfaces in Second Language Knowledge* (pp. 195–226). Amsterdam: John Benjamins.
Young, R. (1989) Ends and means: Methods for the study of interlanguage variation. In M.S. Gass, C. Madden, D. Preston and L. Selinker (eds) *Variation in Second Language Acquisition: Psycholinguistic Issues* (pp. 65–90). Clevedon: Multilingual Matters.
Young, R. (1991) *Variation in Interlanguage Morphology.* New York: Peter Lang.
Zampini, M.L. and Green, K.P. (2001) The voicing contrast in English and Spanish: the relationship between perception and production. In J. Nicol (ed.) *One Mind, Two Languages* (pp. 23–48). Oxford: Blackwell.

Index

Acceptability judgement 174
Allophone 160, 166
Analysis and control 165-66, 170, 173
Anaphora 155-57
Ancient Greek 13-14
Article 5, 11, 62-63, 76, 120, 124-25
Attention 3, 6, 28-32, 35-38, 42-44, 47-50, 52, 55, 57, 61, 65, 74-75, 77-78, 85, 98, 106-15, 120, 129-30, 133-37, 141, 145-47, 152, 158, 162-65, 168-69, 173-74, 215
Auditory structure 11-12

Bilingual 19-20, 23-25, 44, 66, 103, 174
Binding 64, 74, 148, 150-59

Chinese 21, 25, 64, 71, 114, 148-49, 151-59, 178, 208
Chunks 78, 134
Cognition 2, 8, 20, 25, 65-67
Cognitive state 46
Communicative language teaching 28, 32-35, 37, 138
Communicative value 54-55, 58, 97
Comprehension 10-11, 39-40, 47, 49, 52, 75, 81, 101-2, 109, 111, 134, 136-38, 140-41, 143-45, 147, 158, 161, 183, 202
Competition Model 25
Conceptual restructuring 68, 73, 75-77
Conceptual structure 1, 8-10, 12-13, 63
Conceptual system 10, 14, 61-62, 64-65, 67-68, 71-74, 77, 79
Consciousness 1, 3, 6, 10, 64
Critical period 46
Crosslinguistic influence 64, 113

Deaf/Deaf learner 80-82, 85-86, 89-90, 92-93, 95-97, 100, 102-5
Declarative knowledge 29, 75
Definiteness 65-66, 73
Desirable difficulties 39
Developmental sequence 3, 6, 68-69
Developmental sharpening 46
Direct/Indirect assessment 86, 88-89, 90, 95-96

Discourse 62, 64, 71-72, 75, 81, 83, 86-88, 93-94, 96-97, 100, 135, 206-7, 209
Drills 29, 33-34, 40
Dual Knowledge 2-5

Elaboration 6-7, 31-32
English 5, 12, 16-17, 22-25, 33, 36-37, 44, 53-54, 62-64, 66-74, 77, 79-82, 85-90, 93, 96-105, 113-114, 116-28, 130-31, 138-40, 148-49, 151-58, 160-61, 177-82, 185-86, 195, 198, 202-4, 206, 208-9
Equipotentiality 46-47
Error correction 51, 78
Essay coding 82-86
Explicit knowledge 79, 158, 164, 166
Explicitness 6-7, 111, 174
Expressions 33, 62, 79, 205-6, 208-12, 214-15, 217-22
External salience 110

Feedback 33-35, 39, 41, 44, 47, 51, 53-56, 77, 79, 82-84, 100, 104, 110-11
First language acquisition 45-46, 69, 109
Focus on form 1, 3, 7, 43, 45, 47-51, 55-57, 68, 77, 108, 110, 128, 138
Foreign-accentedness 177
Form-based approach 112, 136
Form-meaning connection 34-36, 38, 43, 52, 61, 71, 80, 102, 104, 133, 140, 146-47
Formulas 205-9, 213, 215, 217-21
French 22-24, 33, 44, 51, 101, 113-15, 135, 160, 164, 167-68
Frequency 23, 31, 35, 53-54, 58, 87, 92-94, 111, 117, 136, 139, 181, 216, 220

German 6, 24, 64, 114-15
Grammatical morphemes 20, 47, 49, 58, 61-63, 68-69, 72-73, 77, 109
Grammaticality judgement 19, 66-67, 88, 95-96

Hyper correction 76

Implicit knowledge 69, 75, 79, 164

Index   255

Input enhancement 1, 7, 10, 47-48, 80, 82,
  84-86, 95, 97-101, 104-5, 108-10, 147
Input processing 10, 50, 54, 106, 108, 109,
  112-13, 115, 126-30, 133, 146
Intake 47, 106-9, 133, 140
Internal salience 110-11, 113
Interrogative intonation 199-203

Japanese 24-25, 63, 66-67, 113-14, 116-28,
  130-31, 151, 158, 176-86, 190, 195, 198,
  200, 203-4, 208
Judgement of acceptability (*see*
  Acceptability judgement) 168, 170

Korean 58, 70, 72, 112-20, 123-25, 127,
  131-32, 136, 178, 208
Krashen 2-4, 6-7, 13, 29

L1 influence 72
L2 processing 104, 133-34, 147
Language module 2, 9
Latin 13, 115, 139
Learnability 57, 63-65, 68, 73, 77-78
Learner-external 110
Learner-generated attention 110-13
Learner-internal 110
Learner system 2
Left Branching structure 184, 191
Lexicon 9, 20, 23
Linguistic relativity 61, 64-67, 70, 71, 77
Longitudinal research 100
LOP/levels of processing 30

Mastery 82, 90, 92, 97-99, 176, 201
Meaning-based approach 112, 128, 136
Memory 9-10, 27, 30-32, 35, 39, 41-42, 58,
  107, 133-34, 138, 140, 144-47
Metagrammar 2, 11-13
Metalinguistic ability 1-2, 4, 6, 14, 161-62,
  165, 167, 169, 174
Metasyntactic ability 160-67
Modality 85, 174
Modified output 34
Monitor 4, 6, 13, 41, 141
Mora timing 180-83, 186-89, 196-97, 199-204
Morphological development 45
Moving window 134, 137-39, 141-44, 147

Naturalistic narrative data 182
Negotiation of form 49
Negotiation for meaning 49, 55, 57
Noticing 120, 122, 124, 129-30, 134, 146
Number 18, 21, 25, 31, 33, 39, 41, 43, 47-48,
  54, 57, 64, 66, 68, 70, 73, 79, 86, 92, 95,
  97-99, 122, 125-26, 132, 138, 140, 147, 154,
  160, 167, 174, 186, 194-95, 212, 217-18

Operator-variable binding 148, 155
Output 102, 104, 109-10, 129, 176
Overuse 62, 72, 74-75, 77, 140

Parameter 25, 79, 151-52, 157-58
Perceptual salience 53, 146-67
Phonology 5-6, 24, 53, 81, 161
Phonological structure 9, 11, 12, 15
Plural marking 60, 66-68, 71-73
Plural –s 59, 62, 68-69, 71-73, 75-77
Pragmatics 9, 24, 43, 45, 47, 205-6, 208-9, 218-21
Priming 36-7, 41, 44, 211-12
Procedural knowledge 29, 75
Processing approach 128
PRO-drop 24, 140, 157-58
Production 10-11, 13, 20, 29, 39, 49, 59,
  64-65, 83-84, 86-87, 91-94, 97, 100, 102,
  136, 164, 176-91, 194-96, 198-206, 208-9,
  212, 214-21
Proficiency 37, 54, 58, 66-67, 81-82, 85-86,
  103, 112, 134, 138-41, 145-47, 151, 158,
  165, 180-81, 188, 194-96, 198-204, 206
Prosody hierarchy 177-78

Reading competence 161-62
Recasts 41, 45, 50-61, 63, 68, 74-79, 134
Recognition 1, 8, 23, 25, 96, 103, 136, 138-9,
  141, 161, 205-14, 216-21
Reconstruction 135, 152
Redundant grammatical forms 133-35, 137,
  145-47
Reflexive 148-58
Replication 165-66. 168-70, 173-75
Right Branching structure 184-85, 191, 194,
  202

Salience 35, 40, 47, 53, 58, 109-11, 113, 146, 147
Semantic formulas 205
Semantics 9, 31, 45, 47, 62-64. 68, 70, 78
Shallow processing 47
Socio-economic status/ SES 166, 174
Spanish 16-17, 24-25, 36-38, 44, 62, 64,
  114-15, 135-40, 158, 208
Syntactic structure 9-11, 44, 161, 164-65, 184
Syntactically ambiguous 180, 185, 197, 199
Syntax 5-6, 12, 17, 20, 24, 45, 47, 53, 62, 64,
  81, 102, 127, 161-62, 169, 175

Target language 2, 4, 24, 27, 46, 51-54, 60-62,
  69, 72, 78, 101, 103, 106, 109, 112, 114,
  128, 135-37, 145, 152, 157-59, 164

Task demand 33, 44, 160
Temporal cues 135
Textual enhancement 83-84, 109
Teachability Hypothesis 70
Thinking for speaking 65, 72
Transfer appropriate processing/TAP
  27-28, 30-32, 34-36, 39, 42-44, 96
Type of processing, resource
  allocation/TOPRA 38
Typological proximity 46

Universal Grammar/UG 3, 10, 18, 148-52, 155, 157-59

Validity 4, 66, 68, 72, 89-90, 95-97, 108

Variability 134
Variable 7, 70, 74, 76, 87, 90, 114, 130, 148-50, 153-59, 170
Visual input enhancement 80, 82, 84-86, 95-101, 104-5
Visuogloss 83-86, 90-92, 94, 97-99
Vocabulary 23, 81, 102, 116, 139, 141, 158, 176, 183, 209, 211, 222
Vocabulary Knowledge Scale/VKS 209, 211-212, 216, 218, 221-22
Voice Onset Time/VOT 24
VP-ellipsis 148-49, 150, 153, 155-56

Working memory 9-10, 58, 133-34, 138, 140, 144-47

For Product Safety Concerns and Information please contact our EU Authorised Representative:

Easy Access System Europe

Mustamäe tee 50

10621 Tallinn

Estonia

gpsr.requests@easproject.com

www.ingramcontent.com/pod-product-compliance
Lightning Source LLC
Chambersburg PA
CBHW070557300426
44113CB00010B/1290